Interconnection Networks for Large-Scale Parallel Processing

Theory and Case Studies

The Lexington Books Series in Computer Science

Interconnection Networks for Large-Scale Parallel Processing

Theory and Case Studies

Howard Jay Siegel

School of Electrical Engineering
Purdue University

Lexington Books

D.C. Heath and Company/Lexington, Massachusetts/Toronto

Library of Congress Cataloging in Publication Data

Siegel, Howard Jay.
  Interconnection networks for large-scale parallel processing.

  Bibliography: p.
  Includes index.
    1. Computer networks. 2. Parallel processing (Electronic computers)
3. Electronic data processing—Distributed processing. 4. Computer
architecture. I. Title.
TK5105.5.S54   1985   001.64'404   79-6015
ISBN 0-669-03594-7

Second printing, March 1986.

Published simultaneously in Canada

Printed in the United States of America

International Standard Book Number: 0-669-03594-7

Library of Congress Catalog Card Number: 79-6015

*Dedicated to my family
and
to all those people who,
directly or indirectly, asked:
"How's the book coming?"*

Contents

Figures

Tables

Preface and Acknowledgments

This book is designed to be used both as a textbook for graduate level university courses and as a self-study book for practicing computer scientists/engineers. The book was developed in conjunction with a graduate-level course on parallel processing at Purdue University. Teaching this material for several years has provided me with much insight into the best ways to present it in textbook form. There are 94 figures and 19 tables to aid in the understanding of the interconnection network studies, and there are also over 140 references for further reading.

When using this book in a graduate-level course, the text may be supplemented by articles from the current literature. Three types of articles are recommended for additional reading. First, articles about existing and proposed systems using the types of networks discussed in this book, such as MPP (Batcher 1980, 1982), PASM (Siegel and others 1981), STARAN (Batcher 1977), and Ultracomputer (Gottlieb and others 1983). Second, articles about variations on the types of networks presented here, such as the delta (Patel 1981), gamma (Parker and Raghavendra 1982), and mesh (Nassimi and Sahni 1980) networks. Articles presenting other approaches to network analysis, such as Lawrie (1975), Pradham and Kodandapani (1980), and Wu and Feng (1981), are the third type. Students taking a course based on this book should have at least an undergraduate level background in computer programming, digital logic, and computer architecture.

The book can be used by the practicing computer scientist/engineer in different ways, depending on the information desired. Obviously, the most knowledge will be gained by reading the entire book. Those less concerned with theory can skip the algorithm correctness proofs in chapter 3 and still understand the material. Readers whose interests are just the case studies of multistage networks can obtain the information they want from chapters 1, 2, 5, and 6 (ignoring the references in chapters 5 and 6 to the related theory in chapters 3 and 4).

The study of interconnection networks is an increasingly important area of research, in which a great deal of work has already been done. Therefore, two disclaimers need to be made. First, although there are over 140 references given at the end of the book, the list is not intended to be exhaustive. Some additional sources of information about interconnection networks are mentioned in the "Summary and Further Reading." Second, the approach to analyzing and evaluating networks presented here is not the only one. I have found this approach to be effective in teaching about networks, and once the knowledge has been gained from this book, articles presenting other approaches can be more easily understood.

I want to acknowledge the efforts of the many people who have contributed to this book in various ways. I first thank Jeff Ullman, my Ph.D. thesis advisor, for interesting me in interconnection networks and guiding most of the research in chapter 3. I next thank three of my students whose theses form the basis of much of the material in chapters 5 and 6: George B. Adams III, Robert J. McMillen, and S. Diane Smith. A great deal of time was spent by Leah H. Jamieson, George B. Adams III, Nathaniel J. Davis IV, and Robert J. McMillen, carefully and thoroughly reading the manuscript and giving me numerous useful suggestions. I also thank Norma H. Siegel for providing invaluable editorial assistance. Mickey Krebs diligently translated my scribbled notes and many, many revisions into the "computer composed" manuscript that was sent to the publisher. Sharon Katz supplied artistic advice and transformed my sketches into the figures presented here. The cooperation of Ms. Krebs' and Ms. Katz's supervisor, Andy Hughes, is gratefully acknowledged. I appreciate the support and encouragement given to me by Ben Coates, former head of the School of Electrical Engineering at Purdue University. I also thank my loyal secretary Carol Edmundson for her help. The students who have taken my parallel processing course over the last few years supplied the feedback that enabled me to transform this research material into a textbook. A majority of the research reported in this book was supported by one or more of the following agencies and grants: the Air Force Office of Scientific Research, Air Force Systems Command, under grant number AFOSR-78-3581; the Ballistic Missile Defense Agency, under contract number DASG60-80-C-0022; the National Science Foundation, under grants DCR-74-21939, ECS-80-16580, ECS-81-20896; and the Purdue Research Foundation, under an XL grant. Last, but not least, I thank Ken Thurber for his suggestion that I write this book, and Marsha Forrest, of Lexington Books, for her patience and assistance.

1 Overview

A myriad of tasks require the computational power and speed made possible by parallel processing. Usually, these tasks require fast computation for real-time response and/or the need to process immense data sets. These tasks include weather forecasting, map making, aerodynamic simulations, chemical-reaction simulations, seismic data processing, air-traffic control, satellite-collected imagery analysis, missile guidance, ballistic-missile defense, robot vision, and speech understanding. Parallel-processing systems comprised of a multitude of tightly coupled, cooperating processors can supply the support essential to meeting the computational performance goals for all these applications. This book examines methods to provide communications among the processors of such systems.

The age of very large-scale integration (VLSI) has made feasible large-scale parallel/distributed processing systems. For example, one existing machine, the MPP (Massively Parallel Processor) described by Batcher (1980, 1982) consists of 2^{14} processing elements. A major problem in designing large-scale parallel/distributed systems is the construction of an interconnection network to provide interprocessor communications and, in some cases, memory access for the processors.

The task of interconnecting N processors and N memory modules, where N may be in the range of 2^6 to 2^{16}, is not trivial. The interconnection scheme must provide fast and flexible communications at a reasonable cost. A single shared bus, as shown in figure 1–1, is not sufficient, because it is often desirable to allow all processors to send data to other processors simultaneously (for example, from processor i to processor $i + 1$, $0 \le i < N - 1$). Ideally, each processor should be linked directly to every other processor so that the system is completely connected, as shown for $N = 8$ in figure 1–2. In this example, it could be assumed that each node is a processor with its own memory, or that even-numbered nodes are processors and odd-numbered nodes are memories. Unfortunately, these configurations are highly impractical when N is large because $N - 1$ unidirectional lines are required for each processor. For example, if $N = 2^{10}$, then $2^{10} * (2^{10} - 1) = 1,047,552$ unidirectional links would be needed.

An alternative interconnection scheme that allows all processors to communicate simultaneously is the crossbar network shown in figure 1–3. In this example, the processors communicate through the memories. The network may be viewed as a set of intersecting lines, where interconnections

1

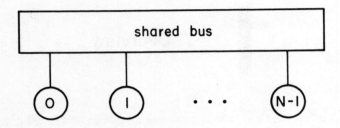

Figure 1–1. A Single Shared Bus Providing Communications for N Devices

between processors and memories are specified by the crosspoint switches at each line intersection (Thurber 1979). The difficulty with crossbar networks is that N^2 crosspoint switches are needed. As a result, the cost of the network grows with N^2, which, given current technology, makes it infeasible for large systems.

To solve the problem of providing fast, efficient communications at a reasonable cost, many different networks between the extremes of the single bus and the completely connected scheme have been proposed in the literature. There is no single network that is generally considered best. The cost-effectiveness of a particular network design depends on such factors as the computational tasks for which it will be used, the desired speed of inter-processor data transfers, the actual hardware implementation of the network, the number of processors in the system, and any cost constraints on the construction. A variety of networks have been proposed and are over-viewed in numerous survey articles and books (see, for example, Anderson and Jensen 1975; Baer 1976, 1980; Enslow 1977; Feng 1981; Hockney and Jeshope 1981; Kuck 1977, 1978; Masson, Gingher, and Nakamura 1979; Siegel, McMillen, and Mueller 1979; Thurber and Masson 1979; Thurber and Wald 1975; Thurber 1978).

This book is an in-depth study of a collection of network designs that can be used to support large-scale parallelism. That is, these networks can provide the communications needed in a parallel-processing system con-sisting of a large number of processors (in the 2^6 to 2^{16} range, for example) that are working together to perform a single overall task. Many of these networks can be used in dynamically reconfigurable machines that can per-form independent multiple tasks, where each task is processed using paral-lelism.

The networks explored here are based on the shuffle-exchange, cube, PM2I (plus-minus 2^i), and Illiac (nearest-neighbor) interconnection pat-terns. They are defined in chapter 2. Chapter 2 also presents models of dif-ferent types of parallel machines. Chapters 3 and 4 are investigations of

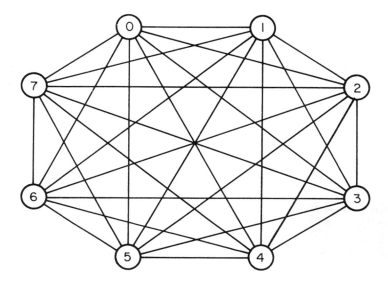

Figure 1-2. A Completely Connected System for $N = 8$

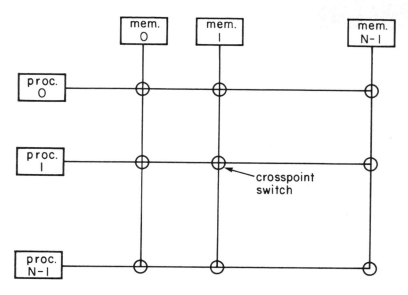

Figure 1-3. A Crossbar Network Connecting N Processors to N Memories

these networks when implemented by a single stage of switches. The capability of each of these networks to permute data among processors is examined in chapter 3. Chapter 4 presents the ways in which these networks can be partitioned for use in reconfigurable systems. Chapters 5 and 6 are studies of two families of multistage networks. The multistage cube/shuffle-exchange networks are examined in chapter 5. In chapter 6, data manipulator type networks, which are multistage implementations of the PM2I connection patterns, are analyzed. Chapters 2, 3, and 4 provide the theoretical foundation for the rest of the book. Chapters 3 and 4 also include case studies of single-stage networks. Chapters 5 and 6 present case studies of multistage networks.

The proposed or existing networks incorporating the shuffle-exchange, cube, PM2I, or Illiac types of connection patterns include the data manipulator (Feng 1974), ADM (Siegel and Smith 1978), IADM (Siegel and McMillen 1981a), gamma (Parker and Raghavendra 1982), omega (Lawrie 1975), perfect shuffle (Stone 1971), mesh (Nassimi and Sahni 1981), generalized-cube (Siegel and McMillen 1981c), extra-stage cube (Adams and Siegel 1982b), SW-banyan (Goke and Lipovski 1973), delta (Patel 1981), flip (Batcher 1976), indirect binary n-cube (Pease 1977), Benes (Benes 1965), and baseline (Wu and Feng 1980). This set of networks encompasses the types used in many current systems and proposed for use in a variety of machine designs, including: MPP (Batcher 1982), DAP (Hunt 1981), CLIP4 (Fountain 1981), BASE 8 (Reeves and Rindfuss 1979), Illiac IV (Bouknight and others 1972), Novel Multiprocessor Array (Okada, Tajimi, and Mori 1982), Omen (Higbie 1972), SIMDA (Wester 1972), RAP (Couranz, Gerhardt, and Young 1974), STARAN (Batcher 1977b), DISP (Filip 1982), CHoPP (Sullivan, Bashkow, and Klappholz 1977), PASM (Siegel and others 1981), PUMPS (Briggs and others 1982), the Ballistic Missile Defense Agency distributing-processing test bed (Siegel and McMillen 1981b), Ultracomputer (Gottlieb and others 1983), Burrough's proposed Flow Model Processor for the Numerical Aerodynamic Simulator (Barnes and Lundstrom 1981), and data-flow machines (Dennis, Boughton, and Leung 1980). Thus, the information in this book will provide knowledge and insights that will aid in the understanding of all of these networks and systems.

2 Interconnection Networks and Parallel-Machine Models

This chapter presents the models of parallel-computation systems and interconnection networks to be used in this book. The interconnection networks section includes the types of connection patterns used in many networks that have been proposed to support large-scale parallelism. The goal of the sections on parallel-machine models is to provide a brief introduction to the ways in which large-scale parallel-processing systems can be organized. The SIMD mode of parallelism is emphasized because it is used as a basis for the interconnection network definitions and the theoretical developments in chapters 3 and 4.

SIMD machines are discussed in three sections. First, the general architecture of typical SIMD machines is examined. Next, examples of the way in which SIMD machines can be used to perform tasks are given. Finally, a formal mathematical model of an SIMD machine is presented. In the following section, the model of SIMD machines is used as a basis for defining the interconnection networks studied in this book. Then there is a discussion of multiple-SIMD machines and their advantages over SIMD machines. A model of MIMD systems and a comparison of the MIMD and SIMD modes of parallelism are given in the next section. The last section of the chapter describes a model of partitionable-SIMD/MIMD machines, which permit the use of SIMD, MIMD, and multiple-SIMD parallelism.

Organization of SIMD Machines

SIMD stands for single-instruction stream–multiple-data stream. Typically, an SIMD machine is a computer system consisting of a control unit, N processors, N memory modules, and an interconnection network. The control unit broadcasts instructions to the processors, and all active (enabled) processors execute the same instruction at the same time. Thus, there is a single instruction stream. Each active processor executes the instruction on data in its own associated memory module. Thus, there are multiple data streams. The interconnection network, sometimes referred to as an alignment or permutation network, allows communication among the processors and memory modules.

These machines are designed to exploit the parallelism of such tasks as matrix operations and such problem domains as image-processing, where

5

the same operation is performed on many different matrix or image elements. The category of SIMD machines was defined in Flynn (1966). General information about SIMD systems can be found in such textbooks as Baer (1980), Hockney and Jeshope (1981), Hwang and Briggs (1984), Stone (1980), and Thurber (1976). Examples of SIMD machines that have been constructed are the Illiac IV (Bouknight and others 1972) and STARAN (Batcher 1974). The word size that each processor in an SIMD machine operates on varies from system to system—for example, the Illiac IV used 64-bit words and STARAN uses 1-bit words. As an example of the possible size of SIMD machines, the recently constructed MPP system includes 2^{14} simple processing units (Batcher 1980, 1982).

One way to view the physical structure of an SIMD machine is as a set of N processing elements interconnected by a network and fed instructions by a control unit. Each *processing element* (*PE*) consists of a processor with its own memory. This configuration, shown in figure 2–1, is called the *processing-element-to-processing-element* organization. The network is unidirectional and connects each PE to all or some subset of the other PEs. A transfer instruction moves data from each PE to one or more of the PEs to which that PE is connected by the network. To move data between two PEs that are not directly connected, the data must be passed through intermediary PEs by executing a programmed sequence of data transfers. For example, assume PE 0 is connected only to PE 1, and PE 1 is connected only to PE 2. To move a data item from PE 0 to PE 2, the data item must pass through PE 1. The processing-element-to-processing-element type of organization is used in the Illiac IV SIMD machine (Barnes and others 1968; Bouknight and others 1972).

An alternative SIMD-machine organization is to position the network between the processors and the memories. This type of configuration, shown in figure 2–2, is called the *processor-to-memory* organization. In this case the interconnection network is bidirectional—it both connects each processor to all or some subset of memories, as well as each memory to all or some subset of processors. A transfer instruction results in data being moved from each processor to one or more of the memories to which that processor is connected by the network, or from each memory to one or more of the processors to which that memory is connected by the network. One processor can transfer data to another processor through any memory to which both are connected. To pass data between two processors, a programmed sequence of data transfers must be executed. This sequence of transfers moves the data from one processor to the other by passing the data through intermediary memories (and possibly processors). For example, assume processor i is connected to memory $i - 1$, memory i, and memory $i + 1$. Then processor 1 can communicate with processor 3 through memory 2. One way for processor 1 to communicate with processor 5 is by using

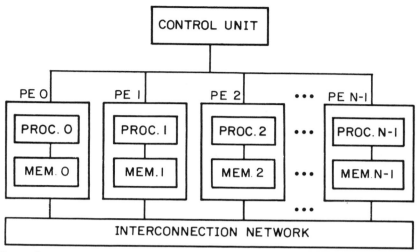

Figure 2–1. Processing-Element-to-Processing-Element SIMD-Machine Configuration with N Processing Elements (PEs)

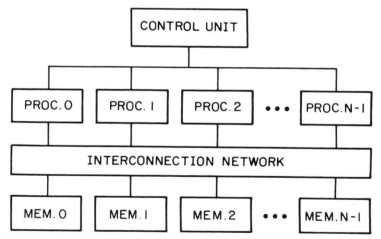

Figure 2–2. Processor-to-Memory SIMD-Machine Configuration with N Processors and N Memories

memory 2, processor 3, and memory 4 as intermediaries. In general, the number of processors and memories does not have to be the same. The processor-to-memory configuration is used in the TRAC partitionable-SIMD/MIMD machine (Kapur, Premkumar, and Lipovski 1980).

Variations of these basic configurations have also been proposed. In the BSP SIMD machine (Kuck and Stokes 1982; Lawrie and Vora 1982), a dual unidirectional network scheme to connect processors and memories was proposed, as shown in figure 2–3. Another variation is used in the STARAN SIMD machine (Batcher 1974, 1976, 1977a, 1977b), where a uni-directional network supports both processor-to-memory and processor-to-processor communications, as shown in figure 2–4.

The processing-element-to-processing-element paradigm will be used in this book. The results presented, however, will be applicable to the other structures. The next section provides examples of the way in which an SIMD machine can be used.

The Use of SIMD Machines

To demonstrate how SIMD machines operate, consider the following simple task. Assume that each of X, Y, and Z is a one-dimensional array (vector) of N elements and that the task to be performed is the elementwise addition of X and Y, storing the result in Z. In a uniprocessor (serial) system, this task can be expressed as:

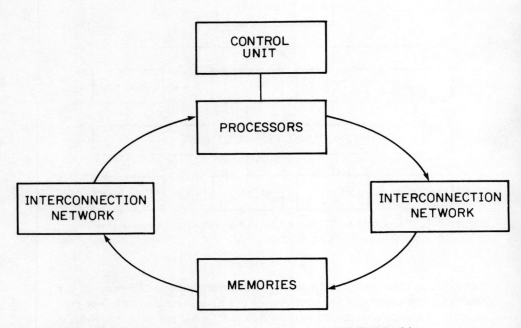

Figure 2–3. Dual Network Processor-to-Memory SIMD-Machine Configuration

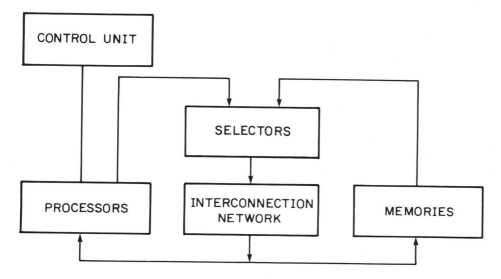

Figure 2-4. Machine Configuration Used in STARAN

$$\text{for } i = 0 \text{ until } N - 1 \text{ do}$$
$$Z(i) \leftarrow X(i) + Y(i)$$

This computation will take N steps on a serial machine because the body of the loop is executed N times.

Assume that X, Y, and Z are stored in an SIMD machine with N PEs, such that $X(i)$, $Y(i)$, and $Z(i)$ are all stored in the memory of PE i, $0 \le i < N$ as shown in figure 2-5. To perform an elementwise addition of the vectors X and Y and store the result in Z, all PEs would execute (simultaneously)

$$Z \leftarrow X + Y$$

with PE i doing the addition of $X(i)$ and $Y(i)$, storing the result in $Z(i)$, for all i, $0 \le i < N$. That is, each PE adds the X and Y elements in its memory and stores the sum in the Z location in its memory. Because there are N elements in each of X, Y, and Z, there are N PEs, each PE does only one addition. Thus, in this case, the SIMD machine does in one step a task requiring N steps on a serial processor.

Consider a variation on this example. Assume the N-step serial task is:

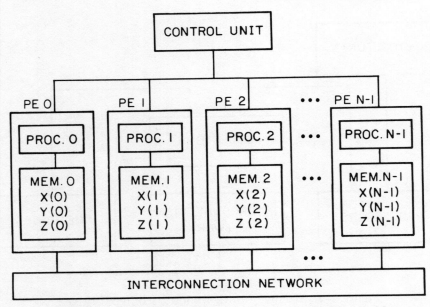

Figure 2-5. Storing Vectors X, Y, and Z in an SIMD Machine

$$\text{for } i = 1 \text{ until } N - 1 \text{ do}$$
$$Z(i) \leftarrow X(i) + Y(i - 1)$$
$$Z(0) \leftarrow X(0)$$

Given the data allocation shown in figure 2–5, an SIMD machine performs this task in three different steps:

1. The value of $Y(i - 1)$ is moved through the interconnection network from PE $i - 1$ to PE i, $1 \le i < N$. Most proposed and existing SIMD interconnection networks allow all of these PEs do this in one parallel data transfer (Siegel 1979a). In other words, while PE 1 sends $Y(1)$ to PE 2, PE 2 sends $Y(2)$ to PE 3, and so on.
2. In PE i, add $X(i)$ to $Y(i - 1)$ and store the result in $Z(i)$, $1 \le i < N$ (PE 0 is inactive).
3. In PE 0, store $X(0)$ in $Z(0)$ (all other PEs are inactive).

This example demonstrates the need for the interconnection network and for methods for selectively activating and deactivating PEs.

A slightly more complex processing example illustrates the concepts involved in using SIMD parallelism for image processing. In particular, the following example explores the smoothing of an image (Siegel and others 1981). Often, an image is smoothed to remove "noise." This algorithm smooths a gray-level black and white (as opposed to color) input image. The algorithm presented has h as an input image and hs as an output image. Assume both h and hs contain 512-by-512 *pixels* (picture elements), for a total of 512^2 pixels each. Each pixel of h is an 8-bit unsigned integer representing one of 256 possible gray levels. The gray level of each pixel indicates how dark that pixel is, where 0 means white and 255 means black. Each point in the smoothed image $hs(i,j)$ is the average of the gray levels of $h(i,j)$ and its eight nearest neighbors, $h(i-1,j-1)$, $h(i-1,j)$, $h(i-1,j+1)$, $h(i,j-1)$, $h(i,j+1)$, $h(i+1,j-1)$, $h(i+1,j)$, and $h(i+1,j+1)$. The top, bottom, left, and right edge pixels of hs are not calculated because their corresponding pixels in h do not have eight adjacent neighbors.

Consider how this task could be implemented on an SIMD machine with $N = 1024$ PEs. Assume that the 1024 PEs are logically arranged as an array of 32-by-32 PEs, where $32 = \sqrt{1024}$, and that the PE addresses (numbers) range from 0 to 1023 (figure 2–6A). Each PE stores a 16-by-16 subimage block of the 512-by-512 image h. Thus, each of the 1024 PEs holds $16^2 = 512^2/1024$ pixels. Specifically, PE 0 stores the pixels in columns 0 to 15 of rows 0 to 15, PE 1 stores the pixels in columns 16 to 31 of rows 0 to 15, and so on. In general, suppose $N = 2^m$ PEs operate on a picture of 2^k-by-2^k pixels. The PEs are logically arranged as a $2^{m/2}$-by-$2^{m/2}$ array, where $m/2$ is an integer, such that each PE stores in its memory a block of pixels of size $2^{k-(m/2)}$-by-$2^{k-(m/2)}$. The smoothed image hs is stored similarly.

For notational purposes, let each PE consider its 16-by-16 subimage array as:

$$h' = \begin{bmatrix} h'(0,0) & \cdots & h'(0,14)\ h'(0,15) \\ & \cdots & \\ h'(15,0) & \cdots & h'(15,15) \end{bmatrix}$$

Each PE treats its block of hs, call it hs', similarly. Also, let the subscripts of $h'(i,j)$ extend to -1 and 16 to aid in calculations across boundaries of two adjacent subimage blocks in different PEs. For example, the pixel to the left of $h'(0,0)$ in PE 1 is $h'(0,-1)$, which is $h'(0,15)$ in PE 0, and the pixel below $h'(15,15)$ in PE 1 is $h'(16,15)$, which is $h'(0,15)$ in PE 33. Therefore, $-1 \le i,j \le 16$.

The algorithm that each PE performs to smooth its pixel $h'(i,j)$ to yield smoothed pixel $hs'(i,j)$ is:

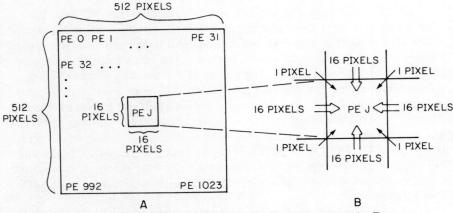

Figure 2–6. Image-Smoothing in an SIMD Environment. A. Data
allocation for smoothing a 512-by-512 image using 1024 PEs.
B. Data transfers needed to smooth edge pixels in each PE

for i = 0 until 15 do

    for j = 0 until 15 do

$$hs'(i,j) \leftarrow [h'(i - 1,j - 1) + h'(i - 1,j) + h'(i - 1,j + 1)$$
$$+ \; h'(i,j - 1) + h'(i,j)$$
$$h'(i,j + 1) + h'(i + 1,j - 1) + h'(i + 1,j)$$
$$+ \; h'(i + 1,j + 1)]/9$$

All PEs execute this algorithm simultaneously, each on its own subimage.
The approach is to perform 1024 16-by-16 pixel-smoothing algorithms in
parallel rather than one 512-by-512 pixel-smoothing algorithm as in the
serial algorithm.

At the edges of each 16-by-16 subimage, data must be transmitted
between PEs to calculate the smoothed value hs'. For example, $h'(0,16)$
must be transferred to the local PE from the PE on its right (except for PEs
31, 63, 95, . . . , 1023—that is, those at the right edge of the logical array of
PEs, because pixels on the edges of the 512-by-512 array h are not
smoothed). The necessary data transfers are shown for PE J in figure 2–6B.
As in the second vector-addition example, transfers between different PEs
can occur simultaneously. For example, when PE $J - 1$ sends its $h'(0,15)$
to PE J (because it is PE J's $h'(0, -1)$), PE J can send its $h'(0,15)$ to PE
$J + 1$, PE $J + 1$ can send its $h'(0,15)$ to PE $J + 2$, and so on.

To perform a smoothing operation on a 512-by-512 image by the parallel smoothing of 1024 subimage blocks of size 16-by-16, $16^2 = 256$ parallel-smoothing operations are performed. As described, the neighbors of the subimage-edge pixels must be transferred in from adjacent PEs. The total number of parallel data element transfers needed is $(4 * 16) + 4 = 68$; 16 for each of the top, bottom, left, and right edges, and four for the corners (see figure 2–6B). The corresponding serial algorithm needs no data transfers between PEs, but $512^2 = 262,144$ smoothing calculations must be performed. If no data transfers were needed, the parallel algorithm would be faster than the serial algorithm by a factor of $262,144/256 = 1024 = N$. If it is assumed that each parallel data transfer requires at most as much time as one smoothing operation, then the time-factor improvement is $262,144/324 = 809$. That is, the parallel algorithm is about three orders of magnitude faster than the serial algorithm. This approximation of the inter-PE transfer time is conservative, because calculating the addresses of the nine pixels for each smoothing operation involves nine multiplications using the subscripts (Gries 1971). Thus, the overhead of the 68 inter-PE transfers that must be performed in the SIMD machine is negligible compared to the reduction from 262,144 to 256 smoothing operations.

These simple examples serve to introduce SIMD programs. Other examples from the image- and speech-processing domains include two-dimensional FFTs (Mueller, Siegel, and Siegel 1980b; Siegel 1981), Hadamard transforms (Krygiel 1976), image correlation (Siegel, Siegel, and Feather 1982), histogramming (Siegel and others 1981), resampling (Warpenburg and Siegel 1982), one-dimensional FFTs (Stone 1971), linear-predictive coding (Siegel and others 1980), and dynamic time warping (Yoder and Siegel 1982). Techniques for evaluating the performance of SIMD algorithms are discussed in Siegel, Siegel, and Swain (1982).

Model of SIMD Machine Architectures

The model of an SIMD machine presented here consists of five parts: processing elements, control-unit instructions, processing-element instructions, masking schemes, and interconnection functions. It is a mathematical model that provides a common formal basis for evaluating and comparing the various components of different SIMD machines. This model is based on the one presented in Siegel (1979b).

Processing Element

Each *processing element* (*PE*) is a processor together with its own memory. It is assumed that the processor contains at least three fast-access general-purpose registers referred to as *A, B,* and *C.* There is also a *data transfer register (DTR).* The DTR of each PE is connected to the DTRs of the other PEs via the interconnection network. When data transfers among PEs occur, it is the DTR contents of each PE that are transferred. There are N PEs, each assigned an address (number) from 0 to $N - 1$, where $N = 2^m$—that is $\log_2 N = m$, as shown in figure 2-1. It is further assumed that each PE has a register *ADDR* which contains the address of that PE. A PE is shown in figure 2-7.

An alternative PE organization would have two DTRs in each processor, one for sending data into the network and one for receiving data from the network. In the following chapters, the single DTR organization is assumed in the various SIMD machine algorithms for two reasons: (1) the algorithms can easily be made to operate for the two DTR organization by adding an instruction to move the data from the PE input DTR to the PE output DTR immediately after each interprocessor data transfer; and (2) the single DTR implementation exhibits interesting problems that the two DTR organization does not, as will be discussed later in chapter 3.

At any given time, each PE is either in the active or the inactive mode.

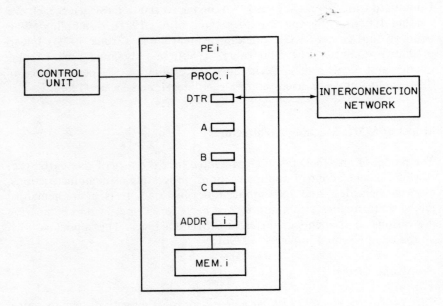

Figure 2-7. Processing Element (PE) *i*

If a PE is *active,* it executes the instructions broadcast to it by the control unit. If a PE is *inactive,* it will not execute the instructions broadcast to it. (*Enabled* and *disabled* are used as synonyms for active and inactive, respectively.) Masking schemes, which are defined later in this section, are used to specify which PEs will be active.

Control-Unit Instructions

The *control unit* stores the SIMD programs, executes control of flow instructions, and broadcasts processing-element instructions to the PEs. An example of a control flow instruction is the loop statement

$$\text{for } i = 0 \text{ until } 15 \text{ do } \ldots$$

in the earlier image-smoothing example. The loop index i is a control-unit variable. It is incremented and compared to the upper limit of 15 by the control unit.

Instructions to be executed by the PEs, such as the smoothing operations in the previous example, are broadcast from the control unit to the PEs. When the control unit broadcasts an instruction, all active PEs execute that same instruction at the same time, each PE operating on data in its own registers or memory The control-unit instructions dictate what instructions are broadcast from the control unit to the PEs.

For the purposes of this general model, these functions are all that need to be assumed about the control unit. The details of control units can differ depending on overall system design and intended machine applications. For example, see the papers about the STARAN (Batcher 1974), Illiac IV (Bouknight and others 1972), PEPE (Vick and Cornell 1978), and PASM (Kuehn, Siegel and Hallenbeck 1982) systems.

Processing-Element Instructions

The *processing-element instructions* component of the SIMD model consists of those operations which each processor can perform on data in its individual memory or registers. All active PEs execute the instruction broadcast by the control unit at the same time, but on different data. It is assumed the set of processing-element instructions includes the capability to move data among the registers. The notation $Z \leftarrow Y$ means the contents of register Y are copied into register Z, where Z and Y could be A, B, C, or DTR. The notation $Z \leftrightarrow Y$ is an abbreviation for two registers exchanging their contents (for example, by using a third register for temporary storage).

Masking Schemes

A *masking scheme* is a method for determining which PEs will be active at a given time. An SIMD machine may have several different masking schemes. The masking scheme provides the system user with a mechanism to enable some PEs and disable others. Each mask partitions the set of PE addresses, the integers $0, 1, \ldots, N - 1$, into two sets: those PEs which are active and those PEs which are inactive. The union of the activated set and the deactivated set must be the set of all PEs. For some masking schemes, the set of PEs that can be activated by a single mask is any member of the "power set" of the integers $0, 1, \ldots, N - 1$—that is, any arbitrary subset of the PEs. For example, one way to specify the desired active or inactive status of the PEs is to use an N-bit vector, where if bit i of the vector is 1, then PE i is activated, and if bit i of the vector is 0, then PE i is deactivated, $0 \le i < N$. This method is used in the Illiac IV SIMD machine where there are 64 PEs and 64-bit words (Stevens 1975). However, when N is large this method becomes cumbersome. For other schemes, the set of PEs that can be activated by a single mask is more restricted. The two masking schemes used here are PE address masks and data-conditional masks.

The *PE address masking* scheme (Siegel 1977) uses an m-position mask to specify which PEs are to be activated, each position of the mask corresponding to a bit position in the binary addresses of the PEs. Each position of the mask will contain either a 0, 1, or X ("don't care"). The only PEs that will be active are those which match the mask in the following way: for all i, $0 \le i < m$, if the mask has a 0 in the ith position, then the PE address must have a 0 in the ith position; if the mask has a 1 in the ith position, then the PE address must have a 1 in the ith position; and if the mask has an X in the ith position, then the PE address may have either a 0 or 1 in the ith position.

For example, if $N = 8$ (so $m = 3$) and the mask is $1X0$, then only PEs 6 (110 in binary) and 4 (100 in binary) would be active. Superscripts are used as repetition factors—for example, $X^3 01^2$ is $XXX011$. Square brackets will be used to denote a mask. Consider the following examples of sets of PEs that can be activated, where $0 \le i < m$:

Even-numbered PEs: $[X^{m-1}0]$

Odd-numbered PEs: $[X^{m-1}1]$

The first 2^i PEs: $[0^{m-i}X^i]$

The last 2^i PEs: $[1^{m-i}X^i]$

Every 2^ith PE beginning with PE 0: $[X^{m-i}0^i]$

Every 2^ith PE beginning with PE J, $J < 2^i$, and $J = j_{i-1} \ldots j_1 j_0$: $[X^{m-i}j_{i-1} \ldots j_1 j_0]$

PE address masks are specified in the SIMD machine program. These masks can be broadcast by the control unit and decoded by each PE, based on its own address. Alternatively, the masks can be decoded by the control unit, which would compute and transmit an active or inactive status bit for each PE (Kuehn, Siegel, and Hallenbeck 1982; Siegel and others 1981). Each processing-element instruction and interconnection function (defined in the next subsection) could be accompanied by a mask specifying which PEs will execute that command. An alternative would be to execute a mask instruction whenever a change in the active status of the PEs is required. A compiler or assembler could be used to convert from one method to the other. For the sake of clarity, each instruction in the algorithms in chapter 3 will be accompanied by a mask. For example, executing:

$$A \leftarrow B + C \qquad [X^{m-1}1]$$

causes each PE with an odd-numbered address to add to contents of B and C and store the sum in A.

PE address masks require only $2m$ bits to be represented in an easily decodable fashion and therefore are a concise way to specify which PEs are to be activated. However, PE address masks are restricted in that an arbitrary subset of PEs cannot necessarily be activated by a single PE address mask because there are 2^N different subsets of the PEs (each of the N PEs can be either active or inactive), while there are only 3^m different PE address masks (each of the m positions can be 0, 1, or X). For example, no single PE address mask exists that can activate PEs 0 and 3, and only those PEs, for $N \geq 4$. Even though PE address masks cannot activate all of the possible 2^N subsets of PEs, they are quite useful because the subsets of PEs to be activated in actual algorithms are generally regular in form, not arbitrary. Variations on PE address masks that increase their flexibility and examples of their use are given in Siegel and others (1981). PE address masks are used in the algorithms in chapter 3.

Another masking scheme is data-conditional masking. *Data-conditional masks* are the implicit result of performing a conditional branch dependent on data local to (that is, stored in) the PEs. Whenever such a conditional statement is broadcast by the control unit, each PE may be executing it with different data, so the outcome may differ from one PE to the next. The notation:

where (data condition) do . . . elsewhere . . .

will be used to indicate a data conditional mask (Mueller, Siegel, and Siegel 1980a). These data-conditional masks are also called *where statements*. They are broadcast by the control unit as part of the instruction stream. As a result of a where statement, each PE sets its own internal flag to activate itself for either the do statements or the elsewhere statements, but not both. Because there is a single instruction stream, the broadcasting of the elsewhere statements follows the do statements; that is, the do and elsewhere statements cannot be executed simultaneously.

For example, as a result of executing the statement:

$$\text{where } A > B \text{ do } C \leftarrow A \text{ elsewhere } C \leftarrow B$$

each PE loads its C register with the maximum of its A and B registers; that is, some PEs execute $C \leftarrow A$ and then the rest execute $C \leftarrow B$. This type of masking is used in such machines as the Illiac IV (Barnes and others 1968; Bouknight and others 1972; Lawrie and others 1975; Stevens 1975) and the PEPE (Crane and others 1972; Wilson 1972). Where statements can be nested using an execution-time control stack (Siegel and Mueller 1978).

Data-conditional masks can be made to activate any set of the PEs. For example, recall that each PE has its own address, an integer from 0 to $N - 1$, stored in a register called ADDR. To force PEs w and y to execute statement S, use the conditional:

$$\text{where } ((ADDR = w) \text{ or } (ADDR = y)) \text{ do } S \text{ elsewhere null.}$$

When the elsewhere is null, it can be omitted.

Because data-conditional statements are an essential part of all programming languages, it is reasonable to assume they would be present in an SIMD machine. They are used, in addition to PE address masks, in chapter 3. The results of chapter 3 would still be valid even if only data-conditional masks were used because if each PE knows its own address, data-conditional masks can be used to simulate PE address masks using no additional interprocessor data transfers.

When PE address masks and data-conditional masks are used together, PE address masks must accompany each instruction in the do and elsewhere blocks. For a PE to be active it must be in active mode as a result of the where statement and also match the PE address mask accompanying the instruction.

Interconnection Networks

An *interconnection network* can be described by a set of interconnection functions. Each *interconnection function* is a bijection (permutation) on the set of PE addresses. When an interconnection function f is applied, PE i sends the contents of its DTR to the DTR of PE $f(i)$. This move occurs for all i simultaneously, for $0 \le i < N$ and PE i active. Saying that an interconnection function is a bijection means that every PE sends data to exactly one PE, and every PE receives data from exactly one PE (assuming all PEs are active). In this model, it is assumed that an inactive PE can receive data from another PE if an interconnection function is executed, but an inactive PE cannot send data. The implications of this assumption in terms of DTR data being overwritten are discussed in the first section of chapter 3.

To pass data from one PE to another PE a programmed sequence of one or more interconnection functions must be executed. This sequence of functions moves the data from one PE's DTR to the other's by a single transfer or by passing the data through intermediary PEs. For example, let one of the interconnection functions f in an interconnection network be defined by $f(P) = P + 1$ modulo N, $0 \le P < N$, where P is a PE address. When f is applied, PE 0 transfers the contents of its DTR to the DTR of PE $f(0) = 1$, PE 1 transfers the contents of its DTR to the DTR of PE $f(1) = 2, \ldots$, and PE $N - 1$ transfers the contents of its DTR to the DTR of PE $f(N - 1) = 0$. These transfers occur simultaneously. To pass data from PE P to PE $P + 2$ modulo N, $0 \le P < N$, f can be executed twice. Another interconnection function in this network might be $g(P) = P - 1$ modulo N, $0 \le P < N$. When g is applied, PE 0 transfers the contents of its DTR to the DTR of PE $g(0) = N - 1$, PE 1 transfers the contents of its DTR to the DTR of PE $g(1) = 0 \ldots$, PE $N - 1$ transfers the contents of its DTR to the DTR of PE $g(N - 1) = N - 2$.

An interconnection function f mathematically maps the address P to the address $f(P)$. For the previous example, f maps the address P to the address $P + 1$ modulo N. Thus, saying an interconnection network *maps the address x to the address y* is equivalent to saying that it causes PE x to pass its data to PE y. The former is a mathematical description, the latter is a physical description.

Interconnection functions are part of an SIMD program, as are processing-element instructions. Each interconnection function specified in an SIMD program is an instruction to perform an inter-PE data transfer. These instructions set the interconnection network switches and transfer the data between PEs. The network switches can be set by the control unit, such as in the STARAN SIMD machine (Batcher 1976), or by the PEs (using such techniques as routing tags, which are discussed in chapters 5 and 6). The four particular interconnection networks defined in the next section (Illiac, PM2I, shuffle-exchange, and cube) will be studied in chapters 3 through 6.

Summary

In summary, an SIMD machine can be formally represented as the five-tuple (N,C,I,M,F), where:

1. N is a positive integer, representing the number of processing elements in the machine.
2. C is the set of control-unit instructions—that is, instructions executed by the control unit to control the flow of the program.
3. I is the set of processing-element instructions—that is, instructions that can be executed by each active PE and act on data within that PE.
4. M is the set of masking schemes, where each mask partitions the set $\{0, 1, \ldots, N - 1\}$ into two disjoint sets, the enabled PEs and the disabled PEs.
5. F is the set of interconnection functions (or the interconnection network), where each function is a bijection on the set $\{0, 1, \ldots, N - 1\}$, which determines the communication links among the PEs.

A particular SIMD machine architecture can be described by specifying N, C, I, M, and F. In this book, $N = 2^m$; C includes "for . . . until . . . step . . . do" instructions for controlling loops in the program; I includes instructions for moving data among the DTR and other registers of the same PE; M includes PE address and data-conditional masks; and F is varied. The assumptions made about the SIMD machine to be used as the model are intentionally minimal so that the material in this book is applicable to a wide range of machines.

The Interconnection Networks

The four types of interconnection networks studied in this book are the Illiac, the PM2I, the shuffle-exchange, and the cube. As indicated in chapter 1, these networks form the basis of a larger number of networks that have been used in systems or proposed in the literature. Interconnection networks can be constructed from a single stage of switches or multiple stages of switches. In a single-stage network, data items may have to be passed through the switches several times before reaching the final destinations. In a multistage network, generally one pass through the multiple (usually m) stages of switches is sufficient to transfer the data items to their final destinations.

The single-stage implementation of interconnection networks is used as a basis for the theoretical development in chapters 3 and 4. Their relation to multistage networks will be discussed in chapters 5 and 6. Conceptually, a a single-stage network can be viewed as N input selectors and N output selectors, as shown in figure 2.8. The way in which the input selectors are connected to the output selectors determines the allowable interconnections.

As a simple example, let an interconnection network consist of just the interconnection functions $f(P) = P + 1$ modulo N and $g(P) = P - 1$ modulo N, $0 \le P < N$, as defined in the last section. Consider a single-stage network implementation of this network based on the model in figure 2–8. Because this network has only two interconnection functions f and g, each input selector has only two outputs and each output selector has only two inputs. Specifically, input selector i has lines to output selectors $i + 1$ modulo N and $i - 1$ modulo N, for each i, $0 \le i < N$. Thus, output selector j gets its input from either input selector $j - 1$ modulo N or input selector $j + 1$ modulo N, for each j, $0 \le j < N$. For example, for $N \ge 4$, input selector 1 has lines to output selector 2 (using f) and output selector 0 (using g), and output selector 1 gets its input from either input selector 0 (using f) or input selector 2 (using g). To move data from, for example, PE k to PE $k + 2$ modulo N, $0 \le k < N$, the data items must pass through the network twice: first from PE k to PE $k + 1$, then from PE $k + 1$ to PE $k + 2$. That is, interconnection function f would be executed twice.

In this section, as each interconnection network is defined, its description as a single-stage network is also given. The relationship of this representation to the associated multistage network representations is described in chapters 5 and 6. The following notation are used: let $N = 2^m$; let

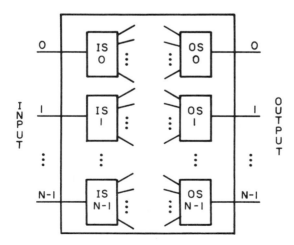

Note: *IS* is input selector; *OS* is output selector.

Figure 2–8. Conceptual View of a Single-Stage Network

the binary representation of an arbitrary PE address P be $p_{m-1}p_{m-2}\cdots$ p_1p_0; let $\bar{p}_i$ be the complement of p_i; and let the integer n be the square root of N. It is assumed throughout the book that $-j$ modulo $N = N - j$ modulo N, for $j > 0$; for example, -4 modulo $16 = 12$ modulo 16.

The Illiac Network

The *Illiac* network consists of four interconnection functions defined as follows:

$$\text{Illiac}_{+1}(P) = P + 1 \text{ modulo } N$$

$$\text{Illiac}_{-1}(P) = P - 1 \text{ modulo } N$$

$$\text{Illiac}_{+n}(P) = P + n \text{ modulo } N$$

$$\text{Illiac}_{-n}(P) = P - n \text{ modulo } N$$

where n (the square root of N) is assumed to be an integer. For example, if $N = 16$, $\text{Illiac}_{+n}(0) = 4$. This network allows PE P to send data to any one of PEs $P + 1$, PE $P - 1$, PE $P + \sqrt{N}$, or PE $P - \sqrt{N}$, arithmetic modulo N. If the PEs are considered as an n-by-n array, then each PE is connected to its north, south, east, and west neighbors, as shown for $N = 16$ in figure 2-9. This network is called the Illiac because it was implemented in the Illiac IV SIMD machine, where $N = 64$ (Barnes and others 1968; Bouknight and others 1972). It is often referred to as a four-nearest-neighbor connection pattern.

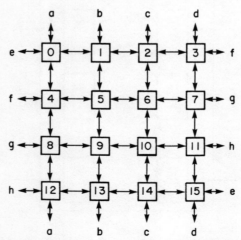

Note: The actual Illiac IV SIMD machine had $N = 64$. Vertical lines are $+\sqrt{N}$ and $-\sqrt{N}$. Horizontal lines are $+1$ and -1.

Figure 2-9. Illiac Network for $N = 16$

Relating this pattern to the conceptual model of a single-stage network shown in figure 2–8, for each i, $0 \leq i < N$, input selector i has lines to output selectors $i + 1$, $i - 1$, $i + \sqrt{N}$, and $i - \sqrt{N}$, modulo N. For each j, $0 \leq j < N$, output selector j gets its inputs from input selectors $j - 1$, $j + 1$, $j - \sqrt{N}$, and $j + \sqrt{N}$, modulo N. Because there is a single instruction stream in an SIMD machine, all active PEs must use the same interconnection function at the same time. For example, if PE 0 is sending data to PE 1, then all active PEs must send data using the Illiac$_{+1}$ connection.

This type of network is included in the MPP (Batcher 1980, 1982) and DAP (Hunt 1981) SIMD systems. It is similar to the eight-nearest-neighbor network used in the CLIP4 (Fountain 1981) and BASE 8 (Reeves and Rindfuss 1979) machines. The "mesh" interconnection network (Nassimi and Sahni 1979, 1980, 1981; Thompson and Kung 1977) is like the Illiac network except there are no "end-around" connections (that is, the connections indicated by the lower-case letters in figure 2–9 are not included). Various properties and capabilities of the Illiac network are discussed in Bouknight and others (1972), Gentleman (1978), Orcutt (1976), and Siegel (1977, 1978, 1979b, 1980).

The Plus-Minus 2^i (PM2I) Network

The *plus-minus 2^i* (*PM2I*) network consists of $2m$ interconnection functions defined by:

$$PM2_{+i}(P) = P + 2^i \text{ modulo } N$$

$$PM2_{-i}(P) = P - 2^i \text{ modulo } N$$

for $0 \leq i < m$. For example, PM2$_{+1}$(2) = 4 if $N > 4$. Because $P + 2^{m-1} = P - 2^{m-1}$, modulo N, for all P, $0 \leq P < N$, the interconnection functions PM2$_{+(m-1)}$ and PM2$_{-(m-1)}$ are equivalent. Figure 2–10 shows the PM2$_{+i}$ interconnections for $N = 8$. Diagrammatically, PM2$_{-i}$ is the same as PM2$_{+i}$ except the direction is reversed.

This network is called the plus-minus 2^i because in terms of mapping source addresses to destinations, it can add or subtract 2^i from the PE addresses; that is, it allows PE P to send data to any one of PE $P + 2^i$ or PE $P - 2^i$, arithmetic modulo N, $0 \leq i < m$. The network is a set of natural arithmetic functions on the PE addresses, allowing 1 to be added or subtracted from any bit position. In particular, the function PM2$_{+i}$ adds 1 to the ith bit position of the addresses and the function PM2$_{-i}$ subtracts 1 from the ith bit position of the addresses (arithmetic modulo N). The PM2I network is a superset of the Illiac network; that is, Illiac$_{+1}$ = PM2$_{+0}$, Illiac$_{-1}$ = PM2$_{-0}$, Illiac$_{+n}$ = PM2$_{m/2}$, and Illiac$_{-n}$ = PM2$_{-m/2}$.

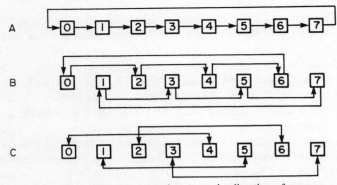

Note: For the PM2$_{-i}$ connections, $0 \leq i \leq 2$, reverse the direction of arrows.

Figure 2–10. PM2I Network for $N = 8$. A. PM2$_{+0}$ connections. B. PM2$_{+1}$ connections. C. PM2$_{+2}$ connections

In terms of the conceptual model of a single-stage network (figure 2–8), for the PM2I network, for each j, $0 \leq j < N$, input selector j is connected to output selectors $j + 2^i$ and $j - 2^i$ modulo N, for all i, $0 \leq i < m$. For each j, $0 \leq j < N$, output selector j gets its input from input selectors $j - 2^i$ and $j + 2^i$ modulo N, for all i, $0 \leq i < m$. As with the Illiac network, all active PEs must use the same PM2I interconnection function at the same time. For example, if one PE is using the $+2^0$ connection, all active PEs must use their $+2^0$ connection.

A similar network is used in the Novel Multiprocessor Array (Okada, Tajima, and Mori 1976, 1982) and is included in the network of the Omen computer (Higbie 1972). The concept underlying the SIMDA machine's interconnection network is similar to that of the PM2I (Wester 1972). The PM2I connection pattern forms the basis for the data manipulator (Feng 1974), ADM (Siegel and Smith 1978), IADM (Siegel and McMillen 1981a), and gamma (Parker and Raghavendra 1982) multistage networks. Various properties of the single-stage PM2I network are discussed in Fishburn and Finkel (1982), Pradhan and Kodandapani (1980), Siegel (1977, 1978, 1979b, 1980), Siegel and Smith (1979), and Smith and Siegel (1979).

The Shuffle-Exchange Network

The *shuffle-exchange* network consists of a shuffle function and an exchange function. The *shuffle* is defined by:

$$\text{shuffle } (p_{m-1}p_{m-2} \cdots p_1 p_0) = p_{m-2}p_{m-3} \cdots p_1 p_0 p_{m-1}$$

and the *exchange* is defined by:

$$\text{exchange}(p_{m-1}p_{m-2}\cdots p_1p_0) = p_{m-1}p_{m-2}\cdots p_1\bar{p}_0$$

For example, shuffle(3) = 6 and exchange(6) = 7, for $N \geq 8$. Shuffling a PE's address is equivalent to taking the left-cyclic end-around shift of its binary representation. The name "shuffle" has its origin in shuffling cards, by perfectly intermixing two halves of a deck, as shown in figure 2-11. Because of this perfect intermixing, the shuffle is often called the perfect shuffle. The exchange interconnection allows each PE to send data to the PE whose address differs from it in only the low-order bit position. This network is shown in figure 2-12 for $N = 8$, where the shuffle interconnections are shown by dashed lines and the exchange interconnections by solid lines. When the shuffle is used as a connection in a single-stage network, it is usually accompanied by an exchange connection. If it were not, both PE 0 and PE $N - 1$ could not communicate with any other PE.

Consider the conceptual model of single-stage networks shown in figure 2-8. For the shuffle-exchange single-stage network, input selector $P = p_{m-1}\cdots p_1p_0$ is connected to output selectors $p_{m-2}\cdots p_1p_0p_{m-1}$

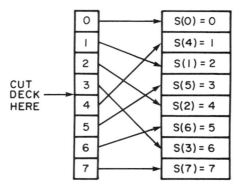

Note: S stands for shuffle.

Figure 2-11. Perfectly Shuffling a Deck of Eight Cards

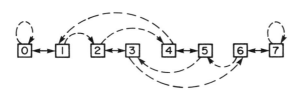

Note: Solid line is exchange; dashed line is shuffle.

Figure 2-12. Shuffle-Exchange Network for $N = 8$

$(= \text{shuffle}(P))$ and $p_{m-1} \ldots p_1 \bar{p}_0 (= \text{exchange}(P))$. Output selector g_{m-1} $\ldots g_1 g_0$ gets its inputs from selectors $g_0 g_{m-1} \ldots g_2 g_1$ and $g_{m-1} \ldots g_1 \bar{g}_0$. As with the other networks, all active PEs must use the same interconnection function at the same time. For example, if one PE shuffles, all active PEs must shuffle.

Mathematical properties of the shuffle are discussed in Golomb (1961) and Johnson (1956). The multistage omega network is a series of m shuffle-exchanges (Lawrie 1975). The shuffle is also included in the networks of the Omen (Higbie 1972) and RAP (Couranz, Gerhardt, and Young 1974) systems. Features of the single-stage shuffle-exchange network are discussed in Chen and others (1981, 1982), Fishburn and Finkel (1982), Gentleman (1978), Lang (1976), Lang and Stone (1976), Nassimi and Sahni (1981, 1982b), Pradhan and Kodandapani (1980), Siegel (1977, 1978, 1979b, 1980), Stone (1971), and Wu and Feng (1981).

The Cube Network

The *cube* network consists of m interconnection functions defined by:

$$\text{cube}_i(p_{m-1} \ldots p_{i+1} p_i p_{i-1} \ldots p_0) = p_{m-1} \ldots p_{i+1} \bar{p}_i p_{i-1} \ldots p_0$$

for $0 \leq i < m$. For example, $\text{cube}_2(7) = 3$. The cube interconnection functions for $N = 8$ are shown in figure 2–13.

This network is called the cube because when the PE addresses are considered as the corners of an m-dimensional cube, using appropriate labels, this network connects each PE to its m neighbors as shown in figure 2–14 for $N = 8$. In this figure, horizontal lines connect vertices whose labels differ in the 0th (low-order) bit position (cube$_0$), diagonal lines connect ver-

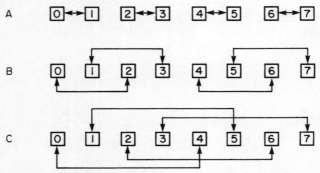

Figure 2–13. Cube Network for $N = 8$. A. Cube$_0$ connections. B. Cube$_1$ connections. C. Cube$_2$ connections

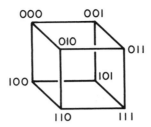

Note: Vertices are labeled from 0 to 7 in binary.

Figure 2-14. Three-Dimensional Cube Structure

tices that differ in the 1st (middle) bit position (cube$_1$), and vertical lines connect vertices that differ in the 2nd (high-order) bit position (cube$_2$).

In terms of mapping souce addresses to destinations, the cube interconnection function cube$_i$ complements the ith bit position of the PE addresses. The cube function cube$_0$ and the shuffle-exchange function exchange are identical. The cube network is a generalization of the exchange in that the exchange allows the complementing of the 0th bit position and the cube allows the complementing of any of the bit positions. That is, the cube network allows each PE to communicate with any of the m PEs whose addresses differ from it in any one bit position. This network is a set of natural logic functions on the PE addresses, allowing any bit position to be complemented.

Using the conceptual model of single-stage networks in figure 2-8, the cube network input selector $p_{m-1} \ldots p_1 p_0$ is connected to output selectors $p_{m-1} \ldots p_{i+1} \bar{p}_i p_{i-1} \ldots p_0$, for all i, $0 \le i < m$. Output selector $g_{m-1} \ldots g_1 g_0$ gets its inputs from input selectors $g_{m-1} \ldots g_{i+1} \bar{g}_i g_{i-1} \ldots g_0$, for all i, $0 \le i < m$. As in the other networks, only one cube interconnection function (that is, cube$_i$ for a fixed value of i) can be used at a time.

The cube network forms the underlying structure of many multistage networks, such as the SW-banyan ($S = F = 2$) (Goke and Lipovski 1973), STARAN flip (Batcher 1976; Bauer 1974), Beneš (Beneš 1965), indirect binary n-cube (Pease 1977), generalized cube (Siegel and McMillen 1981c; Siegel and Smith 1978), and the extra-stage cube (Adams and Siegel 1982b). The interconnection scheme proposed for use in the CHoPP MIMD machine (Sullivan, Bashkow, and Kappholz 1977) is based on the single-stage cube network. Various properties of the single-stage cube network are discussed in Fishburn and Finkel (1982), Nassimi and Sahni (1981, 1982a, 1982b), and Siegel (1977, 1978, 1979b, 1980).

Summary

Four single-stage interconnection networks have been defined: Illiac, PM2I, shuffle-exchange, and cube. In chapter 3, the capabilities and limitations of these four networks are compared by using each network to perform the connections defined by the other networks. This comparison will aid in developing an understanding of and intuition for the use of these networks. Chapter 4 describes the theory underlying the partionability of these networks into independent subnetworks. Multistage cube/shuffle-exchange networks and multistage PM2I networks are studied in chapters 5 and 6, respectively. In addition to SIMD machines, interconnection networks play an important role in other models of parallel architectures. These classes of architectures—multiple-SIMD, MIMD, and partitionable-SIMD/MIMD—are defined in the following sections.

Multiple-SIMD Machines

A *multiple-SIMD machine* is a parallel-processing system that can be dynamically reconfigured to operate as one or more independent virtual SIMD machines of various sizes. A multiple-SIMD system consists of N processors, N memory modules, an interconnection network, and Q control units, where $Q < N$. The processors, memories, and interconnection network can be organized in different ways, as they can in an SIMD machine (see the second section of this chapter). A general model of a multiple-SIMD machine, based on the processing-element-to-processing-element structure, is shown in figure 2–15. Each of the multiple control units can be connected to some subset of the PEs. If PE i and PE j are assigned to different control units, they are no longer following the same instruction stream and will act independently. By assigning PEs to control units, independent virtual SIMD machines of various sizes can be created. Examples of proposed systems capable of operating in the multiple-SIMD mode are MAP (Nutt 1977a, 1977b), PASM (Siegel, Mueller, and Smalley 1978; Siegel and others 1981), PM4 (Briggs and others 1979), and TRAC (Sejnowski and others 1980). The Illiac IV was originally designed to be a multiple-SIMD system (Barnes and others 1968). As one example of machine size, the proposed MAP machine involves eight control units and 1024 processors.

A multiple-SIMD system offers several possible advantages over an SIMD system with a similar number of PEs, including (Siegel and others 1981):

1. Fault detection. When high reliability is needed, three partitions can run the same program on the same data and compare results.

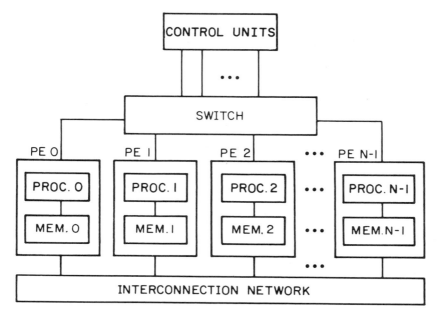

Figure 2–15. General Model of a Multiple-SIMD System

2. Fault tolerance. If a single PE fails, only those virtual SIMD machines (partitions) that include the failed PE are affected. The rest of the system can continue to function.
3. Multiple simultaneous users. Because there can be multiple independent virtual SIMD machines, there can be multiple simultaneous users of the system, each executing a different SIMD program.
4. Program development. Rather than trying to debug an SIMD program on, for example, 1024 PEs, a user can debug the program on a smaller-size virtual SIMD machine of 32 or 64 PEs.
5. Efficiency. If a task requires only $N/2$ of N available PEs, the other $N/2$ can be used for another task.
6. Subtask parallelism. Two or more independent SIMD subtasks that are part of the same job can be executed in parallel, sharing results if necessary.

As a result, a multiple-SIMD system is preferable in many environments to an SIMD system. If the virtual SIMD machines that can be formed in a multiple-SIMD system are to be independent, the network they share must be partitionable into independent subnetworks. As shown in chapter 4, the cube and PM2I single-stage networks can be partitioned to support multiple-SIMD parallelism. Chapter 5 and 6 show that the multistage cube/shuffle-exchange and multistage PM2I networks, respectively, can also support multiple-SIMD partitioning.

MIMD Machines

The acronym *MIMD* stands for *multiple-instruction stream–multiple-data stream*. Typically, an MIMD machine consists of N processors, N memory modules, and an interconnection network. Each of the N processors follows its own program. Thus, there are multiple instruction streams. Each processor fetches its own data on which to operate. Thus, there are multiple data streams, as in an SIMD system. The interconnection network provides communications among the processors and memory modules. While in an SIMD system all active processors use the interconnection network at the same time (that is, synchronously), in an MIMD system, because each processor is executing its own program, inputs to the network arrive independently (that is, asynchronously). Examples of MIMD systems that have been constructed are Cm* (Jones and others 1977; Swan and others 1977; Swan, Fuller, and Siewiorek 1977) and C.mmp (Wulf and Bell 1972). As an example of the possible size of an MIMD machine, the proposed CHoPP MIMD machine design is intended to support as many as 10^6 processors (Sullivan, Bashkow, and Klappholz 1977).

MIMD machines can be organized in the processing-element-to-processing-element configuration (for example, CHoPP) or in the processor-to-memory configuration (for example, C.mmp), indicated in figures 2–16 and 2–17, respectively. When using the processor-to-memory configuration, a local memory or cache can be associated with each processor—for example, as in Ultracomputer (Gottlieb and others 1983).

Basically, an MIMD machine includes a collection of independent processors that can be used to work together to do tasks faster than a single processor. More information about MIMD systems and their use can be found in such textbooks as Baer (1980), Hwang and Briggs (1984), and Stone (1980).

The MIMD mode of parallelism differs from the SIMD mode in that the processors in an MIMD system operate asynchronously with respect to each other, unlike the lock-step synchronous operation of all of the active processors in an SIMD machine. This increased flexibility of MIMD systems comes at the increased costs of overhead to perform synchronization when it is necessary (it is not implicit, as in SIMD systems) and of designing programs for each of the N processors (there may not be a single program, as in SIMD operation). However, certain problem domains are not appropriate to the single-instruction stream limitations of SIMD machines, and therefore justify MIMD costs.

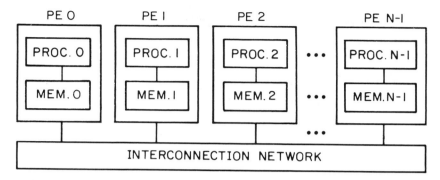

Figure 2–16. Processing-Element-to-Processing-Element MIMD-Machine Configuration with *N* Processing Elements

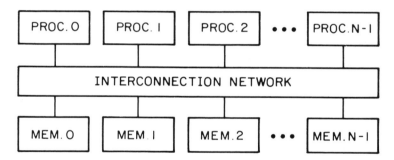

Figure 2–17. Processor-to-Memory MIMD-Machine Configuration with *N* Processors and *N* Memories

The single-stage interconnection networks presented earlier in this chapter can be used in an MIMD environment. For example, the use of the shuffle-exchange in an MIMD system is proposed and evaluated in Chen, Yew, and Lawrie (1982), and the cube is employed in the proposed CHoPP MIMD machine (Sullivan, Bashkow, and Kappholz 1977). In addition, the multistage cube/shuffle-exchange type of networks presented in chapter 5 has been proposed for use in MIMD systems—for example, in Ultracomputer (Gottlieb and others 1983), as has the multistage PM2I type of networks presented in chapter 6—such as the ADM network (McMillen and Siegel 1982c).

Partitionable-SIMD/MIMD Machines

A *partitionable-SIMD/MIMD machine* is a parallel-processing system that can be dynamically reconfigured to operate as one or more independent virtual SIMD and/or MIMD machines of various sizes. A partitionable-SIMD/MIMD machine has the same components as a multiple-SIMD machine except that each processor can follow its own instructions (MIMD operation) in addition to being capable of accepting an instruction stream from a control unit (SIMD operation). Like multiple-SIMD machines, the N processors, N memory modules, and interconnection network of a partitionable-SIMD/MIMD system can be partitioned to form independent virtual machines. In this case, each virtual machine can be an SIMD machine or an MIMD machine. Examples of proposed partitionable-SIMD/MIMD systems are PASM (Siegel, Mueller, and Smalley 1978; Siegel and others 1981), PM4 (Briggs and others 1979), and TRAC (Kapur, Premkumar, and Lipovski 1980; Premkumar and others 1980; and Sejnowski and others 1980). As an example of machine size, the proposed PASM system is designed for 1024 processors.

The processors, memories, and interconnection network can be organized in different ways, as they can in an SIMD machine. For example, PASM uses the processing-element-to-processing-element architecture and TRAC uses the processor-to-memory organization. The advantages of multiple-SIMD machines listed earlier also apply to partitionable-SIMD/MIMD systems, where each virtual machine (partition) can operate in either the SIMD or the MIMD mode of parallism. In addition, in a partitionable-SIMD/MIMD machine the same set of processors can switch between the SIMD and MIMD modes of parallelism when performing a task. For example, SIMD mode could be used to preprocess an image (for example, to remove noise or fill gaps) and then MIMD mode could be used to do a pattern-recognition task on the preprocessed image. Partitionable-SIMD/MIMD machines are very flexible parallel-processing systems. The networks capable of supporting multiple-SIMD machines listed earlier can also be adapted for use in partitionable-SIMD/MIMD systems.

Conclusions

In this chapter, the interconnection networks were defined and models of four types of parallel-processing systems were presented: SIMD, multiple-SIMD, MIMD, and partitionable-SIMD/MIMD. The SIMD model was examined in the most detail because it is the basis for chapters 3 and 4. Systems capable of operating in the multiple-SIMD and partitionable-SIMD/MIMD modes of parallelism are the motivation for the network partitionability analyses presented in chapter 4. The multistage networks examined in chapters 5 and 6 are capable of operating in any of these four parallel computation environments. For more information about these different types of parallel architectures, see the textbooks and papers cited throughout this chapter.

3 Single-Stage Network Comparisons

This chapter examines the ability of each of the four networks defined in chapter 2 to perform the interconnections contained in the other networks. The task of using network 1 to perform the connections that are part of network 2 is referred to as *simulating* network 2 with network 1. In other words, if network 1 was implemented on a given SIMD machine, and a network 2 connection was required for a particular computational algorithm, network 1 would have to simulate the actions of network 2. The techniques used in this chapter can be generalized and applied to simulating connections other than those in the four networks previously defined.

The ability of an interconnection network to simulate (that is, perform) the actions of other interconnection networks is important to SIMD machine designers who must select a set of interconnection functions to implement in hardware. The number of functions they include is constrained by such factors as cost and hardware complexity. Therefore, the designers must consider the ability of the chosen network to simulate other interconnection functions that may be necessary for the machine to perform various computational tasks. For example, if the shuffle-exchange network is implemented, and a cube interconnection is required, it is of interest to know how long it will take the shuffle-exchange to simulate a cube connection.

Methods for proving lower and upper time bounds on SIMD-machine interconnection network simulation algorithms are presented. The *lower bound* gives a minimum number of parallel data transfers (interconnection-function executions) required to perform the simulation. The *upper bound* is the maximum number of transfers needed and is based on the time complexity of an actual algorithm that performs the simulation. Each algorithm involves the movement of N data items among the N PEs.

If L is a lower bound on a simulation, it is impossible to do the simulation in fewer than L transfers (that is, at least L steps are needed). A lower bound must be proved to be true by some mathematical argument. If U is an upper bound on a simulation, there exists an algorithm to do the simulation in U steps (that is, at most U steps are needed). No more than U steps are needed because an algorithm that can do it in U steps is given.

Obviously, $L \leq U$. When $L = U$, the bounds are tight. If $L < U$, then there is a gap between the bounds, which means that either there is a better lower bound L', $L' > L$; or a better upper bound U', $U' < U$ (that is, a faster algorithm); or both. Thus, closing the gap involves finding a better lower-bound proof and/or a better simulation algorithm. Once the gap is closed, the bounds are tight.

If $L \neq U$, L is referred to as *a* lower bound and U is referred to as *an* upper bound (there exists a better lower and/or upper bound). When $L = U$, L is referred to as *the* lower bound and U is referred to as *the* upper bound (no better bounds exist). Thus, when the bounds are tight it means that the best possible (upper-bound) algorithm has been found. When there is a gap, there is room for improvement in the lower-bound analysis or in the upper-bound algorithm or both. As a result, it is important to determine the lower bound in addition to constructing an algorithm.

Just as there is, in general, no automatic way to generate a regular computer program, there is no automatic way to generate an upper-bound simulation algorithm or a lower-bound analysis. Various examples of techniques that can be used to calculate bounds are given by examining the time required for each of the networks in chapter 2 to simulate the others. These specific simulations are used because each of the networks discussed here has been proposed in some form in the literature and shown to be useful. A system designer will know the lower bound on the number of data transfers needed if a network presented here were implemented and it was then found necessary to simulate the actions of one of the other networks that has been defined. The designer is also provided with algorithms to perform the simulations. The material in this chapter is based on Siegel (1977, 1979b).

A somewhat different problem from that of one network simulating another is the ability of a network to perform any arbitrary interconnection function. Arbitrary functions have been examined for the four networks in Siegel (1978). The technique used associates a tag with each data item to be transferred; the tag specifies the destination PE. These tags and their associated data are then sorted, using a parallel bitionic sorting scheme (Batcher 1968; Knuth 1973). This approach is not taken here. In this chapter, the ability of a network to simulate a specific (as opposed to arbitrary) interconnection function is examined. The algorithm presented to perform the simulation of a specific interconnection function requires significantly less time than it would take to perform the same interconnection function using the sorting approach.

All the lower-bound results in this chapter are valid for all models of SIMD machines; that is, they can be used for any set of masking schemes and any set of machine instructions. There are no restrictions on the model. The interconnection function of the network to be simulated that requires the most time to simulate will determine the lower time bound for the simulation of that network. Furthermore, when an interconnection function is simulated, its effect on all PEs must be simulated. The lower bounds are in terms of the number of times interconnection functions must be executed to perform the simulation.

All upper-bound algorithm results are in terms of the model presented in chapter 2, where $N = 2^m$, C includes instructions for loop control, I includes instructions for moving data between the DTR and the other registers of the same PE, $M = \{PE$ address masks, data-conditional masks$\}$, and F will vary. (Recall that data-conditional statements can be used to simulate PE address masks without using any additional inter-processor data transfers.) The interconnection function is to be simulated as if it were executed with all PEs being active. The process for removing this restriction is shown later in this chapter.

Each upper bound is based on the time complexity of the algorithm presented to do that simulation. Each algorithm is described and proved correct. Some of the algorithm-correctness proofs use the technique of proof by induction (see Stone 1973 or McCoy 1975). The chapter also provides an example of how each simulation algorithm operates.

The simulation-algorithm execution times are dominated by the inter-PE transfers that are needed, as can be seen by considering the way in which various instructions can be implemented. The instructions in the simulation algorithms can be divided into three categories: control-unit operations (in C), register-to-register operations (in I), and interprocessor data transfers (in F). Control-unit operations, such as incrementing a count register in the control unit for a "for loop," can be done, in general, in parallel (overlapped) with the previously broadcast PE instruction, thus taking no additional time. Register-to-register operations within a PE probably involve a single chip or, at worst, adjacent chips. The interprocessor data transfers involve setting the controls of the interconnection network and passing data among the PEs, involving board-to-board, and probably rack-to-rack distances. Furthermore, if there is a sequence of data transfers and the two DTR model is implemented to reduce clocking problems, an input-DTR-to-output-DTR move will be required after each transfer. Thus, unless the number of register-to-register operations is much greater than the number of interprocessor data transfers, the time for the interprocessor transfers will be the dominating factor in determining the execution time of the simulation algorithm.

When an interconnection function is executed with all PEs in the active state, no DTR data is destroyed; rather, it is transferred to another DTR. However, if some PEs are inactive, their DTR contents can be destroyed (that is, overwritten and not transferred)—the problem referred to in chapter 2 of the single-DTR organization that the two-DTR organization does not pose. For example, when $N = 8$, the data-transfer instruction shuffle [001] will overwrite and destroy the DTR contents of PE 2. To prevent the loss of the data in the DTR of PE 2, a copy of it must be saved before executing the data-transfer instruction. The combinations of PE address masks and interconnection functions that will destroy data are evaluated in Siegel (1977). In the correctness proofs of the algorithms in this chapter, it will be shown that no needed data is destroyed by interprocessor data transfers.

The following analyses provide a lower bound and upper bound on the time required to perform each simulation. In most cases these bounds are tight or there is a gap of only 1; that is, the lower and upper bounds are approximately equal.

The following ground rules are used in these analyses:

1. When simulating the interconnection function f, the data originally in the DTR of PE P must be transferred to the DTR of PE $f(P)$, $0 \le P < N$.
2. The bounds are in terms of the number of executions of interconnection functions required to perform the simulation.
3. The particular interconnection function of the network to be simulated that requires the most time to simulate will determine the time bounds for the simulation of that network.

The following notation and terminology are used. Superscripts will be used as repetition factors in both the specification of PE address masks and in PE addresses themselves; for example, PE number $0^{m-(i+1)}10^i$ is PE number 2^i. A 0 superscript implies the null string—for example, if $j = 0$ then $0^{m-j}1^j = 0^m$. Recall that the transferring of data from PE a to PE b will also be referred to as mapping the address a to b, because the interconnections have been defined as mathematical functions on the PE addresses. For example, the cube$_0$ function maps the address 5 to 4 (cube$_0(5) = 4$), which means that data from PE 5 are sent to PE 4. Similarly, for $N \ge 16$, the PM2$_{+3}$ function maps the address 1 to 9 (PM2$_{+3}(1) = 9$), which means the data from PE 1 are sent to PE 9. The notation network 1 $\rightarrow$ network 2 means the case where network 1 is used to simulate network 2. In the algorithms ":" indicates a comment. When discussing the algorithms, Si is used as an abbreviation for statement i of the algorithm.

The results to be derived are summarized in table 3–1; the entries in row a and column b are lower and upper bounds on the time required for network a to simulate b. Both the lower-bound analyses and upper-bound algorithms and correctness proofs will vary in technique and complexity—some will appear obvious, others will take a good deal of thought to understand.

Lower- and Upper-Bound Results Using the PM2I Network

This section provides lower and upper bounds on the number of inter-PE data transfers required by the PM2I network to simulate the cube, Illiac,

Table 3-1
Lower and Upper Bounds on Network Simulation Times

		PM2I	Cube	Illiac	Shuffle-Exchange
PM2I	lower	—	2	1	m
	upper	—	2	1	$m + 1$
Cube	lower	m	—	m	m
	upper	m	—	m	m
Illiac	lower	$n/2$	$(n/2) + 1$	—	$2n - 4$
	upper	$n/2$	$(n/2) + 1$	—	$2n - 1$
Shuffle-Exchange	lower	$2m - 1$	$m + 1$	$2m - 1$	—
	upper	$2m$	$m + 1$	$2m$	—

Note: The entries in row a and column b are lower and upper bounds on the time required for network a to simulate network b.

and shuffle-exchange networks, as well as algorithms to perform these simulations. Each simulation algorithm is preceded by a description of the approach used and followed by a formal proof that the algorithm is correct.

Lower Bound on PM2I → Cube

For cube_i, $0 \leq i < m - 1$:

It will be shown that at least two steps are required by demonstrating that one step is insufficient. A single PM2I function cannot simulate cube_i for i in this range. Consider $\text{cube}_i(0^m) = 0^{m-(i+1)}10^i$ and $\text{cube}_i(1^m) = 1^{m-(i+1)}01^i$, for $0 \leq i < m - 1$. The only PM2I function that can map 0^m to $0^{m-(i+1)}10^i$ is PM2_{+i}, $0 \leq i < m - 1$. However, $\text{PM2}_{+i}(1^m) = 0^{m-i}1^i \neq \text{cube}_i(1^m)$, $0 \leq i < m - 1$. Thus, no single PM2I function can have the effect of cube_i on the addresses 0^m and 1^m, so the simulation must take at least two steps. In other words, since no single PM2I function is equivalent to cube_i, at least two PM2I transfers are required.

For cube_{m-1}:

The simulation of cube_{m-1} is a special case. The time required is one step because $\text{cube}_{m-1} = \text{PM2}_{+(m-1)}$. In terms of mappings, they both complement the high-order bit position of the addresses:

$$\text{cube}_{m-1}(p_{m-1}p_{m-2} \cdots p_1 p_0) = \bar{p}_{m-1}p_{m-2} \cdots p_1 p_0$$
$$= \text{PM2}_{+(m-1)}(p_{m-1}p_{m-2} \cdots p_1 p_0)$$

Upper Bound on PM2I → Cube

For $cube_i$, $0 \le i < m - 1$:

The following algorithm to simulate $cube_i$ first uses the $PM2_{+i}$ in $S1$ to map addresses of the form $P = p_{m-1} \ldots p_{i+1} 0 p_{i-1} \ldots p_0$ to $cube_i(P) = p_{m-1} \ldots p_{i+1} 1 p_{i-1} \ldots p_0$. The $PM2_{+i}$ in $S1$ also maps addresses of the form $P = p_{m-1} \ldots p_{i+1} 1 p_{i-1} \ldots p_0$ to addresses of the form $P' = p_{m-1} \ldots p_{i+1} 0 p_{i-1} \ldots p_0 + 2^{i+1}$ modulo N. Executing $PM2_{-(i+1)}$ in $S2$ maps this to $P' - 2^{i+1} = p_{m-1} \ldots p_{i+1} 0 p_{i-1} \ldots p_0 = cube_i(P)$.

Algorithm to simulate $cube_i$, $0 \le i < m - 1$:

$(S1)$ $PM2_{+i}$ $[X^m]$:all PEs execute $PM2_{+i}$

$(S2)$ $PM2_{-(i+1)}$ $[X^{m-(i+1)} 0 X^i]$:active PEs execute $PM2_{-(i+1)}$

The algorithm uses only two transfers.

Table 3–2 demonstrates the operation of this algorithm for $cube_1$ ($i = 1$) when $N = 8$ ($m = 3$). For example, the data from the DTR of PE 3 ($= 011$) is moved to PE 5 ($= 101$) by $S1$, and then, because 5 matches the mask ($[X0X]$), to PE 1 ($= 001$) by $S2$. The data movement from PE 3 to PE 1 ($= cube_1(3)$) is shown by the dotted line in table 3–2.

Correctness proof:

Case 1:   Consider PE addresses of the form $p_{m-1} \ldots p_{i+1} 0 p_{i-1} \ldots p_0$. These PEs execute $PM2_{+i}$ in $S1$. $PM2_{+i}(p_{m-1} \ldots p_{i+1} 0 p_{i-1}$

Table 3–2
PM2I → Cube$_i$ Simulation
(i = 1, N = 8)

PE	Initial DTR Contents	S1 DTR Contents	S2 DTR Contents
000	000	110	010
001	001	111	011
010	010	000	000
011	011	001	001
100	100	010	110
101	101	011	111
110	110	100	100
111	111	101	101

Note: It is assumed that initially the DTR of PE P contains the integer P, $0 \le P < 8$.

$\cdots p_0) = p_{m-1} \cdots p_{i+1} 1 p_{i-1} \cdots p_0 = \text{cube}_i (p_{m-1} \cdots p_{i+1} 0 p_{i-1} \cdots p_0)$. Since $p_i = 1$, these PEs do not match the mask in $S2$ (will not execute PM2$_{-(i+1)}$). Furthermore, PEs that do match the mask in $S2$ will send data to PEs with a 0 in the ith address-bit position. Thus, the data remains in the DTR of PE $p_{m-1} \cdots p_{i+1} 1 p_{i-1} \cdots p_0$, as it should.

Case 2: Consider PE addresses of the form $p_{m-1} \cdots p_{i+1} 1 p_{i-1} \cdots p_0$. These PEs execute PM2$_{+i}$ in $S1$. PM2$_{+i}(p_{m-1} \cdots p_{i+1} 1 p_{i-1} \cdots p_0) = (p_{m-1} \cdots p_{i+1} 0 p_{i-1} \cdots p_0) + 2^{i+1}$. Since $p_i = 0$, these PEs match the mask in $S2$. Thus, PM2$_{-(i+1)}$ is executed. By subtracting 2^{i+1} the desired result is attained; specifically:

$$\text{PM2}_{-(i+1)}(\text{PM2}_{+i}(p_{m-1} \cdots p_{i+1} 1 p_{i-1} \cdots p_0))$$

$$= \text{PM2}_{-(i+1)}(p_{m-1} \cdots p_{i+1} 0 p_{i-1} \cdots p_0 + 2^{i+1})$$

$$= p_{m-1} \cdots p_{i+1} 0 p_{i-1} \cdots p_0$$

$$= \text{cube}_i(p_{m-1} \cdots p_{i+1} 1 p_{i-1} \cdots p_0)$$

The data transfer in $S2$ does not destroy any DTR data because data are sent to PEs whose addresses are of the form $X^{m-(i+1)} 0 X^i$ (PEs with a 0 in the ith address-bit position), which are also active and sending data.

For cube$_{m-1}$:

To do the simulation use PM2$_{+(m-1)}$, since cube$_{m-1}$ = PM2$_{+(m-1)}$.

Lower and Upper Bounds on PM2I → Illiac

The Illiac network is a subset of the PM2I network. Specifically, Illiac$_{+1}$ = PM2$_{+0}$, Illiac$_{-1}$ = PM2$_{-0}$, Illiac$_{+n}$ = PM2$_{+(m/2)}$, and Illiac$_{-n}$ = PM2$_{-(m/2)}$. Therefore the lower and upper bounds are 1.

Lower Bound on PM2I → Shuffle-Exchange

For the shuffle:

Assume all arithmetic is modulo N. It will first be shown that the shuffle has the effect of adding $N - 1$ distinct integers to the set of PE addresses. It will then be shown that the PM2I network requires m steps to do this process.

For $0 \le P < N/2$, P is of the form $0 p_{m-2} \cdots p_1 p_0$, and shuffle (P) is of the form $p_{m-2} \ldots p_1 p_0 0$—that is, shuffle$(P) = 2P$. For $N/2 \le P' < N$, P' is of the form $1 \, p'_{m-2} \ldots p'_1 p'_0$, and shuffle$(P')$ is of the form $p'_{m-2} \ldots p'_1 p'_0 1$—that is shuffle$(P') = 2P' + 1$. Thus, for $0 \le P < N/2$, shuffle $(P) - P = P$, and for $N/2 \le P' < N$, shuffle$(P') - P' = P' + 1$. For example, for $N = 8$, shuffle$(2) - 2 = 2$ and shuffle$(5) - 5 = 6$. Thus, the former case adds the integers 0 to $(N/2) - 1$ to the set of PE addresses and the latter case adds the integers $(N/2) + 1$ to N. Note that $N = 0$ modulo N. Therefore, a single execution of the shuffle adds $N - 1$ distinct integers (modulo N) to the set of PE addresses (the only integer between 0 and $N - 1$ not added is $N/2$).

The physical interpretation of adding $N - 1$ distinct integers (modulo N) to the set of PE addresses is that a single execution of the shuffle moves the DTR data of the PEs $N - 1$ different distances. Specifically, the distances are 0 for data from PE 0, 1 for data from PE 1, 2 for data from PE 2, $\ldots$, $(N/2) - 1$ for data from PE $(N/2) - 1$, $(N/2) + 1$ for data from PE $N/2$, $(N/2) + 2$ for data from PE $(N/2) + 1, \ldots, N - 1$ for data from PE $N - 2$; that is, the DTR data from PE P, $0 \le P < N/2$, are moved a distance of P, and the DTR data from PE P', $N/2 \le P' < N$, are moved a distance of $P' + 1$. By using this property as a measure, it can be shown that a lower bound on the number of steps it takes for the PM2I to simulate the shuffle is $\lceil \log_2(N - 1) \rceil = m$. ($\lceil k \rceil$ is the ceiling of k—that is, the smallest integer greater than or equal to k.)

Each execution of a PM2I function can add to the set of PE addresses either an integer modulo N, if the PE is active, or nothing, if the PE is inactive. (Subtracting 2^i modulo N is equivalent to adding $N - 2^i$ modulo N.) Thus, the number of distinct integers added to the PE addresses after y executions of distinct PM2I functions is at most 2^y because each execution can add something (2^i or $N - 2^i$) or nothing (0).

For example, for $N = 8$, PM2$_{+2}$ can be used to move the data originally from PEs 4, 5, 6, and 7 a distance of 4, while moving the data originally from PEs 0, 1, 2, and 3 a distance of 0. Then, PM2$_{+1}$ can be used to move the data originally from PEs 6 and 7 a total distance of 6, and the data originally from PEs 2 and 3 a distance of 2. Finally, the use of PM2$_{+0}$ can result in the data originally from PE 1 being moved a distance of 1, the data originally from PE 3 a total distance of 3, the data originally from PE 5 a total distance of 5, and the data from PE 7 a total distance of 7. Thus, the data originally from PE i have been moved a distance of i, $0 \le i \le 7$. Alternatively, it may be said that a total of i has been added to address i, $0 \le i \le 7$.

For the PM2I network to add $N - 1$ distinct integers to the set of PE addresses, as a single execution of the shuffle does, at least $\lceil \log_2(N - 1) \rceil = m$ steps are required. Therefore, for the PM2I to simulate the action of the shuffle at least m transfers are needed.

For the exchange:

Recall that the exchange = $cube_0$. Thus, the exchange, like $cube_0$, requires at least two steps to be simulated because it is not equivalent to any single PM2I function.

Upper Bound on PM2I → Shuffle-Exchange

For the shuffle:

To understand the concept underlying the algorithm to perform the shuffle, again consider the distance the shuffle moves a data item. As stated in the lower-bound analysis, the data item originally in the DTR of PE P, $0 \leq P < N/2$, is moved to shuffle(P) = $2P$, a distance of shuffle(P) − $P = P$. The data item originally in the DTR of PE P', $N/2 \leq P' < N$, is moved to shuffle(P') = $2P' + 1$ modulo N, a distance of shuffle(P') − $P' = P' + 1$. This is shown in table 3–3 for $N = 8$. The algorithm uses the $PM2_{+0}$, $PM2_{+1}$, $PM2_{+2}$, . . . , $PM2_{+m-1}$, and $PM2_{+0}$ interconnection functions, in that order, to move the DTR data from PE P a distance of P, $0 \leq P < N/2$, and the DTR data from PE P' a distance of $P' + 1$ modulo N, $N/2 \leq P' < N$, as is also shown for $N = 8$ in table 3–3. Specifically, for $0 \leq P < N/2$, the data item originally in PE P is moved by $PM2_{+i}$ if $p_i = 1$, $0 \leq i < m$, moving it from P to $2P$. For $N/2 \leq P' < N$, the data item originally in PE P' is moved by $PM2_{+i}$ if $p'_i = 1$, $0 \leq i < m$, moving it from P' to $2P'$, and then by $PM2_{+0}$, moving it from $2P'$ to $2P' + 1$. Note that the first column in table 3–3 shows the origin PE for the data items, from which the data are moved by the PM2I functions.

In the following algorithm, during steps $S3$ to $S5$, for $1 \leq j < m - 1$, all of the data of interest are in even-numbered PEs. After $S5$ has been executed for $j = m - 1$, the data from PE P has been moved to PE $2P$ modulo N by using a subset of $PM2_{+0}$, $PM2_{+1}$, . . . , $PM2_{+m-1}$, in that order. Similarly, the data from PE P' are moved to PE $2P'$. Then, $S6$ executes $PM2_{+0}$ to move data from PE $2P'$ to $2P' + 1$. This algorithm is from Seban and Siegel (1983).

Algorithm to simulate the shuffle:

($S1$) $A \leftarrow$ DTR [$X^{m-1}0$]   :even PEs save DTR contents
                                                   in A register

($S2$) $PM2_{+0}$ [$X^{m-1}1$]   :odd PEs send DTR data +1
                                                   to even PEs

($S3$) for $j = 1$ until $m - 1$ do

Table 3–3
The Concept Underlying the PM2I $\to$ Shuffle Algorithm
(N = 8)

Origin PE Number	Distance Moved by Shuffle	Distance Moved by PM2I				Total
0 = 000	+0	—	—	—	—	+0
1 = 001	+1	+1	—	—	—	+1
2 = 010	+2	—	+2	—	—	+2
3 = 011	+3	+1	+2	—	—	+3
4 = 100	+5	—	—	+4	+1	+5
5 = 101	+6	+1	—	+4	+1	+6
6 = 110	+7	—	+2	+4	+1	+7
7 = 111	+0	+1	+2	+4	+1	+0
		$PM2_{+0}$	$PM2_{+1}$	$PM2_{+2}$	$PM2_{+0}$	

Note: The distance the data item in the DTR of each PE is moved by the shuffle and by the PM2I network simulating the shuffle is shown.

$(S4)$ $\qquad$ $A \leftrightarrow \text{DTR} [X^{m-j-1} 1 X^{j-1} 0]$ $\qquad$:even PEs, jth bit = 1, switch A and DTR

$(S5)$ $\qquad$ $PM2_{+j} [X^{m-1} 0]$ $\qquad$:even PEs send DTR data $+ 2^j$

$(S6)$ $PM2_{+0} [X^{m-1} 0]$ $\qquad$:half of data sent from even PEs to odd PEs

$(S7)$ DTR $\leftarrow A [X^{m-1} 0]$ $\qquad$:reload DTR from A register in even PEs

The algorithm uses $m + 1$ inter-PE data transfers and $m + 1$ register-to-register moves.

Table 3–4 demonstrates the operation of this algorithm for $N = 8$ $(m = 3)$. For example, consider the data item initially in the DTR of PE 5 $(= 101)$. PE 5 does not match the mask in $S1$ $([XX0])$. PE 5 does match the mask in $S2$ $([XX1])$ and the data are moved to PE $PM2_{+0}(5) = 6 (= 110)$. PE 6 does match the mask in $S4$ when $j = 1$ $([X10])$ and the data are moved to the A register of PE 6. The data are unaffected by $S5$ when $j = 1$ (because they are not in the DTR). PE 6 does match the mask in $S4$ when $j = 2$ $([1X0])$ and the data are moved to the DTR of PE6. PE 6 does match the mask in $S5$ when $j = 2$ $([XX0])$ and the data are moved to the DTR of PE $PM2_{+2}(6) = 2$. PE 2 does match the mask in $S6$ $([XX0])$ and the data are moved to the DTR of PE $PM2_{+0}(2) = 3$. PE 3 does not match the mask in $S7$ $([XX0])$. Thus, the data originally from PE 5 are moved to PE 3 = shuffle(5) as shown by the dotted line in table 3–4.

Table 3-4
PM2I → Shuffle Simulation
(N = 8)

PE	Initial DTR Contents	S1 A Contents	S2 DTR Contents	S4 j=1 A Contents	S4 j=1 DTR Contents	S5 j=1 DTR Contents	S4 j=2 A Contents	S4 j=2 DTR Contents	S5 j=2 DTR Contents	S6 DTR Contents	S7 DTR Contents
000	000	000	111	000	111	110	000	110	100	100	000
001	001	—	—	—	—	—	—	—	—	100	100
010	010	010	001	001	010	111	001	111	101	101	001
011	011	—	—	—	—	—	—	—	—	101	101
100	100	100	011	100	011	010	010	100	110	110	010
101	101	110	101	101	110	011	011	101	—	110	110
110	110	—	—	—	—	—	—	—	111	111	011
111	111	—	—	—	—	—	—	—	—	111	111

Note: It is assumed that initially the DTR of PE P contains the integer P, $0 \le P < 8$.

Correctness proof: Assume all arithmetic is modulo N. The induction hypothesis (to be proven correct) is that after executing $PM2_{+j}$ in $S2$ (for $j = 0$) or $S5$ (for $1 \le j < m$) the data originally in the DTR of PE $Q = q_{m-1} \ldots q_1 q_0$ will currently be in PE $P = p_{m-1} \ldots p_1 p_0 = (q_{m-1} \ldots q_{j+2} q_{j+1}) * 2^{j+1} + (q_j \ldots q_1 q_0) * 2$. (When $j = 0$, $P = (q_{m-1} \ldots q_2 q_1) * 2 + (q_0) * 2$.) The data will be in the A register if $q_j = 0$ and in the DTR if $q_j = 1$.

Thus, when $j = m - 1$, the data originally from PE Q is in PE $(q_{m-1} \ldots q_1 q_0) * 2$. The data item in the DTR of PE $(q_{m-1} \ldots q_1 q_0) * 2$ is moved to PE $(q_{m-1} \ldots q_1 q_0) * 2 + 1$ by $S6$; this move is correct because this data item is from a PE where $q_j = q_{m-1} = 1$, so shuffle$(Q) = 2 * Q + 1$. The data item in the A register of PE $(q_{m-1} \ldots q_1 q_0) * 2$ is moved to the DTR of that PE by $S7$; this move is correct because this data item is from a PE where $q_j = q_{m-1} = 0$, so shuffle$(Q) = 2 * Q$.

To complete the correctness proof it must be shown that the induction hypothesis is true.

BASIS: $j = 0$.

Case 1:   The data item is originally from the DTR of PE $Q = q_{m-1} \ldots q_2 q_1 0$.
This data item is moved to the A register of that PE by $S1$. Because $q_0 = 0$, $Q = (q_{m-1} \ldots q_2 q_1) * 2 + (q_0) * 2 = P$. These data are not moved by $S2$. They remain in the A register and $q_0 = 0$. Thus, the induction hypothesis is true for $j = 0$ for this case.

Case 2:   The data item is originally from the DTR of PE $Q = q_{m-1} \ldots q_2 q_1 1$.
This data item is not moved by $S1$. It is moved to the DTR of PE $P = Q + 1$ by $PM2_{+0}$ in $S2$. Because $q_0 = 1$, $Q + 1 = q_{m-1} \ldots q_2 q_1 1 + 1 = (q_{m-1} \ldots q_2 q_1) * 2 + 2 = (q_{m-1} \ldots q_2 q_1) * 2 + (q_0) * 2 = P$. The data item is in the DTR and $q_0 = 1$. Thus, the induction hypothesis is true for $j = 0$ for this case.

INDUCTION STEP: Assume true for $j = k - 1$ and show true for $j = k$.

Case 1:   The data item is originally from the DTR of PE $Q = q_{m-1} \ldots q_2 q_1 q_0$, where $q_{k-1} = 0$.
From the induction hypothesis when $j = k - 1$, this data item is in the A register of PE $P = p_{m-1} \ldots p_1 p_0 = (q_{m-1} \ldots q_{k+1} q_k) * 2^k + (q_{k-1} \ldots q_1 q_0) * 2$.

Subcase 1a: $p_k = 1$. The A register data are moved to the DTR of PE P by $S4$ and then to the DTR of PE $P + 2^k$ by $S5$. Recall $P = p_{m-1}$

$\ldots p_1 p_0 = (q_{m-1} \ldots q_{k+1} q_k) * 2^k + (q_{k-1} \ldots q_1 q_0) * 2.$
Because $q_{k-1} = 0$, $(0 q_{k-2} \ldots q_1 q_0) * 2 < 2^k$. Thus, if $p_k = 1$, it
must be that $q_k = 1$. Because $q_k = 1$, $P + 2^k =$

$$(q_{m-1} \ldots q_{k+1} 1) * 2^k + (q_{k-1} \ldots q_1 q_0) * 2 + 2^k$$
$$= (q_{m-1} \ldots q_{k+1}) * 2^{k+1} + 2^k + (q_{k-1} \ldots q_1 q_0) * 2 + 2^k$$
$$= (q_{m-1} \ldots q_{k+1}) * 2^{k+1} + (1 q_{k-1} \ldots q_1 q_0) * 2$$
$$= (q_{m-1} \ldots q_{k+1}) * 2^{k+1} + (q_k q_{k-1} \ldots q_1 q_0) * 2$$

Furthermore, the data is in the DTR and $q_k = 1$. Thus, the induction hypothesis is true for $j = k$ for this subcase.

Subcase 1b: $p_k = 0$. The A register data is kept in the A register of PE P and not moved by $S4$ or $S5$. As in subcase 1a, since $q_{k-1} = 0$, $(0 q_{k-2} \ldots q_1 q_0) * 2 < 2^k$. Thus, if $p_k = 0$, it must be that $q_k = 0$. Since $q_k = 0$, $P =$

$$(q_{m-1} \ldots q_{k+1} 0) * 2^k + (q_{k-1} \ldots q_1 q_0) * 2$$
$$= (q_{m-1} \ldots q_{k+1}) * 2^{k+1} + (q_k \ldots q_1 q_0) * 2$$

Furthermore, the data is in the A register and $q_k = 0$. Thus, the induction hypothesis is true for $j = k$ for this subcase.

Case 2: The data item is originally from the DTR of PE $Q = q_{m-1} \ldots q_1 q_0$, where $q_{k-1} = 1$.
From the induction hypothesis when $j = k - 1$, this data item is in the DTR of PE $P = p_{m-1} \ldots p_1 p_0 = (q_{m-1} \ldots q_{k+1} q_k) * 2^k + (q_{k-1} \ldots q_1 q_0) * 2$.

Subcase 2a: $p_k = 1$. The DTR data is moved to the A register of PE P by $S4$ and is not moved by $S5$. Recall $p_{m-1} \ldots p_1 p_0 = (q_{m-1} \ldots q_{k+1} q_k) * 2^k + (q_{k-1} \ldots q_1 q_0) * 2$. Since $q_{k-1} = 1$, $(q_{k-1} \ldots q_1 q_0) * 2 = 2^k + (q_{k-2} \ldots q_1 q_0) * 2$. Thus, if $p_k = 1$, it must be that $q_k = 0$. Since $q_k = 0$, $P =$

$$(q_{m-1} \ldots q_{k+1} 0) * 2^k + (q_{k-1} \ldots q_1 q_0) * 2$$
$$= (q_{m-1} \ldots q_{k+1}) * 2^{k+1} + (q_k \ldots q_1 q_0) * 2$$

Furthermore, the data is in the A register and $q_k = 0$. Thus, the induction hypothesis is true for $j = k$ for this subcase.

Subcase 2b: $p_k = 0$. The DTR data is kept in the DTR of PE P (not moved by $S4$). It is then moved to the DTR of PE $P + 2^k$ by $S5$. Since $q_{k-1} = 1$, $(q_{k-1} \ldots q_1 q_0) * 2 = 2^k + (q_{k-2} \ldots q_1 q_0) * 2$. Thus, if $p_k = 0$, it must be that $q_k = 1$. Since $q_k = 1$, $P + 2^k =$

$(q_{m-1} \cdots q_{k+1}) * 2^{k+1} + (q_k q_{k-1} \cdots q_1 q_0) * 2$ as in subcase 1a. Furthermore, the data is in the DTR and $q_k = 1$. Thus the induction hypothesis is true for $j = k$ for this subcase.

These cases complete the proof that the induction hypothesis is true.

No data of interest are destroyed by the inter-PE data transfers. The transfer in $S2$ overwrites no relevant data since such data are saved in the A registers in $S1$. The transfers in $S5$, for $1 \le j < m$ move data among the even-numbered PEs (that is, all even-numbered PEs transfer data simultaneously) so no data are overwritten. Finally, the transfer in $S6$ overwrites data in the DTRs of the odd-numbered PEs; however, all data of interest are in the even-numbered PEs at that point.

This completes the correctness proof. All the data have been moved as the shuffle would have moved them.

For the exchange:

To do the simulation, use the PM2I $\rightarrow$ cube$_0$ algorithm because exchange = cube$_0$.

Lower- and Upper-Bound Results
Using the Cube Network

This section provides lower bounds on the number of inter-PE transfers required by the cube network to simulate the PM2I, Illiac, and shuffle-exchange networks. As in the previous section, algorithms to perform the simulations are described and proved correct.

Lower Bound on Cube → PM2I

The time required for the cube to simulate $PM2_{+i}$ or $PM2_{-i}$ is $m - i$. To prove this, the Hamming distance is used as a measure to determine the distance between a PE address and the address to which it is mapped. If the function H is the Hamming distance, then $H(a,b)$ is the number of bit positions in which a and b differ (Lin 1970). By definition, $H(a,\text{cube}_i(a)) = 1$, $0 \le i < m$, $0 \le a < N$. But for $0 \le i < m$, $PM2_{+i}(1^m) = 0^{m-i}1^i$ and $PM2_{-i}(0^m) = 1^{m-i}0^i$, so $H(1^m, PM2_{+i}(1^m)) = H(0^m, PM2_{-i}(0^m)) = m - i$. Since $PM2_{+i}$ and $PM2_{-i}$ do not affect the low-order i bits, these distances are the maximum achievable with this measure. Thus, when $i = 0$, $PM2_{+i}$ and $PM2_{-i}$ can each map an address to another that is at a Hamming distance of m. Since the cube functions can map addresses only a distance 1 for each execution, at least m steps are required for the cube to simulate the PM2I.

Upper Bound on Cube → PM2I

For PM2$_{+i}$, $0 \leq i \leq m - 2$ (PM2$_{-i}$ is similar):

Consider mapping the address P to $P + 2^i$. Bit j, $j = m - 1, m - 2$, . . . , $i + 1$, of P will be complemented by PM2$_{+i}$ if and only if bits $j - 1$ through i are ones. For example, consider $P = 00110$. For $i = 1$, PM2$_{+1}(00110) = 01000$. Bit 4 is not complemented because bits 3, 2, and 1 are not all ones. Bit 3 is complemented because bits 2 and 1 are ones. Bit 2 is complemented because bit 1 is a one. When j in $S1$ is $m - 1, m - 2, \ldots,$ $i + 1$, the algorithm simulates this action of the "carry" generated by PM2$_{+i}$ by executing cube$_j$ with the mask $[X^{m-j}1^{j-i}X^i]$ (only addresses with ones in bit positions $i, i + 1, \ldots, j - 1$ will match this mask). When $j = i$ the mask in $S1$ is $[X^{m-i}1^0X^i] = [X^m]$. Thus, all addresses match the mask, and cube$_i$ is executed complementing the ith bit of all addresses, as would PM2$_{+i}$.

Algorithm to simulate PM2$_{+i}$, $0 \leq i < m - 1$:

($S1$) for $j = m - 1$ step -1 until i do

   cube$_j$ $[X^{m-j}1^{j-i}X^i]$:complement bits that PM2$_{+i}$ would

The algorithm uses $m - i$ transfers. Thus, the maximum number of transfers needed to simulate PM2I is m (which occurs when $i = 0$).

   Table 3–5 demonstrates the operation of this algorithm for PM2$_{+1}$ ($i = 1$) when $N = 8$ ($m = 3$). For example, the data from the DTR of PE 6 ($= 110$) are moved to PE 2 ($= 010$) when $j = 2$ (because 6 matches the mask $[X1X]$), and then to PE 0 ($= 000 = $ PM2$_{+1}(6)$) when $j = 1$ (because the mask is $[X^m]$), as shown by the dotted line.

Correctness proof: Without loss of generality, consider the PE address $p_{m-1} \cdots p_i \cdots p_0$, where the sequence of ones starting with p_i is of length k, $0 \leq k \leq m - i$ (that is, $p_{i+k-1} \cdots p_{i+1}p_i = 1 \ldots 11$).

Case 1:   Consider PE addresses where $p_i = 0$; that is, $k = 0$.
         Let P be a PE address of this form. For $j = m - 1, m - 2, \ldots,$
         $i + 1$, this address will not match the mask. $S1$ maps P to p_{m-1}
         $\cdots p_{i+1}1p_{i-1} \cdots p_0 = $ PM2$_{+i}(P)$ when $j = i$.

Table 3–5
Cube → PM2$_{+i}$ Simulation
(i = 1, N = 8)

PE	Initial DTR Contents	S1 j = 2 DTR Contents	S1 j = 1 DTR Contents
000	000	000	·110
001	001	001	111
010	010	·110·	000
011	011	111	001
100	100	100	010
101	101	101	011
110	110··	010	100
111	111	011	101

Note: It is assumed that initially the DTR of PE *P* contains the integer *P*, $0 \leq P < 8$.

Case 2:   Consider PE addresses where $p_i = 1$, so $m - i \geq k > 0$, and the address is of the form $p_{m-1} \cdots p_{i+k+1} 01^k p_{i-1} \cdots p_0$. When $j = m - 1, m - 2, \ldots, i + k + 1$, this address does not match the mask (because $p_{i+k} = 0$). When $j = i + k, i + k - 1,$ $\ldots, i$, this address matches the mask (because $p_{i+k-1} \cdots p_{i+1}$ $p_i = 1 \ldots 11$) and cube$_j$ is executed. Thus, $p_{m-1} \cdots p_{i+k+1} 01^k$ $p_{i-1} \cdots p_0$ is mapped to $p_{m-1} \cdots p_{i+k+1} \overline{01^k} p_{i-1} \cdots p_0 =$ $p_{m-1} \cdots p_{i+k+1} 10^k p_{i-1} \cdots p_0 = \text{PM2}_{+i}(p_{m-1} \cdots p_{i+k+1} 01^k$ $p_{i-1} \cdots p_0)$.

No transfers in this simulation destroy data because whenever cube$_j$ is executed the mask's *j*th position is *X*. In other words, when PE $P = p_{m-1}$ $\cdots p_{j+1} p_j p_{j-1} \cdots p_0$ sends data using cube$_j$, PE cube$_j(P) = p_{m-1} \cdots$ $p_{j+1} \bar{p}_j p_{j-1} \cdots p_0$ is also active and also sends its data.

For PM2$_{\pm m-1}$:

To do the simulation use cube$_{m-1}$ because cube$_{m-1} = \text{PM2}_{\pm(m-1)}$ (see the PM2I → cube analysis in the previous section).

Lower and Upper Bounds on Cube → Illiac

This follows from the cube → PM2I and PM2I → Illiac analyses. The lower and upper bounds of *m* occur when the cube network is used to simulate Illiac$_{\pm 1}$.

Lower Bound on Cube → Shuffle-Exchange

For the shuffle:

When the shuffle is applied to address $0^{m-(j+1)}10^j$ it is mapped to $0^{m-(j+2)}10^{j+1}$, changing the value of bit position j, $0 \leq j < m$. This change occurs for all j, $0 \leq j < m$, simultaneously. For example, when $m = 4$ ($N = 16$), shuffle(0001) = 0010, shuffle(0010) = 0100, shuffle(0100) = 1000, and shuffle(1000) = 0001. Thus, the shuffle changes all m bit positions when applied to the set of all PE addresses. For the cube to have this effect, all m cube functions must be executed at least once. Therefore, at least m transfers are required.

For the exchange:

By definition, $cube_0$ = exchange. Thus, only one transfer is required.

Upper Bound on Cube → Shuffle-Exchange

For the shuffle:

To understand how this algorithm works, carefully compare the following algorithm to the example in figure 3–1, which shows, for $N = 16$, how the data item originally in the DTR of PE $P = p_{m-1} \cdots p_1 p_0$ is moved to the DTR of PE shuffle(P) = $p_{m-2} \cdots p_1 p_0 p_{m-1}$.

In general, $S1$ moves the initial DTR contents of all N PEs into the $N/2$ PEs where the high-order bit of the address equals the low-order bit: half in the A registers, half in the DTRs. (In $S1$ the elsewhere statement is broadcast after the do statement.) The data remain in these PEs while $S3$ and $S4$ are executed for $j = 1, 2, \ldots, m - 2$. For j in this range, all the action takes place in PEs where the high-order bit of the address equals the low-order bit. In $S3$ the data are switched between the A register and DTR before each execution of $cube_j$ (in $S4$) depending on whether the jth address bit of the PE equals the $(j - 1)$st. The following explanation demonstrates the reasons.

As illustrated in figure 3–1, after $S4$ is executed for $j = 1$, the data originally in the DTR of PE $p_3 p_2 p_1 p_0$ are in PE $p_3 p_2 p_0 p_3$; in the A register if $p_1 = p_0$, in the DTR if $p_1 \neq p_0$. That is, the low-order bits have been shuffled. Let ADDR(i) be the ith bit of ADDR. Before executing $S4$ for $j = 2$ (that is, executing $cube_2$), $S3$ switches the data between the A register and the DTR if ADDR(2) $\neq$ ADDR(1)—that is, $p_2 \neq p_0$. To understand why this switch occurs, consider the following cases.

Case 1:   Consider PE $P' = p_3 p_2 p_0 p_3$, where $p_2 = p_0$ (the data are not switched).

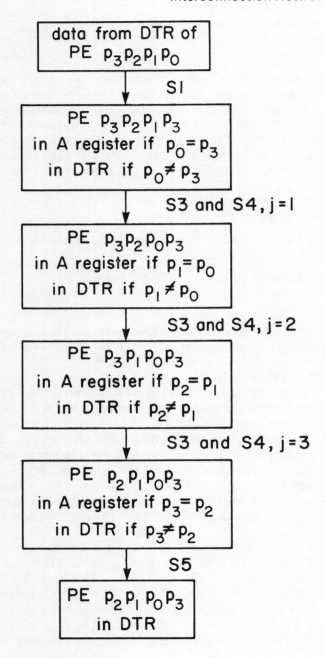

Figure 3-1. Data Flow in the Cube → Shuffle Algorithm when $N = 16$

The data in the A register of this PE should be moved to a PE whose ADDR(2) = p_1. The data in the A register of this PE were originally from a PE where $p_1 = p_0$. These data should stay in PE P', where $p_2 = p_0$ because $p_2 = p_0 = p_1$ = ADDR(2) (that is, $p_3 p_2 p_0 p_3 = p_3 p_1 p_0 p_3$).

The data in the DTR of this PE should be moved to a PE whose ADDR(2) = p_1. The data in the DTR of this PE were originally from a PE where $p_1 \neq p_0$. In P', $p_2 = p_0$, so ADDR(2) = $p_1 = \bar{p}_0 = \bar{p}_2$. These data should be moved by cube$_2$ in $S4$ to PE cube$_2(P')$ (that is, $p_3 \bar{p}_2 p_0 p_3 = p_3 p_1 p_0 p_3$).

Case 2:   Consider PE $P' = p_3 p_2 p_0 p_3$, where $p_2 \neq p_0$ (the data are switched).

The data in the A register of this PE should be moved to a PE whose ADDR(2) = p_1. The data in the A register of this PE originally came from a PE where $p_1 = p_0$. In P', $p_2 \neq p_0$, so ADDR(2) = $p_1 = p_0 = \bar{p}_2$. These data should be moved to the DTR by $S3$ and then moved to PE cube$_2(P')$ by $S4$ (that is, $p_3 \bar{p}_2 p_0 p_3 = p_3 p_1 p_0 p_3$).

The data in the DTR of this PE should be moved to a PE whose ADDR(2) = p_1. The data in the DTR of this PE originally came from a PE where $p_1 \neq p_0$. In P', $p_2 \neq p_0$, so ADDR(2) = $p_1 = \bar{p}_0 = p_2$. These data should be moved by $S3$ into the A register so that they will remain in this PE because $p_3 p_2 p_0 p_3 = p_3 p_1 p_0 p_3$.

After $S4$ is executed for $j = m - 2$, the data originally from PE p_{m-1} $\ldots p_1 p_0$ are in PE $p_{m-1} p_{m-3} \cdots p_1 p_0 p_{m-1}$ (in the A register or DTR). When $j = m - 1$, $S4$ (cube$_{m-1}$) sends half of the data to the DTRs of PEs where the high- and low-order address bits differ. The data originally from PE P are now in shuffle(P). $S5$ moves the data in PEs where the high-order address bit equals the low-order bit from the A register into the DTR, completing the simulation.

Algorithm to simulate the shuffle:

($S1$) where ADDR $(m - 1)$ = ADDR(0)   :high-order bit equals low-order bit

         do $A \leftarrow$ DTR $[X^m]$:save DTR data in A register
         elsewhere cube$_0$ $[X^m]$:send DTR data

($S2$) for $j = 1$ until $m - 1$ do

($S3$)   where ADDR(j) $\neq$ ADDR($j - 1$)
         do $A \longleftrightarrow$ DTR $[X^m]$:switch data

($S4$)   cube$_j$ $[X^m]$:send data

($S5$) where ADDR($m - 1$) = ADDR(0)
     do DTR $\leftarrow$ A [X^m]   :load DTR from A register

The algorithm uses m inter-PE data transfers, $m + 1$ where-statements, and $m + 1$ register-to-register moves.

    Table 3–6 demonstrates the operation of this algorithm when $N = 8$ ($m = 3$). For example, the data in DTR of PE 6 (= 110) are moved to the DTR of PE 7 (= 111) by $S1$, to the DTR of PE 5 (= 101) by $S4$ when $j = 1$, to the A register of PE 5 (= 101) by $S3$ when $j = 2$, and to the DTR of PE 5 (= 101) by $S5$. The data movement from PE 6 to PE 5 (= shuffle(6)) is shown by the dotted line.

Correctness proof: After the execution of $S1$, the DTR data from PE $P = p_{m-1} \cdots p_1 p_0$ *will be in PE* $p_{m-1} \cdots p_2 p_1 p_{m-1}$; in the A register if $p_{m-1} = p_0$, in the DTR if $p_{m-1} \neq p_0$. All the data being shuffled are now in PEs where the high-order and low-order address bits are equal. In the loop $S2$, $S3$, and $S4$, after cube$_j$ is executed, $j = 1, 2, \ldots, m - 2$, the data from PE P will be in PE $p_{m-1} \cdots p_{j+1} p_{j-1} \cdots p_1 p_0 p_{m-1}$ (the low-order $j + 1$ bits will be shuffled as illustrated in figure 3–1). If $p_j = p_{j-1}$, the data will be in the A register; if $p_j \neq p_{j-1}$, they will be in the DTR. Thus, when $j = m - 2$, the data from PE P will be in PE $p_{m-1} p_{m-3} \cdots p_1 p_0 p_{m-1}$; in the A register if $p_{m-2} = p_{m-3}$ or in the DTR if $p_{m-2} \neq p_{m-3}$. This can be proved by induction on j. The following cases consider only PEs where the high-order and low-order address bits are equal.

BASIS: $j = 1$.

Case 1: Consider the A register and DTR contents of the PE where ADDR(1) = ADDR(0).
    (a) A register: The data from PE P, where $p_{m-1} = p_0$, are in the A register of PE $p_{m-1} \cdots p_2 p_1 p_{m-1}$ (as a result of $S1$) and remain there. This is correct: $p_{m-1} \cdots p_2 p_1 p_{m-1} = p_{m-1} \cdots p_2 p_0 p_{m-1}$ because $p_1 = $ ADDR(1) = ADDR(0) $ = p_{m-1} = p_0$.
    (b) DTR: The data from PE P, where $p_{m-1} \neq p_0$, are in the DTR of PE $p_{m-1} \cdots p_2 p_1 p_{m-1}$ (as a result of $S1$) and are sent by $S4$ to PE $p_{m-1} \cdots p_2 \bar{p}_1 p_{m-1}$. This transfer is correct: $p_{m-1} \cdots p_2 \bar{p}_1 p_{m-1} = p_{m-1} \cdots p_2 p_0 p_{m-1}$ because $\bar{p}_1 = \overline{\text{ADDR(1)}} = \overline{\text{ADDR(0)}} = \bar{p}_{m-1} = p_0$.

Case 2: Consider the A register and DTR contents of the PE where ADDR(1) $\neq$ ADDR(0).

Table 3-6
Cube → Shuffle Simulation
(N = 8)

PE	Initial DTR Contents	S1 A Contents	S1 DTR Contents	S3 j = 1 A Contents	S3 j = 1 DTR Contents	S4 j = 1 DTR Contents	S3 j = 2 A Contents	S3 j = 2 DTR Contents	S4 j = 2 DTR Contents	S5 DTR Contents
000	000	000	001	000	001	010	000	010	—	000
001	001	—	001	001	—	011	001	011	100	100
010	010	010	011	011	010	001	001	011	100	001
011	011	—	011	—	011	—	—	—	101	101
100	100	—	100	—	100	—	—	—	010	010
101	101	101	100	100	101	110	110	100	011	110
110	110	—	110	110	—	100	110	100	011	011
111	111	111	110	111	110	101	111	101	—	111

Note: It is assumed that initially the DTR of PE P contains the integer P, $0 \leq P < 8$.

(a) A register: The data from PE P, where $p_{m-1} = p_0$, are in the A register of PE $p_{m-1} \ldots p_2 p_1 p_{m-1}$ (as a result of $S1$). Data are sent to the DTR of this PE by $S3$ and then sent by $S4$ to the DTR of PE $p_{m-1} \ldots p_2 \bar{p}_1 p_{m-1}$. This transfer is correct: $p_{m-1} \ldots p_2 \bar{p}_1 p_{m-1} = p_{m-1} \ldots p_2 p_0 p_{m-1}$ because $\bar{p}_1 = \overline{\text{ADDR}(1)} = \text{ADDR}(0) = p_{m-1} = p_0$.

(b) DTR: The data from PE P, where $p_{m-1} \neq p_0$, are in the DTR of PE $p_{m-1} \ldots p_2 p_1 p_{m-1}$ (as a result of $S1$). The data are moved to the A register of that PE by $S3$. This move is correct: $p_{m-1} \ldots p_2 p_1 p_{m-1} = p_{m-1} \ldots p_2 p_0 p_{m-1}$ because $p_1 = \text{ADDR}(1) = \overline{\text{ADDR}(0)} = \bar{p}_{m-1} = p_0$.

INDUCTION STEP: Assume the hypothesis is true for $j = i$, and consider $j = i + 1$.

Case 1: Consider the A register and DTR contents of the PE where $\text{ADDR}(i + 1) = \text{ADDR}(i)$.

(a) A register: From the induction hypothesis, the data from PE P, where $p_i = p_{i-1}$, are in the A register of PE $p_{m-1} \ldots p_{i+1} p_{i-1} \ldots p_1 p_0 p_{m-1}$. When $j = i + 1$ these data remain there. This is correct: $p_{m-1} \ldots p_{i+2} p_{i+1} p_{i-1} \ldots p_1 p_0 p_{m-1} = p_{m-1} \ldots p_{i+2} p_i p_{i-1} \ldots p_1 p_0 p_{m-1}$ because $p_{i+1} = \text{ADDR}(i + 1) = \text{ADDR}(i) = p_{i-1} = p_i$.

(b) DTR: From the induction hypothesis, the data from PE P, where $p_i \neq p_{i-1}$, are in the DTR of PE $p_{m-1} \ldots p_{i+1} p_{i-1} \ldots p_1 p_0 p_{m-1}$. When $j = i + 1$ the data are sent by $S4$ to PE $p_{m-1} \ldots \bar{p}_{i+1} p_{i-1} \ldots p_1 p_0 p_{m-1}$. This transfer is correct: $p_{m-1} \ldots p_{i+2} \bar{p}_{i+1} p_{i-1} \ldots p_1 p_0 p_{m-1} = p_{m-1} \ldots p_{i+2} p_i p_{i-1} \ldots p_1 p_0 p_{m-1}$ because $\bar{p}_{i+1} = \overline{\text{ADDR}(i + 1)} = \overline{\text{ADDR}(i)} = \bar{p}_{i-1} = p_i$.

Case 2: Consider the A register and DTR contents of the PE where $\text{ADDR}(i + 1) \neq \text{ADDR}(i)$.

(a) A register: From the induction hypothesis, the data from PE P, where $p_i = p_{i-1}$, are in the A register of PE $p_{m-1} \ldots p_{i+1} p_{i-1} \ldots p_1 p_0 p_{m-1}$. When $j = i + 1$, the data are sent to the DTR of this PE by $S3$ and then sent by $S4$ to the DTR of PE $p_{m-1} \ldots \bar{p}_{i+1} p_{i-1} \ldots p_1 p_0 p_{m-1}$. This transfer is correct: $p_{m-1} \ldots p_{i+2} \bar{p}_{i+1} p_{i-1} \ldots p_1 p_0 p_{m-1} = p_{m-1} \ldots p_{i+2} p_i p_{i-1} \ldots p_1 p_0 p_{m-1}$ because $\bar{p}_{i+1} = \overline{\text{ADDR}(i + 1)} = \text{ADDR}(i) = p_{i-1} = p_i$.

(b) DTR: From the induction hypothesis, the data from PE P, where $p_i \neq p_{i-1}$, are in the DTR of PE $p_{m-1} \ldots p_{i+1} p_{i-1} \ldots p_1 p_0 p_{m-1}$. When $j = i + 1$, the data are moved to the A register of this PE by $S3$ and remain there. This move is correct:

$$p_{m-1}\cdots p_{i+2}p_{i+1}p_{i-1}\cdots p_1p_0p_{m-1} = p_{m-1}\cdots \overline{p_{i+2}p_ip_{i-1}}$$
$$\cdots p_1p_0p_{m-1} \text{ because } p_{i+1} = \text{ADDR}(i+1) = \overline{\text{ADDR}(i)} =$$
$$\bar{p}_{i-1} = p_i.$$

Consider the final actions of $S3$ and $S4$ when $j = m - 1$, followed by $S5$.

Case 1: Consider the A register and DTR contents of the PE where $\text{ADDR}(m - 1) = \text{ADDR}(m - 2)$.

(a) A register: From the previous analysis, the data from PE P, where $p_{m-2} = p_{m-3}$, are in the A register of $p_{m-1}p_{m-3}\cdots p_1p_0 p_{m-1}$. These data remain in the A register in $S3$ and are moved to the DTR of that PE in $S5$ because $\text{ADDR}(m - 1) = \text{ADDR}(0) = p_{m-1}$. This result is correct: $p_{m-1}p_{m-3}\cdots p_1p_0p_{m-1} = p_{m-2} p_{m-3}\cdots p_1p_0p_{m-1}$ because $p_{m-1} = \text{ADDR}(m-1) = \text{ADDR}(m-2) = p_{m-3} = p_{m-2}$.

(b) DTR: From the foregoing analysis, the data from PE P, where $p_{m-2} \ne p_{m-3}$, are in the DTR of $p_{m-1}p_{m-3}\cdots p_1p_0p_{m-1}$. These data are sent to PE $\bar{p}_{m-1}p_{m-3}\cdots p_1p_0p_{m-1}$ in $S4$ and are not overwritten in $S5$ (because for PE $\bar{p}_{m-1}p_{m-3}\cdots p_1p_0p_{m-1}$, $\text{ADDR}(m-1) \ne \text{ADDR}(0)$). This result is correct: $\bar{p}_{m-1}p_{m-3} \cdots p_1p_0p_{m-1} = p_{m-2}p_{m-3}\cdots p_1p_0p_{m-1}$ because, using ADDR to refer to the PE containing the data prior to this execution of $S4$, $\bar{p}_{m-1} = \overline{\text{ADDR}(m-1)} = \overline{\text{ADDR}(m-2)} = \bar{p}_{m-3} = p_{m-2}$.

Case 2: Consider the A register and DTR contents of the PE where $\text{ADDR}(m - 1) \ne \text{ADDR}(m - 2)$.

(a) A register: From the preceding induction proof, the data from PE P, where $p_{m-2} = p_{m-3}$ are in the A register of PE $p_{m-1}p_{m-3}\cdots p_1p_0p_{m-1}$. $S3$ moves these data to the DTR and $S4$ moves them to PE $\bar{p}_{m-1}p_{m-3}\cdots p_1p_0p_{m-1}$, where the data remain; the data are not overwritten by $S5$ because for PE $\bar{p}_{m-1}p_{m-3}\cdots p_1p_0p_{m-1}$, $\overline{\text{ADDR}(m-1)} = \text{ADDR}(0)$. This result is correct: $\bar{p}_{m-1}p_{m-3}\cdots p_1p_0p_{m-1} = p_{m-2}p_{m-3}\cdots p_1p_0p_{m-1}$ because, using ADDR to refer to the PE containing the data prior to this execution at $S4$, $\bar{p}_{m-1} = \overline{\text{ADDR}(m-1)} = \text{ADDR}(m-2) = p_{m-3} = p_{m-2}$.

(b) DTR: From the preceding analysis, the data from PE P, where $p_{m-2} \ne p_{m-3}$, are in the DTR of PE $p_{m-1}p_{m-3}\cdots p_1p_0p_{m-1}$. These data are saved in the A register in $S3$ and moved back to the DTR in $S5$ because $\text{ADDR}(m - 1) = \text{ADDR}(0) = p_{m-1}$. This result is correct: $p_{m-1}p_{m-3}\cdots p_1p_0p_{m-1} = p_{m-2}p_{m-3}\cdots p_1p_0p_{m-1}$ because $p_{m-1} = \text{ADDR}(m-1) = \overline{\text{ADDR}(m-2)} = \bar{p}_{m-3} = p_{m-2}$.

For the exchange:

To do the simulation use $cube_0$ because $cube_0$ = exchange by definition.

Lower- and Upper-Bound Results Using the Illiac Network

Lower bounds on the number of inter-PE transfers required by the Illiac network to simulate the PM2I, cube, and shuffle-exchange networks are given in this section. Algorithms to perform these simulations are described and proved correct.

Lower Bound on Illiac → PM2I

Let $d(a,b) = |a - b|$, the absolute difference between a and b. Let $j = (m/2) - 1$. Then $2^j = 2^{(m/2)-1} = (2^{m/2})/2 = n/2$. Then $d(0,PM2_{+j}(0)) = n/2$. It will now be shown that at least $n/2$ Illiac transfers are required to move data this distance.

For $0 \leq a < N$, $d(a, \text{Illiac}_{+n}(a)) = d(a, \text{Illiac}_{-n}(a)) = n$, so the interconnection functions Illiac_{+n} and Illiac_{-n} cannot be used to move a distance of $n/2$ in less than $(n/2) + 1$ steps because if $\text{Illiac}_{\pm n}$ is used, at least $n/2$ additional $\text{Illiac}_{\pm 1}$ transfers would be required. For example, if Illiac_{+n} were used to map 0 to $n/2$, it would have to be followed by $n/2$ executions of Illiac_{-1}. Therefore, the interconnection functions Illiac_{+n} and Illiac_{-n} cannot be used to move a distance of $n/2$ in $n/2$ steps or less. Only Illiac_{+1} and Illiac_{-1} can be used if less than $(n/2) + 1$ steps are to be used. For $0 \leq a < N$, $d(a, \text{Illiac}_{+1}(a)) = d(a, \text{Illiac}_{-1}(a)) = 1$. The only way to map 0 to $n/2$ in $n/2$ steps is to execute Illiac_{+1} $n/2$ times. Thus, $n/2$ steps are required. The case for $PM2_{-j}(1^m)$ is similar.

Upper Bound on Illiac → PM2I

The correctness proofs of these algorithms clearly explain how they operate.

For $PM2_{+i}$, $0 \leq i < m/2$ ($PM2_{-i}$ is similar):

Algorithm to simulate $PM2_{+i}$, $0 \leq i < m/2$:

($S1$) for $j = 1$ until 2^i do Illiac_{+1} $[X^m]$:all PEs execute Illiac_{+1} 2^i times

This algorithm uses 2^i transfers. When $i = (m/2) - 1$ the maximum of $2^{(m/2)-1} = n/2$ transfers occurs.

Table 3-7 demonstrates the operation of this algorithm for $PM2_{+1}$ ($i = 1$) and $N = 16$. For example, the data from the DTR of PE 6 are moved to PE 7 ($= 6 + 1$) when $j = 1$ and to PE 8 ($= 7 + 1$) when $j = 2$. The movement of data from PE 6 to PE 8 ($= PM2_{+1}(6)$) is shown by the dotted line.

Correctness proof: Executing Illiac$_{+1}$ 2^i times is equivalent to executing $PM2_{+i}$, $0 \leq i < m/2$. This can be expressed formally, where (Illiac$_{+1}$)^j means execute Illiac$_{+1}$ j times, as (Illiac$_{+1}$)$^{2^i}(a) = PM2_{+i}(a) = a + 2^i$ modulo N, $0 \leq a < N$, $0 \leq i < m/2$.

For $PM2_{+i}$, $m/2 \leq i < m$ ($PM2_{-i}$ is similar):

Algorithm to simulate $PM2_{+i}$, $m/2 \leq i < m$:

($S1$) for $j = 1$ until $2^i/n$ do Illiac$_{+n}$ [X^m]   :all PEs execute Illiac$_{+n}$ $2^i/n$ times

This algorithm uses $2^i/n$ transfers. When $i = m - 1$ the maximum of $2^{m-1}/n = n/2$ transfers occurs.

Table 3–7
Illiac $\rightarrow$ PM2$_{+i}$ Simulation
(i = 1, N = 16)

PE	Initial DTR Contents	j = 1 DTR Contents	j = 2 DTR Contents
0000	0000	1111	1110
0001	0001	0000	1111
0010	0010	0001	0000
0011	0011	0010	0001
0100	0100	0011	0010
0101	0101	0100	0011
0110	0110·········	0101	0100
0111	0111	········0110·········	0101
1000	1000	0111	·······0110
1001	1001	1000	0111
1010	1010	1001	1000
1011	1011	1010	1001
1100	1100	1011	1010
1101	1101	1100	1011
1110	1110	1101	1100
1111	1111	1110	1101

Note: It is assumed that initially the DTR of PE P contains the integer P, $0 \leq P < 16$.

Table 3–8 demonstrates the operation of this algorithm for $PM2_{+3}$ ($i = 3$) and $N = 16$ ($n = 4$). For example, the data from the DTR of PE 6 are moved to PE 10 ($= 6 + 4$) when $j = 1$ and then to PE 14 ($= 10 + 4$) when $j = 2$. The data movement from PE 6 to PE 14 ($= PM2_{+3}(6)$) is shown by the dotted line in the table.

Correctness proof: Executing $Illiac_{+n}$ $2^i/n$ times is equivalent to executing $PM2_{+i}$, $m/2 \le i < m$. Formally, $(Illiac_{+n})^{2^i/n}(a) = PM2_{+i}(a) = a + 2^i$ modulo N, $0 \le a < N$, $m/2 \le i < m$.

Lower Bound on Illiac → Cube

As in the Illiac → PM2I analysis, let $d(a,b) = |a - b|$, the absolute difference between a and b, and let $j = (m/2) - 1$. Thus, $d(0, cube_j(0)) = n/2$. At least $(n/2) + 1$ steps are required by the Illiac to move this distance. From the Illiac → PM2I study, the only way to map 0 to $n/2$ in less than $(n/2) + 1$ steps using the Illiac network is by executing $Illiac_{+1}$ $n/2$ times, which means the action of $cube_j$ on 0 can be simulated, but $cube_j(n/2) = 0$, and no subsequence of $(Illiac_{+1})^{n/2}$ can perform this mapping. Thus, to simulate the effect of $cube_j$ on both 0 and $n/2$, at least $(n/2) + 1$ steps are required.

Table 3–8
Illiac → PM2$_{+i}$ Simulation
(i = 3, N = 16)

PE	Initial DTR Contents	j = 1 DTR Contents	j = 2 DTR Contents
0000	0000	1100	1000
0001	0001	1101	1001
0010	0010	1110	1010
0011	0011	1111	1011
0100	0100	0000	1100
0101	0101	0001	1101
0110	0110	0010	1110
0111	0111	0011	1111
1000	1000	0100	0000
1001	1001	0101	0001
1010	1010	0110	0010
1011	1011	0111	0011
1100	1100	1000	0100
1101	1101	1001	0101
1110	1110	1010	0110
1111	1111	1011	0111

Note: It is assumed that initially the DTR of PE P contains the integer P, $0 \le P < 16$.

Upper Bound on Illiac → Cube

For cube$_i$, $0 \leq i \leq (m/2) - 2$:

The algorithm performs the simulation for PE addresses with a 0 in the ith bit position and for addresses with a 1 in the ith bit position separately. $S2$ moves the data from PEs whose addresses are of the form $p_{m-1} \cdots p_{i+1} 0 p_{i-1} \cdots p_0$ to the corresponding PEs of the form $p_{m-1} \cdots p_{i+1} 1 p_{i-1} \cdots p_0$ by adding 2^i ($=$ (Illiac$_{+1}$)$^{2^i}$). These data items are saved in the A registers of PEs $p_{m-1} \cdots p_{i+1} 1 p_{i-1} \cdots p_0$ in $S3$ and restored to the DTRs in $S5$. This step completes the simulation for data originally in PEs with a 0 in the ith bit position of their addresses. To perform the simulation for PEs with a 1 in the ith bit position of their addresses, $S1$ saves the original DTR data of PEs whose addresses are of the form $p_{m-1} \cdots p_{i+1} 1 p_{i-1} \cdots p_0$ in their respective A registers. If this step were not taken, these data would be overwritten by $S2$. $S3$ moves the original DTR data of PEs of the form $p_{m-1} \cdots p_{i+1} 1 p_{i-1} \cdots p_0$ from their A registers back into their DTRs. $S4$ then moves these data to the corresponding PEs of the form $p_{m-1} \cdots p_{i+1} 0 p_{i-1} \cdots p_0$ by subtracting 2^i ($=$ (Illiac$_{-1}$)$^{2^i}$). This move completes the simulation for data originally in PEs with a 1 in the ith bit position of their addresses.

Algorithm to simulate cube$_i$, $0 \leq i \leq (m/2) - 2$:

$(S1)$ $A \leftarrow$ DTR $[X^{m-(i+1)} 1 X^i]$:PEs with $p_i = 1$ save DTR data in A register

$(S2)$ for $j = 1$ until 2^i do Illiac$_{+1}$ $[X^m]$:all PEs execute Illiac$_{+1}$ 2^i times

$(S3)$ $A \leftrightarrow$ DTR $[X^{m-(i+1)} 1 X^i]$:PEs with $p_i = 1$ switch DTR and A data

$(S4)$ for $j = 1$ until 2^i do Illiac$_{-1}$ $[X^m]$:all PEs execute Illiac$_{-1}$ 2^i times

$(S5)$ DTR $\leftarrow$ A $[X^{m-(i+1)} 1 X^i]$:PEs with $p_i = 1$ reload DTR with A register data

The algorithm uses $2 * 2^i$ transfers and three register-to-register operations. Thus, the maximum number of transfers needed to simulate cube$_i$, for $0 \leq i \leq (m/2) - 2$, is $2 * 2^{(m/2)-2} = n/2$ (which occurs when $i = (m/2) - 2$).

Table 3–9 demonstrates the operation of this algorithm for cube$_0$ ($i = 0$) and $N = 16$ ($m = 4$). For example, the data from the DTR of PE 6 are moved to PE 7 ($= 6 + 1$) by $S2$ when $j = 1$, saved in the A register by $S3$ (since 7 ($= 0111$) matches the mask $[XXX1]$), and reloaded into the DTR of PE 7 ($=$ cube$_0$(6)) by $S5$ (since 7 matches $[XXX1]$) as shown by the dotted line.

Table 3-9
Illiac → Cube$_i$ Simulation
(i = 0, N = 16)

PE	Initial DTR Contents	S1 A Contents	S2 j = 1 DTR Contents	S3 A Contents	S3 DTR Contents	S4 j = 1 DTR Contents	S5 DTR Contents
0000	0000	—	1111	—	1111	0001	0001
0001	0001	0001	0000	0000	0001	0001	0000
0010	0010	—	0001	—	0001	0011	0011
0011	0011	0011	0010	0010	0011	0011	0010
0100	0100	—	0011	—	0011	0101	0101
0101	0101	0101	0100	0100	0101	0101	0100
0110	0110	—	0101	—	0101	0111	0111
0111	0111	0111	0110	0110	0111	0111	0110
1000	1000	—	0111	1000	0111	1001	1001
1001	1001	1001	1000	—	1001	1001	1000
1010	1010	—	1001	1010	1001	1011	1011
1011	1011	1011	1010	—	1011	1011	1010
1100	1100	—	1011	1100	1011	1101	1101
1101	1101	1101	1100	—	1101	1101	1100
1110	1110	—	1101	1110	1101	1111	1111
1111	1111	1111	1110	—	1111	1111	1110

Note: It is assumed that initially the DTR of PE P contains the integer P, $0 \leq P < 16$.

Correctness proof:

Case 1: Consider the DTR data originally in PE P, where $p_i = 0$.
This PE address does not match the mask in $S1$ since $p_i = 0$. This
address is mapped to (Illiac$_{+1}$)$^{2^i}$ $(p_{m-1} \cdots p_{i+1} 0 p_{i-1} \cdots p_0) =$
$p_{m-1} \cdots p_{i+1} 0 p_{i-1} \cdots p_0 + 2^i = p_{m-1} \cdots p_{i+1} 1 p_{i-1} \cdots p_0$
by $S2$, thus transferring the data from the DTR of PE P to the
DTR of PE $P + 2^i = p_{m-1} \cdots p_{i+1} 1 p_{i-1} \cdots p_0$. This PE
matches the mask in $S3$ (since $p_i = 1$), and these data are saved in
the A register of the PE. This PE matches the mask in $S5$ (since
$p_i = 1$), and so these data are moved from the A register back into
the DTR. Thus, the DTR data originally in PE $P = p_{m-1} \cdots$
$p_{i+1} 0 p_{i-1} \cdots p_0$ terminate in the DTR of PE $p_{m-1} \cdots$
$p_{i+1} 1 p_{i-1} \cdots p_0 = \text{cube}_i(P)$.

Case 2: Consider the DTR data originally in PE P, where $p_i = 1$.
This PE matches the mask in $S1$ (since $p_i = 1$) and the DTR data
is saved in the A register at the PE. This PE matches the mask in
$S3$ (since $p_i = 1$) and the data in the A register are moved back to
the DTR. $S4$ then moves these data from PE P to PE (Illiac$_{-1}$)$^{2^i}$
$(p_{m-1} \cdots p_{i+1} 1 p_{i-1} \cdots p_0) = p_{m-1} \cdots p_{i+1} 1 p_{i-1} \cdots p_0 -$
$2^i = p_{m-1} \cdots p_{i+1} 0 p_{i-1} \cdots p_0$. This PE does not match the
mask in $S5$ (since $p_i = 0$). Thus, the DTR data originally in PE
$P = p_{m-1} \cdots p_{i+1} 1 p_{i-1} \cdots p_0$ terminate in the DTR of PE
$p_{m-1} \cdots p_{i+1} 0 p_{i-1} \cdots p_0 = \text{cube}_i(P)$.

For cube$_{(m/2)-1}$:

This algorithm is similar to one used in the PM2I $\rightarrow$ cube analysis,
when $i = (m/2) - 1$ (recall $2^{(m/2)-1} = n/2$). $S1$ adds $2^{(m/2)-1}$ by executing
Illiac$_{+1}$ $n/2$ times and $S2$ subtracts any "carry" by executing Illiac$_{-n}$ in
PEs where address bit $(m/2) - 1$ is 0.

Algorithm to simulate cube$_{(m/2)-1}$:

($S1$) for $j = 1$ until $n/2$ do Illiac$_{+1}$ $[X^m]$:all PEs execute Illiac$_{+1}$ $n/2$ times

($S2$) Illiac$_{-n}$ $[X^{m/2} 0 X^{(m/2)-1}]$:PEs whose $(m/2)$ $-$ 1st bit is 0
                                                        execute Illiac$_{-n}$

The algorithm uses $(n/2) + 1$ transfers. This is the cube function that takes
the longest to simulate and determined the lower bound as described earlier.
If the algorithm used for simulating cube$_i$, $0 \leq i \leq (m/2) - 2$, were used
for this case ($i = (m/2) - 1$), $2 * 2^{(m/2)-1} = n$ transfers would be required.
Table 3–10 demonstrates the operation of this algorithm for cube$_1$

Table 3–10
Illiac → Cube$_i$ Simulation
(i = 1, N = 16)

PE	Initial DTR Contents	S1 j = 1 DTR Contents	S1 j = 2 DTR Contents	S2 DTR Contents
0000	0000	1111	1110	0010
0001	0001	0000	1111	0011
0010	0010	0001	0000	0000
0011	0011	0010	0001	0001
0100	0100	0011	0010	0110
0101	0101	0100	0011	0111
0110	0110	0101	0100	0100
0111	0111	0110	0101	0101
1000	1000	0111	0110	1010
1001	1001	1000	0111	1011
1010	1010	1001	1000	1000
1011	1011	1010	1001	1001
1100	1100	1011	1010	1110
1101	1101	1100	1011	1111
1110	1110	1101	1100	1100
1111	1111	1110	1101	1101

Note: It is assumed that initially the DTR of PE P contains the integer P, $0 \leq P < 16$.

$(i = 1)$ and $N = 16$ $(n = 4, m = 4)$. For example, the data from the DTR of PE 6 are moved to PE 7 $(= 6 + 1)$ by $S1$ when $j = 1$, to PE 8 $(= 7 + 1)$ by $S1$ when $j = 2$, and then to PE 4 $(= 8 - 4)$ by $S2$ (since 4 $(= 0100)$ matches the mask $[XX0X]$). The data movement from PE 6 to PE 4 $(= \text{cube}_1(6))$ is shown by the dotted line.

Correctness proof:

Case 1:   Consider PE P, where $p_{(m/2)-1} = 0$.
            $S1$ maps P to $P + n/2 = \text{cube}_{(m/2)-1}(P)$. The $(m/2) - $ 1st bit is now 1, so it does not execute $S2$.

Case 2:   Consider PE P, where $p_{(m/2)-1} = 1$.
            $S1$ maps P to $P + n/2$. The $(m/2) - $ 1st bit is now 0, so $S2$ is executed, mapping $P + n/2$ to $P - n/2 = \text{cube}_{(m/2)-1}(P)$.

$S2$ does not destroy data because only PEs with a 0 in the $(m/2) - $ 1st bit position will send and receive data.

For cube$_i$, $m/2 \leq i \leq m - 2$:

This algorithm is analogous to the algorithm for cube$_i$, $0 \leq i \leq (m/2) - 2$. The difference here is that because $i \geq m/2$ (that is, $2^i \geq n$), the Illiac$_{+n}$ and Illiac$_{-n}$ are used instead of Illiac$_{+1}$ and Illiac$_{-1}$, respectively.

Algorithm to simulate cube_i, $m/2 \le i \le m - 2$:

($S1$) $A \leftarrow \text{DTR} \ [X^{m-(i+1)} 1 X^i]$:PEs with $p_i = 1$ save DTR data in A register

($S2$) for $j = 1$ until $2^i/n$ do $\text{Illiac}_{+n} \ [X^m]$:all PEs execute Illiac_{+n} $2^i/n$ times

($S3$) $A \leftrightarrow \text{DTR} \ [X^{m-(i+1)} 1 X^i]$:PEs with $p_i = 1$ switch DTR and A data

($S4$) for $j = 1$ until $2^i/n$ do $\text{Illiac}_{-n} \ [X^m]$:all PEs execute Illiac_{-n} $2^i/n$ times

($S5$) $\text{DTR} \leftarrow A \ [X^{m-(i+1)} 1 X^i]$:PEs with $p_i = 1$ reload DTR with A register data

The algorithm uses $2 * (2^i/n)$ transfers and there are three register-to-register operations. Thus, the maximum number of transfers needed to simulate cube_i, for $m/2 \le i \le m - 2$, is $2 * (2^{m-2}/n) = n/2$ (which occurs when $i = m - 2$).

Table 3–11 demonstrates the operation of this algorithm for cube_2 ($i = 2$) and $N = 16$. For example, the data from the DTR of PE 6 are moved to the A register by $S1$ (since 6 ($= 0110$) matches the mask $[X 1 X X]$), back to the DTR by $S3$ (because 6 matches $[X 1 X X]$), and then to PE 2 ($= 6 - 4$) by $S4$. The data movement from PE 6 to PE 2 ($= \text{cube}_2(6)$) is shown by the dotted line.

Correctness proof: The correctness proof is analogous to the case where $0 \le i \le (m/2) - 2$. In this case, $(\text{Illiac}_{+n})^{2^i/n}(a) = a + 2^i$ modulo N and $(\text{Illiac}_{-n})^{2^i/n}(a) = a - 2^i$ modulo N, $0 \le a < N$, $m/2 \le i \le m - 2$.

For cube_{m-1}:

Use the Illiac $\rightarrow \text{PM2}_{+(m-1)}$ algorithm described previously in the Illiac $\rightarrow$ PM2I analysis, because $\text{PM2}_{+(m-1)}(a) = \text{cube}_{m-1}(a)$, $0 \le a < N$. This algorithm requires $n/2$ transfers.

Lower Bound on Illiac $\rightarrow$ Shuffle-Exchange

For the shuffle:

The lower bound for the Illiac network to simulate the shuffle is $2(n - 2)$ transfers. This bound is derived from results about mesh interconnection networks and mesh interconnection with "orthogonal wraparound." The details, which are in Nassimi and Sahni (1980), are beyond the scope of this book.

Table 3–11
Illiac → Cube$_i$ Simulation
(i = 2, N = 16)

PE	Initial DTR Contents	S1 A Contents	S2 j = 1 DTR Contents	S3 A Contents	S3 DTR Contents	S4 j = 1 DTR Contents	S5 DTR Contents
0000	0000	—	1100	—	1100	0100	0100
0001	0001	—	1101	—	1101	0101	0101
0010	0010	—	1110	—	1110	0110	0110
0011	0011	—	1111	—	1111	0111	0111
0100	0100	0100	0000	0000	0100	0100	0000
0101	0101	0101	0001	0001	0101	0101	0001
0110	0110	0110	0010	0010	0110	0110	0010
0111	0111	0111	0011	0011	0111	0111	0011
1000	1000	—	0100	—	0100	1100	1100
1001	1001	—	0101	—	0101	1101	1101
1010	1010	—	0110	—	0110	1110	1110
1011	1011	—	0111	—	0111	1111	1111
1100	1100	1100	1000	1000	1100	1100	1000
1101	1101	1101	1001	1001	1101	1101	1001
1110	1110	1110	1010	1010	1110	1110	1010
1111	1111	1111	1011	1011	1111	1111	1011

Note: It is assumed that initially the DTR of PE P contains the integer P, $0 \leq P < 16$.

For the exchange:

The exchange function requires at least two steps to be simulated because it is not equivalent to any single Illiac function.

Upper Bound on Illiac → Shuffle-Exchange

For the shuffle:

The algorithm to perform the shuffle using the Illiac network is constructed by replacing each PM2I interconnection function in the PM2I → shuffle algorithm discussed earlier with Illiac interconnection functions. For $S2$, use $\text{Illiac}_{+1} [X^{m-1}1]$ because $\text{Illiac}_{+1} = \text{PM2}_{+0}$ by definition. Similarly, for $S6$, use $\text{Illiac}_{+1} [X^{m-1}0]$. To do $S5$, first recall that only the even-numbered PEs contain the data of concern (after $S2$ is executed and before $S6$ is executed). Therefore, it is acceptable to use $\text{PM2}_{+j} [X^m]$ in $S5$, since any data movement among the odd-numbered PEs is ignored (and overwritten by $S6$). To perform $\text{PM2}_{+j} [X^m]$ for $1 \leq j < m$ with the Illiac network, the Illiac → PM2I algorithms presented previously are used. These substitutions result in the following algorithm.

Algorithm to simulate the shuffle:

$(S1)$ $A \leftarrow \text{DTR} [X^{m-1}0]$

$(S2)$ $\text{Illiac}_{+1} [X^{m-1}1]$

$(S3)$ for $j = 1$ until $(m/2) - 1$ do

$(S4)$ $\quad A \leftrightarrow \text{DTR} [X^{m-j-1}1 X^{j-1}0]$

$(S5)$ $\quad$ for $i = 1$ until 2^j do $\text{Illiac}_{+1} [X^m]$ $\quad$:PM2_{+j}

$(S3')$ for $j = m/2$ until $m - 1$ do

$(S4')$ $\quad A \leftrightarrow \text{DTR} [X^{m-j-1}1 X^{j-1}0]$

$(S5')$ $\quad$ for $i = 1$ until $2^j/n$ do $\text{Illiac}_{+n} [X^m]$ $\quad$:PM2_{+j}

$(S6)$ $\text{Illiac}_{+1} [X^{m-1}0]$

$(S7)$ $\text{DTR} \leftarrow A [X^{m-1}0]$

The total number of Illiac transfers needed is:

for $S2$: 1

for $S6$: 1

for $S5$: $\displaystyle\sum_{j=1}^{(m/2)-1} 2^j = 2^{m/2} - 2 = n - 2$

$$\text{for } S5': \sum_{j=m/2}^{m-1} 2^j/n = \sum_{j=m/2}^{m-1} 2^{j-(m/2)} = \sum_{j=0}^{(m/2)-1} 2^j = n - 1$$

Thus, the grand total is $2n - 1$ transfers. The number of register to register moves is still $m + 1$.

Table 3-12 demonstrates the operation of this algorithm for $N = 16$. For example, the data from the DTR of PE 5 are moved to the DTR of PE 6 ($= 5 + 1$) by $S2$, to the A register of PE 6 by $S4$ when $j = 1$, to the DTR of PE 6 by $S4'$ when $j = 2$, to the DTR of PE 10 ($= 6 + 4$) by $S5'$ when $j = 2$ and $i = 1$, to the A register of PE 10 by $S4'$ when $j = 3$, and the DTR of PE 10 by $S7$. The data movement from PE 5 to PE 10 ($= \text{shuffle}(5)$) is shown by the dotted line.

Correctness proof: The correctness of this algorithm follows from the correctness proofs of the PM2I $\rightarrow$ shuffle and Illiac $\rightarrow$ PM2I algorithms described previously.

For the exchange:

Use the Illiac $\rightarrow$ cube algorithm, for $i = 0$ because exchange $= \text{cube}_0$. This simulation is demonstrated in table 3-9.

Lower- and Upper-Bound Results Using the Shuffle-Exchange Network

In this section lower bounds on the number of inter-PE transfers required by the shuffle-exchange network to simulate the PM2I, cube, and Illiac networks are given. As in the previous sections, an algorithm to perform each simulation is described and proved correct.

Lower Bound on Shuffle-Exchange $\rightarrow$ PM2I

$\text{PM2}_{+i}(1^m) = 0^{m-i}1^i$ and $\text{PM2}_{-i}(0^m) = 1^{m-i}0^i$. To map 1^m to $0^{m-i}1^i$ a sequence of $m - i$ ones must be mapped to $m - i$ zeroes. Recall that the shuffle function can only rotate the bits of an address; therefore given the address 1^m it cannot change any ones to zeroes. The exchange function can map ones to zeroes, but the bit that is to be changed must be in the 0th bit position when the exchange is executed. To map 1^m to $0^{m-i}1^i$, a 1 must be rotated into the 0th bit position, mapped to a 0, and then shuffled to the $(m - 1)$st bit position. Thus, at least $m - 1$ shuffles will be required to per-

Table 3-12
Illiac → Shuffle Simulation
(N = 16)

PE DTR	S1 A	S2 DTR	S4 j=1 A	S4 j=1 DTR	S5 j=1 i=1 DTR	S5 j=1 i=2 DTR	S4' j=2 A	S4' j=2 DTR	S5' j=2 i=1 DTR	S4' j=3 A	S4' j=3 DTR	S5' j=3 i=1 DTR	S5' j=3 i=2 DTR	S6 DTR	S7 DTR
0000	0000	1111	0000	1111	–	1110	0000	1110	1100	0000	1100	1010	1000	1000	1000	0000
0001	–	0000	–	–	1111	–	–	–	1101	–	–	1011	–	–	1000	1000
0010	0010	0001	0001	0010	–	1111	0001	1111	1101	0001	1101	1011	1001	1001	1001	0001
0011	–	0010	–	0011	0010	–	0011	0100	1110	0010	1110	1100	1010	–	1001	1001
0100	0100	0011	0100	–	–	0010	0000	0100	1110	0011	1010	1100	1010	1010	1010	0010
0101	–	0100	–	0101	0010	–	1000	–	0101	–	1001	–	1101	–	1010	1010
0110	0110	0101	0110	–	–	0011	1001	0110	0100	0101	1011	1101	1101	1011	1011	0011
0111	–	0110	–	0111	0111	–	1001	1001	0110	0110	1011	1100	1110	–	1011	1011
1000	1000	0111	1000	–	–	1010	1010	1000	0110	0111	1000	0101	1001	1100	1100	0100
1001	–	1000	–	1001	1010	–	1010	1010	0111	–	1010	0110	1000	–	1100	1100
1010	1010	1001	1001	1010	–	1011	1010	1011	0111	1010	1010	0111	1001	1101	1101	0101
1011	–	1010	–	1011	1011	–	1011	0111	0100	1011	0111	1111	1001	1110	1101	1101
1100	1100	1011	1100	–	–	1010	1010	1100	–	–	1001	1111	1111	1110	1110	0110
1101	–	1100	–	1101	1010	–	1011	1101	0101	0101	1011	–	1101	–	1110	1110
1110	1110	1101	1101	1110	–	1011	–	–	–	–	1011	1001	1001	1111	1111	0111
1111	–	1110	–	–	1110	–	–	–	–	–	–	0111	1111	–	1111	1111

Note: It is assumed that initially the DTR of PE *P* contains the integer *P*, $0 \le P < 16$.

form this mapping. To change $m - i$ ones to $m - i$ zeroes, at least $m - i$ exchanges must be executed, one to map each 1 to a 0. The case for mapping 0^m to $1^{m-i}0^i$ is similar. Therefore, it takes at least $2m - (i + 1)$ steps for the shuffle-exchange to simulate PM2$_{\pm i}$. When $i = 0$, at least $2m - 1$ steps are required to perform the simulation.

Upper Bound on Shuffle-Exchange → PM2I

For PM2$_{+i}$, $0 \leq i < m$ (PM2$_{-i}$ is similar):

The algorithm to perform this simulation uses the same approach as in the cube → PM2I algorithm described earlier. The difference between the two algorithms is the result of the fact that for the exchange function of the shuffle-exchange network to complement a bit it must be first shuffled (rotated) into the 0th bit position.

Consider the task of mapping the address P to $P + 2^i$ modulo N. The algorithm works by complementing the jth bit of an address, $j = m - 1$, $m - 2, \ldots, i + 1$, if the $(j - 1)$st through ith bits are all ones, thus simulating the action of the carry when PM2$_{+i}$ is applied. This is done by $S1$, $S2$, and $S3$. If the original address was $p_{m-1} \ldots p_j 11 \ldots 1 p_{i-1} \ldots p_0$, then p_j will be occupying the 0th bit position and p_{j-1} to p_i will be occupying the $(m - 1)$st to $(m - (j - i))$th bit positions when p_j is complemented by the exchange in $S3$. The algorithm statement $S3$ then complements the ith bit when $j = i$. The low-order i bits $p_{i-1} \ldots p_1 p_0$ are not changed, since they are unaffected by PM2$_{+i}$. $S4$ performs i shuffles so that, in conjunction with the $m - i$ shuffles in $S1$ and $S2$, a total of m shuffles are executed, restoring the address bits to their original positions. In the following algorithm the shuffle in $S4$ is never executed if $i = 0$.

Algorithm to simulate PM2$_{+i}$, $0 \leq i < m$:

($S1$) for $j = m - 1$ step -1 until i do   :execute $S2$ and $S3$ $m - i$ times for carry and p_i

($S2$)   shuffle $[X^m]$:all PEs execute shuffle

($S3$)   exchange $[1^{j-i}X^{m-(j-i)}]$:if original $p_{j-1} \ldots p_{i+1}$ $p_i = 1 \ldots 11$ do exchange

($S4$) for $j = i - 1$ step -1 until 0 do   :all PEs do i shuffles
        shuffle $[X^m]$

The algorithm uses m shuffles and $m - i$ exchanges. The maximum number of transfers is $2m$ and occurs when $i = 0$.

Table 3-13 demonstrates the operation of this algorithm for PM2$_{+1}$ ($i = 1$) and $N = 8$ ($m = 3$). For example, the DTR contents of PE 6

Table 3-13
Shuffle-Exchange → PM2$_{+i}$ Simulation
(i = 1, N = 8)

PE	Initial DTR Contents	S2 j = 2 DTR Contents	S3 j = 2 DTR Contents	S2 j = 1 DTR Contents	S3 j = 1 DTR Contents	S4 j = 0 DTR
000	000	000	000	000	110	110
001	001	100	100	110	000	111
010	010	001	001	100	010	000
011	011	101	101	010	100	001
100	100	010	110	001	111	010
101	101	110	010	111	001	011
110	110	011	111	101	011	100
111	111	111	011	011	101	101

Note: It is assumed that initially the DTR of PE P contains the integer P, $0 \leq P < 8$.

$(= 110 = p_2p_1p_0)$ are moved to PE 5 $(= 101 = p_1p_0p_2)$ by $S2$ and to PE 4 $(= 100 = p_1p_0\bar{p}_2)$ by $S3$ when $j = 2$ (since 5 matches the mask $[1\,XX]$), to PE 1 $(= 001 = p_0\bar{p}_2p_1)$ by $S2$ and to PE 0 $(= 000 = p_0\bar{p}_2p_1)$ by $S3$ when $j = 1$ (because the mask is $[X^m]$), and stop in PE 0 $(= 000 = \bar{p}_2 p_1p_0)$ as a result of $S4$. The data movement from PE 6 to PE 0 $(= PM2_{+1}$ (6)) is shown by the dotted line.

Correctness proof: Induction on the algorithm variable j is used to prove that after $S2$ and $S3$ are executed, if the addresses were to be rotated left j times, as they would be by the shuffle functions in $S2$ and $S4$, then bits $m - 1$ through j and bits $i - 1$ through 0 would contain the desired value; that is, the simulation will be finished for these bits. In other words, $P = p_{m-1} \cdots p_1p_0$ is mapped to $p_{j-1} \cdots p_{i+1}p_ip'_{i-1} \cdots p'_1p'_0p'_{m-1} \cdots p'_{i+1}p'_i$, where $P + 2^i$ modulo $N = p'_{m-1} \cdots p'_1p'_0$. Thus, when $j = i$, the simulation will be complete, except for the i shuffles in $S4$. That is, when $j = i$, P will be mapped to $p'_{i-1} \cdots p'_1p'_0p'_{m-1} \cdots p'_{i+1}p'_i$, which when shuffled i times by $S4$ is $p'_{m-1} \cdots p'_1p'_0$.

BASIS: $j = m - 1$.

Case 1. Consider a PE address originally of the form $p_{m-1}1^{m-(i+1)}p_{i-1} \cdots p_0$. The shuffle in $S2$ maps this address to the corresponding address of the form $1^{m-(i+1)}p_{i-1} \cdots p_0p_{m-1}$. This address matches the mask in $S3$ (since the high-order $j - i = m - (i + 1)$ bits are all ones), and so the exchange is executed, complementing p_{m-1}. That is, it is mapped to $1^{m-(i+1)}p_{i-1} \cdots p_0\bar{p}_{m-1} = 1^{m-(i+1)}p'_{i-1} \cdots p'_0p'_{m-1}$. If this address is rotated left $j = m - 1$

times it becomes $\bar{p}_{m-1}1^{m-(i+1)}p_{i-1} \cdots p_0$. This satisfies the induction hypothesis since $PM2_{+i}$ would have this effect on the $(m-1)$st bit position. Bits $i-1$ to 0 remain unchanged.

Case 2: Consider a PE address originally *not* of the form $p_{m-1}1^{m-(i+1)}$ $p_{i-1} \cdots p_0$. This address is shuffled once by $S2$, mapping it to $p_{m-2} \cdots p_1 p_0 p_{m-1} = p_{m-2} \cdots p_{i+1}p_ip'_{i-1} \cdots p'_0p'_{m-1}$. This result does not match the mask in $S3$ because the high-order $j - i = m - (i + 1)$ bits are not all ones. Therefore, after rotating left $m - 1$ times, the original address is unchanged. This result is correct, because p_{m-1} would not be changed by $PM2_{+i}$ unless p_{m-2} through p_i were all ones.

INDUCTION STEP: Assume true for $j = k$. Show true for $j = k - 1$.

Case 1: Consider a PE address originally of the form:

$$p_{m-1} \cdots p_{k-1}1^{k-(i+1)}p_{i-1} \cdots p_0$$

From the induction hypothesis it is known that after $S3$ is executed with $j = k$ this address will be mapped to:

$$p_{k-1}1^{k-(i+1)}p'_{i-1} \cdots p'_0p'_{m-1} \cdots p'_k$$

where p'_{m-1} through p'_k and p'_{i-1} through p'_0 contain their proper final values (but need to be rotated left k times). When $j = k - 1$ the address is shuffled by $S2$ to:

$$1^{k-(i+1)}p'_{i-1} \cdots p'_0p'_{m-1} \cdots p'_kp_{k-1}$$

This address matches the mask in $S3$ because the high-order $j - i = k - (i + 1)$ bits are all ones. Therefore, p_{k-1} is complemented, as it would be by $PM2_{+i}$, since bits p_{k-2} through p_i are all ones. That is, it is mapped to $1^{k-(i+1)}p'_{i-1} \cdots p'_0p'_{m-1} \cdots$ $p'_k\bar{p}_{k-1} = 1^{k-(i+1)}p'_{i-1} \cdots p'_0p'_{m-1} \cdots p'_kp'_{k-1}$. If this address is left-rotated $j = k - 1$ times, then bits $m - 1$ through $j = k - 1$ will contain their final values. Bits $i - 1$ through 0 remain unchanged.

Case 2: Consider a PE address not of the form given in Case 1. From the induction hypothesis it is known that after $S3$ is executed with $j = k$ this address will be mapped to:

$$p_{k-1} \cdots p_{i+1}p_ip'_{i-1} \cdots p'_0p'_{m-1} \cdots p'_k$$

where p'_{m-1} through p'_k and p'_{i-1} through p'_0 contain their proper final values. When $j = k - 1$ the address is shuffled by $S2$ to:

$$p_{k-2} \cdots p_{i+1} p_i p'_{i-1} \cdots p'_0 p'_{m-1} \cdots p'_k p_{k-1}$$

This address will not match the mask in $S3$ because the high-order $j - i = k - (i + 1)$ bits are not all ones. Thus, p_{k-1} is unchanged, as it should be, since no carry would reach it (that is, $p_{k-1} = p'_{k-1}$). If this address is left-rotated $j = k - 1$ times, the bit positions will contain the proper values.

The exchanges in $S3$ do not destroy data because whenever they are executed the 0th position of the accompanying mask is X. In other words, if $p_{m-1} \cdots p_1 p_0$ is sending data, so is $p_{m-1} \cdots p_1 \bar{p}_0$.

Lower Bound on Shuffle-Exchange → Cube

Consider the mapping $\text{cube}_{m-1}(10^{m-3}11) = 0^{m-2}11$. For the shuffle-exchange network to perform this mapping at least one exchange must be executed because the number of ones in the address decreases as a result of the mapping. Obviously, at least one shuffle is required (to move the 1 out of the high-order bit position). The number of shuffles must exceed $m - 2$ or else the 1 that was originally in bit position 1 (next to the rightmost) will be moved to some position between 2 and $m - 1$, which should be occupied by a 0. However, 1 exchange and $m - 1$ shuffles are not sufficient. If the exchange is used first, followed by $m - 1$ shuffles, then $10^{m-3}11$ will be mapped to $010^{m-3}1 \neq 0^{m-2}11$. If the exchange is not used first, the $m - 1$ shuffles will move the 1 that was originally in position 0 to position $m - 1$, which should be a 0. Therefore, at least $m + 1$ steps are required for this simulation. Similar arguments can be made to show that $m + 1$ steps are required to simulate $\text{cube}_i, 0 < i < m - 1$.

Upper Bound on Shuffle-Exchange → Cube

For cube_0:

To do the simulation use the exchange function because exchange = cube_0 by definition.

For $\text{cube}_i, 0 < i < m$:

Consider mapping the address $p_{m-1} \cdots p_i \cdots p_0$ to $p_{m-1} \cdots \bar{p}_i \cdots p_0$.

The addresses must be shuffled (the bit position must be left-rotated) $m - i$ times before the exchange can be used to complement the ith bit position. After the exchange is used, the address must be shuffled i times to return the bits of each of the addresses to their proper positions.

Algorithm to simulate cube$_i$, $0 < i < m$:

(S1) for $j = 1$ until $m - i$ do   shuffle $[X^m]$:all PEs execute $m - i$ shuffles

(S2) exchange $[X^m]$:all PEs execute exchange

(S3) for $j = 1$ until i do   shuffle $[X^m]$:all PEs execute i shuffles

The algorithm uses m shuffles and 1 exchange.

Table 3–14 demonstrates the operation of this algorithm for cube$_1$ ($i = 1$) and $N = 8$. For example, the data from the DTR of PE 6 ($= 110 = p_2 p_1 p_0$) are moved to PE 5 ($= 101 = p_1 p_0 p_2$) and then to PE 3 ($= 011 = p_0 p_2 p_1$) by S1, then to PE 2 ($= 010 = p_0 p_2 \bar{p}_1$) by S2, and finally to PE 4 ($= 100 = p_2 \bar{p}_1 p_0$) by S3. The data movement from PE 6 to PE 4 ($=$ cube$_1$ (6)) is shown by the dotted line.

Correctness proof: Consider the PE address $p_{m-1} \ldots p_i \ldots p_0$. cube$_i(p_{m-1} \ldots p_i \ldots p_0) = p_{m-1} \ldots \bar{p}_i \ldots p_0$. Applying the shuffle $m - i$ times in S1 maps the address $p_{m-1} \ldots p_i \ldots p_0$ to $p_{i-1} \ldots p_0 p_{m-1} \ldots p_i$. Applying the exchange in S2 maps this to $p_{i-1} \ldots p_0 p_{m-1} \ldots \bar{p}_i$. Applying the shuffle i times in S3 maps $p_{i-1} \ldots p_0 p_{m-1} \ldots \bar{p}_i$ to $p_{m-1} \ldots \bar{p}_i \ldots p_0$. Formally stated, where shuffle^i means apply the shuffle i times:

$$\text{shuffle}^i(\text{exchange } (\text{shuffle}^{m-i}(p_{m-1} \ldots p_i \ldots p_0)))$$

$$= p_{m-1} \ldots p_{i+1} \bar{p}_i p_{i-1} \ldots p_0$$

Lower and Upper Bounds on Shuffle-Exchange → Illiac

These bounds follow from the earlier shuffle-exchange → PM2I and PM2I → Illiac analyses. The lower bound is $2m - 1$ and the upper bound is $2m$ (which occur for Illiac$_{\pm 1}$).

Upper Time Bounds with Some PEs Inactive

The simulation algorithms presented in this chapter assumed that all PEs were executing the interconnection function to be simulated. They were based on the premise that the interconnection function being simulated was

Table 3–14
Shuffle-Exchange → Cube$_i$ Simulation
(i = 1, N = 8)

PE	Initial DTR Contents	S1 j = 1 DTR Contents	S1 j = 2 DTR Contents	S2 DTR Contents	S3 j = 1 DTR Contents
000	000	000	000	010	010
001	001	100	010	000	011
010	010	001	100	110	000
011	011	101	110	100	001
100	100	010	001	011	110
101	101	110	011	001	111
110	110	011	101	111	100
111	111	111	111	101	101

Note: It is assumed that initially the DTR of PE *P* contains the integer *P*, $0 \le P < 8$.

broadcast with a mask equal to $[X^m]$ and was not inside a conditional statement; that is, the simulation was done assuming that all PEs were active. For example, if the shuffle was being simulated, it was simulated as if each PE executed the shuffle function. But if the actual instruction was shuffle [001], only PE 1 should pass its data. Similarly, if the instruction was embedded in a conditional statement, such as:

$$\text{where } y = 0 \text{ do} \qquad \text{shuffle } [X^m]$$

only PEs whose contents of location *y* equal 0 should execute the shuffle.

It will now be shown that if network *k* can simulate interconnection function *f* when all PEs are active, *k* can also simulate *f* when certain PEs are inactive as a result of PE address and/or data-conditional masking. In the next subsection, the case when *f* is executed with an arbitrary PE address mask, but is not embedded in a conditional statement, is considered. The case when *f* is executed with an arbitrary PE address mask and it is embedded in a conditional statement is considered in a subsequent subsection.

Using a PE Address Mask

This subsection examines the case where the interconnection function being simulated is executed with an arbitrary PE address mask $[R]$, but is not inside a conditional statement. If a network *k* can simulate interconnection function *f* executed with mask $[X^m]$, then it can simulate *f* executed with arbitrary PE address mask $[R]$ using no additional inter-PE data transfers.

To simulate $f[R]$ the mask $[R]$ is broadcast from the control unit to all PEs as data and stored in the vector MASK. The DTR contents of each PE are saved in register C. Then $f[X^m]$ is simulated. Each PE then computes f^{-1} (f inverse) of its address, where f^{-1} is the function such that $f^{-1}(f(P)) = P$, $0 \leq P < N$. For example, $(PM2_{+0})^{-1} = PM2_{-0}$, since $PM2_{-0}(PM2_{+0}(P)) = (P + 2^0) - 2^0 = P$, $0 \leq P < N$. This address is computed because $f^{-1}(ADDR)$ gives the address of the PE that would send data to PE ADDR when f is executed. For example, $(PM2_{+0})^{-1}(7) = 6$ since $PM2_{+0}(6) = 7$. PE ADDR should receive new data in its DTR if PE $f^{-1}(ADDR)$ is active (that is, it matches $[R]$). PE ADDR should restore its original DTR contents from its register C if PE $f^{-1}(ADDR)$ is not active (does not match $[R]$). Thus, after computing $f^{-1}(ADDR)$, each PE compares the result with $[R]$, which is stored in MASK. In PEs where it does not match, the original DTR contents saved in C are reloaded into the DTR because these PEs would not have received data as a result of $f[R]$.

For example, for $N = 8$, if $PM2_{+0}[XX1]$ is being simulated, then $f^{-1} = (PM2_{+0})^{-1} = PM2_{-0}$ and $R = XX1$. $PM2_{+0}[X^m]$ is simulated in all PEs. Now consider what happens in, for example, PEs 2 and 3. In PE 2, $PM2_{-0}(2) = 1$ is compared to $[XX1]$. It matches, and so the data that were sent from PE 1 to PE 2 remain in PE 2's DTR, as they should. In PE 3, $PM2_{-0}(3) = 2$ is compared to $[XX1]$. It does not match, and so the data in the DTR that were sent from PE 2 to PE 3 are overwritten with PE 3's original DTR contents (which were saved in PE 3's C register), as they should.

The following algorithm demonstrates how this sequence can be performed in the general case. If necessary, the contents of any PE registers to be used by the simulation algorithm can be saved and restored since those PEs which do not match $[R]$ should not change the contents of these registers. In the algorithm, let MASK(i) be the ith position of the mask $[R]$, let f^{-1} be the inverse of f (the interconnection function to be simulated), and let INVERSE(i) be the ith bit of INVERSE.

$C \leftarrow DTR \quad [X^m]$:save original DTR contents in register C

simulation of $f[X^m]$:use algorithm from earlier sections in this chapter

INVERSE $\leftarrow f^{-1}(ADDR) [X^m]$:each PE computes f^{-1} of its address

for $i = 0$ until $m - 1$ do

    where ((INVERSE(i) $\neq$ MASK(i)) and (MASK(i) $\neq X$))
                                   :compare f^{-1} to MASK

        do DTR $\leftarrow C [X^m]$:restore original data if no match

Now consider how to compute INVERSE $\leftarrow f^{-1}$(ADDR) $[X^m]$ for each interconnection function in the four networks defined in chapter 2. Let ADDR(i) be the ith bit of ADDR. Recall that $\bar{y}$ is the complement of y. In each of the following cases, the instructions given are used to replace INVERSE $\leftarrow f^{-1}$(ADDR) $[X^m]$ in the preceding algorithm.

Case 1:   PM2I.

For PM2_{+i}, $0 \leq i < m$, where $(\text{PM2}_{+i})^{-1} = \text{PM2}_{-i}$:

INVERSE $\leftarrow$ ADDR $-$ 2^i modulo N $[X^m]$

For PM2_{-i}, $0 \leq i < m$, where $(\text{PM2}_{-i})^{-1} = \text{PM2}_{+i}$:

INVERSE $\leftarrow$ ADDR $+$ 2^i modulo N $[X^m]$

Case 2:   Cube.

For cube_i, $0 \leq i < m$, where $(\text{cube}_i)^{-1} = \text{cube}_i$:

INVERSE $\leftarrow$ ADDR $[X^m]$

INVERSE(i) $\leftarrow$ $\overline{\text{ADDR}(i)}$ $[X^m]$

Case 3:   Illiac.

For Illiac_{+1}, where $(\text{Illiac}_{+1})^{-1} = \text{Illiac}_{-1}$:

INVERSE $\leftarrow$ ADDR $-$ 1 modulo N $[X^m]$

For Illiac_{-1}, where $(\text{Illiac}_{-1})^{-1} = \text{Illiac}_{+1}$:

INVERSE $\leftarrow$ ADDR $+$ 1 modulo N $[X^m]$

For Illiac_{+n}, where $(\text{Illiac}_{+n})^{-1} = \text{Illiac}_{-n}$:

INVERSE $\leftarrow$ ADDR $-$ n modulo N $[X^m]$

For Illiac_{-n}, where $(\text{Illiac}_{-n})^{-1} = \text{Illiac}_{+n}$:

INVERSE $\leftarrow$ ADDR $+$ n modulo N $[X^m]$

Case 4:   Shuffle-exchange.

For the exchange, where $(\text{exchange})^{-1} = \text{exchange}$:

INVERSE $\leftarrow$ ADDR $[X^m]$

INVERSE(0) $\leftarrow$ $\overline{\text{ADDR}(0)}$ $[X^m]$

For the shuffle:

INVERSE $\leftarrow$ right cyclic shift (ADDR) $[X^m]$

In summary, if network k can simulate interconnection function f executed with mask $[X^m]$, it can simulate f executed with arbitrary PE address mask $[R]$ using no additional inter-PE data transfers, but requiring

$O(m)$ (a constant times m) machine operations and extra space. This requirement is met by having each PE save a copy of its DTR data, simulating f with all PEs active, and then having those PEs where f^{-1} of their address does not match $[R]$ restore their original DTR data. The value of f^{-1} for each PE could be stored or easily computed. In the next section, the simulation of $f[R]$ when it is embedded in one or more nested conditional statements is considered.

Using Conditional and PE Address Masks

This subsection examines the case where the interconnection function to be simulated is executed with a PE address mask inside a conditional statement. It will be shown that an upper bound on this task is twice the number of inter-PE data transfers that are required to perform the simulation when all PEs are active. If either a single bit position (for example, the high-order bit position) or a particular data word value (for example, all ones) is reserved for use as a tag, the simulation can be done in the same number of inter-PE data transfers as the simulation when all PEs are active.

Before presenting this method, consider the task of executing a conditional statement on an SIMD machine. To implement conditional masks each PE must have a flag (or set of flags if nested conditional statements are allowed) to indicate whether the PE is active for the current do or elsewhere block. Let the set of flags be called the *PE status word,* and the location where it is stored be called the *status-word register*. Without loss of generality, assume that bit 0 of the status-word register indicates the current active or inactive status for the PE. With these assumptions, it can be shown that if a network k can simulate interconnection function f executed with PE address mask $[X^m]$ using y interprocessor data transfers, then k can simulate the effect of f executed with arbitrary PE address mask $[R]$ within a conditional statement using at most $2y$ interprocessor data transfers.

In general, the routines described earlier used to simulate $f[X^m]$ assume that all PEs are active. Thus, the simulation routine in the previous subsection cannot simply replace $f[R]$ within the conditional statement because all PEs will not necessarily be active within that do or elsewhere block. Therefore, to use the simulation routine in the previous section, all PEs must be activated. When the simulation is completed, those PEs which were inactive before the simulation must again be deactivated. To accomplish this, the PE status word is saved in register B, and the status-word register is loaded to indicate the PE is active. The simulation is performed and then the PE status word saved in register B is reloaded into the status-word register. It is assumed that a PE can read from and write into its status-word register while active or inactive.

A tag bit, TAG, is used to identify the data from PEs that would be active if $f[R]$ was executed within the conditional. TAG is set to 1 in those PEs which would actually be executing f, and set to 0 in the PEs which would be inactive and so would not be executing f. The simulation $f[X^m]$ is modified so that each time that the original DTR contents of PEs are transferred, TAG is also transferred. In this way, each TAG bit remains associated with the proper DTR contents. Initially all PEs save a copy of their DTR contents. When the simulation of $f[X^m]$ is completed, those PEs whose DTR contents have a TAG = 0 associated with them reload their original DTR contents because they received data from a PE that was supposed to be inactive.

The following algorithm can be used to simulate $[R]$ when it is embedded in one or more conditional statements.

$(S1)$ $B \leftarrow$ status-word register $[X^m]$:each PE saves its status word in its B register

$(S2)$ status-word register $\leftarrow$ active $[X^m]$:set all PEs to active

$(S3)$ TAG $\leftarrow$ 0 $[X^m]$:initialize TAG to 0 in all PEs

$(S4)$ where $B(0) = 1$ do TAG $\leftarrow$ 1 $[R]$:set TAG to 1 in originally active PEs

$(S5)$ $A \leftarrow$ DTR $[X^m]$:save original DTR data in A register in all PEs

$(S6)$ modified simulation of $f[X^m]$:modification is sending TAG with data

$(S7)$ where TAG = 0 do DTR $\leftarrow$ A $[X^m]$:if sending PE inactive, restore DTR data

$(S8)$ status-word register $\leftarrow$ B $[X^m]$:restore original PE status-word value

As in the previous subsection, it may be necessary to save and later restore the contents of all PE registers used by the simulation.

Let g be an arbitrary function in network k and let $[Q]$ be an arbitrary PE address mask, where $g[Q]$ is used in the algorithm to simulate $f[X^m]$. Then to construct the modified simulation of $f[X^m]$ by network k in $S6$ above replace each occurrence of the form $g[Q]$ in the simulation with:

$g[Q]$:send data item

$C \leftarrow$ DTR $[X^m]$:save data g just sent

DTR $\leftarrow$ TAG $[X^m]$:load TAG to be sent

$g [Q]$:send TAG

TAG $\leftarrow$ DTR $[X^m]$:save new TAG g just sent

DTR $\leftarrow$ C $[X^m]$:load data g sent into DTR

This sequence will keep each PE's DTR data together with their associated TAG.

In this algorithm the number of data transfers required to perform the simulation is twice that needed to perform the simulation if the interconnection function being simulated were not embedded within a conditional statement because the tag bit was transferred in addition to the DTR contents. If there is a reserved bit or a reserved bit configuration for DTR data, the simulation can be done using no additional interprocessor data transfers.

A *reserved bit* is a bit position in the data word to be transferred that is to be used only by the simulation algorithm (for example, the high-order bit). The contents of this bit will be destroyed by the simulation algorithm, so it cannot be used by the programmer, compiler, or otherwise. Bits can be reserved in two ways. One way is to restrict the use of one of the W bits of any data word that is to be transferred through the interconnection network. This restriction would apply only on data words when they are being transferred. Another way is to implement the DTR and fast-access registers with $W + 1$ bit positions. This alternative allows the use of tag bits without restricting the use of the W bits of the data words.

In the simulation algorithm use the reserved bit as TAG. Thus, each time the original DTR data are transferred, TAG is also transferred. Replace $S6$ in the earlier algorithm with "simulation of $f[X^m]$."

A *reserved bit configuration* is similar to a reserved bit, except that instead of using a single bit position of a word, a single value of the word (for example, all bits equal 1) is used. That is, instead of restricting one of W bit positions (or requiring a $W + $ 1st bit for the registers), one of 2^W bit configurations is restricted. This restriction would apply only on data words when they are being transferred.

To see how a reserved bit configuration would be used in a simulation algorithm, let this reserved bit configuration be rbc. Replace $S6$ and $S7$ in the earlier algorithm with:

where TAG = 0 do DTR $\leftarrow$ rbc $[X^m]$:DTR data from inactive PE is
                                                     rbc

simulation of $f[X^m]$

where DTR = rbc do DTR $\leftarrow$ A $[X^m]$:restore original DTR data

Thus, in this case the data that were originally in DTRs of PEs that were active and matched mask $[R]$ were tagged by not being rbc.

Summary

The simulation routines in the preceding sections assume all PEs are executing the interconnection function to be simulated. Further, these routines assume that all PEs are active and able to participate in the simulation algorithm. This section showed how to simulate an interconnection function that is to be executed by only those PEs which match an arbitrary PE address mask. The method requires no additional inter-PE data transfers. The case when the interconnection function to be simulated is being executed with an arbitrary PE address mask and is within a conditional (where) statement was also considered in this section. A procedure for performing the simulation using a tag bit to identify valid data was given. Twice the number of data transfers normally needed are required so that the tag can be passed with the data. This technique requires no additional inter-PE data transfers if there is a reserved bit or reserved bit configuration.

Conclusions

Lower and upper bounds on the time required for each of the cube, PM2I, shuffle-exchange, and Illiac networks to simulate the other networks were presented. To find the lower bounds of these simulation algorithms, one must consider which operations occur in parallel and find ways to describe these actions mathematically. To construct the simulation algorithms, the parallel flow of N data words through N PEs must be understood. It must be determined which data may be destroyed by a data transfer that is not representable as a bijection on the PE addresses and save that data in such a way that it can be later identified and used. Furthermore, special actions must be taken when the interconnection to be simulated is executed with some PE disabled. To prove that the algorithms are correct, standard mathematical techniques, such as induction and case analysis, were adapted for use in parallel-program analysis. In addition, the approach of considering the simulation problem as a task to map one integer or class of integers to another integer or another class of integers was taken, as opposed to viewing the process strictly as one of transferring data among PEs.

The methods presented in this chapter may be generalized and used to compare other networks. These techniques were demonstrated by examples because there are currently no good algorithms for generating such lower-bound proofs, simulation algorithms, or SIMD algorithm-correctness proofs.

The results of this chapter have both theoretical and practical value. Theoretically, they add to the body of knowledge and understanding about the properties of the cube, PM2I, shuffle-exchange, and Illiac networks. Practically, the algorithms can actually be used to perform the various interconnection functions on a system that has implemented one of these networks. Furthermore, the lower-bound proofs derive the minimum number of transfers required to do each simulation; that is, it is impossible to do a simulation in fewer transfers than the lower bound.

No attempt is made to claim that any one network is best as a result of the analysis in this chapter. One factor that will influence the decision of which network to implement in the system is the types of computations for which the system will be primarily used. For example, for a simple image-processing smoothing algorithm such as the one presented in chapter 2, the eight nearest-neighbor interconnection scheme, with only eight interconnection functions ($+1$, -1, $+n$, $-n$, $+n-1$, $+n+1$, $-n-1$, and $-n+1$), may be the most efficient. The number of PEs in the system is another important factor. For small N, a crossbar switch may be acceptable. Other factors include computational speed and cost requirements. Assuming a general-purpose SIMD machine, where N is large, the various networks have advantages and disadvantages, independent of the previous factors.

The Illiac network is much more limited in simulation capabilities than its superset the PM2I network, although it has the advantage of having only four interconnection functions, as compared to the $2m - 1$ distinct functions of the PM2I network. However, if a designer wants the capabilities of the PM2I network, but cannot afford $2m - 1$ interconnection functions, a compromise can be made. Any number of PM2I functions can be eliminated and simulated by the remaining functions. For example, the number of functions may be reduced from $2m - 1$ to m (assuming m is even) by eliminating PM2$_{\pm i}$ for all odd i. The functions PM2$_{\pm(i-1)}$ (i odd) could be executed twice when one of the eliminated functions is needed. Thus, the PM2I network presents more design alternatives than the Illiac network and can be reduced to the Illiac network.

The cube and PM2I networks are conceptually similar, with the cube connection pattern based on a logical neighborhood and the PM2I pattern based on a modulo N addition or subtraction neighborhood. The cube network uses almost half as many interconnection functions as the PM2I network. However, the cube network requires m steps to simulate PM2$_{\pm 0}$, a commonly used connection, whereas the PM2I network requires only two steps to simulate any cube function. Furthermore, the number of connections in the cube networks cannot be reduced as it can with the PM2I network. Because of these considerations, the PM2I network may be preferable in the general case.

The shuffle-exchange network has the advantage of requiring only two interconnection functions, with which it can simulate the other networks discussed using at most $2m$ steps. If the system architect is concerned with minimizing hardware costs and is willing to use $2m$ transfers for the various interconnection patterns that were shown would require that amount (such as PM2$_{\pm 0}$), the shuffle-exchange network is an excellent choice. If the main concern of the system architect is computational speed, without unreasonable expense, a good choice is a PM2I-shuffle hybrid network consisting of the $2m - 1$ PM2I functions and a shuffle function that could simulate any of the functions discussed in at most two steps. Such a hybrid network would offer great flexibility and speed.

In conclusion, the results of this chapter provide information to aid the SIMD-machine architect in selecting an interconnection network that will be best suited to the needs of the system. The methods presented here provide tools for the designer to use to evaluate and compare other networks and hybrids of networks.

4 Partitioning Single-Stage Networks

This chapter analyzes the partitionability of the single-stage networks defined in chapter 2. The *partitionability* of an interconnection network is the ability to divide the network into independent subnetworks of different sizes (Siegel 1980). Each subnetwork of size $N' < N$ must have all of the interconnection capabilities of a complete network of that same type built to be of size N'. A partitionable network can be characterized by any limitations on the way in which it can be subdivided.

Multiple-SIMD systems use partitionable interconnection networks to dynamically reconfigure the system into independent SIMD machines of various sizes. Recall from chapter 2 that a multiple-SIMD machine is a parallel-processing system that can be structured as one or more independent SIMD machines. If PE i and PE j are assigned to different control units, they may not be following the same instruction stream and can act independently. If the virtual SIMD machines that can be formed in a multiple-SIMD system are to be independent, the network they share must be partitionable into independent subnetworks. The multiple-SIMD model is the framework for the analyses in this chapter.

The partitioning properties of a single-stage network can also be used in an MIMD environment, where every processor executes its own instructions (see chapter 2). For example, the CHoPP MIMD machine (Sullivan, Bashkow, and Kappholz 1977) uses a single-stage cube network. The results in this chapter can be used to partition such a system into independent subsystems. These results are obviously also applicable to the partitionable-SIMD/MIMD systems discussed in chapter 2.

In this chapter, interconnection functions are related to permutations and the cycle notation for representing permutations are presented. The cube, Illiac, PM2I, and shuffle-exchange single-stage networks are redefined in terms of their permutation-cycle structure and their partitionability is evaluated. This material is based on Siegel (1980). It is used to study the partitionability of multistage networks in chapters 5 and 6.

Single-Stage Networks as Permutations

Formally, an interconnection network is defined to be a set of interconnection functions. Each interconnection function is a bijection on the set of

85

input/output addresses, the integers from 0 to $N - 1$. A *bijection* is a one-to-one and onto mapping. *One-to-one* means that a PE receives data from exactly one PE when an interconnection function is executed (assuming all PEs are active). Mathematically, one-to-one implies (in this case) that an integer in the set of PE addresses is mapped to by exactly one integer in the set when an interconnection function is applied. For example, consider the exchange function. PE 0 receives data from PE 1; no other PE can send data to PE 0 using the exchange. Analogously, 0 is mapped to by 1 (exchange(1) = 0); no other integer can be mapped to 0 (if exchange(i) = 0, then $i = 1$).

Onto means that every PE receives data from some other PE when an interconnection function is executed (assuming all PEs are active). Mathematically, onto implies (in this case) that every integer in the set of PE addresses is mapped to by some integer in the set when an interconnection function is applied. For example, again consider the exchange function. PE $P = p_{m-1} \ldots p_1 p_0$ receives data from PE exchange(P) = $p_{m-1} \ldots p_1 \bar{p}_0$, $0 \le P < N$; every PE receives data. Analogously, P is mapped to by exchange(P), $0 \le P < N$; every PE address is mapped to by some integer in the set.

A *permutation* is another name for a bijection that is from a set onto the same set, as is the case for interconnection functions. In other words, an interconnection function f permutes the ordered list $0, 1, \ldots, N - 1$ into $f(0), f(1), \ldots, f(N - 1)$. For example, for $N = 8$, the exchange interconnection function permutes the ordered list 0, 1, 2, 3, 4, 5, 6, 7 to exchange(0), exchange(1), . . . , exchange(7), which is 1, 0, 3, 2, 5, 4, 7, 6.

A *cyclic notation* can be used to represent the interconnection function f as a permutation. The permutation is represented as the product of cycles, where a cycle of the form:

$$(j_0 \ j_1 \ j_2 \ \cdots \ j_{k-1} \ j_k)$$

means $f(j_0) = j_1, f(j_1) = j_2, \ldots, f(j_{k-1}) = j_k$, and $f(j_k) = j_0$. The length of this cycle is $k + 1$. The physical interpretation of this cycle is that input j_0 is connected to output j_1, input j_1 is connected to output j_2, . . . , input j_{k-1} is connected to output j_k, and input j_k is connected to output j_0. For example, if the interconnection function p is defined to be $p(i) = i + 1$ modulo 8, then the permutation p is represented by the single cycle:

$$p = (\ 0\ 1\ 2\ 3\ 4\ 5\ 6\ 7\ )$$

Some permutations are represented by two or more disjoint cycles (two cycles are disjoint if they have no elements in common). For example, if the interconnection function q is defined to be $q(i) = i + 2$ modulo 8, then the permutation q is represented by two cycles:

$$q = (0\ 2\ 4\ 6)(1\ 3\ 5\ 7)$$

The permutation cycle structure corresponds to the loops in the physical connections of an interconnection function, which can be observed by comparing the cycle structure for q with its physical connections shown in figure 4-1.

The *product* of two or more permutations is the composition of the bijections (interconnection functions) that define the permutations. If p and q are permutations, then pq represents the effect of first applying p and then applying q. For the examples of p and q above:

$$pq = (0\ 3\ 6\ 1\ 4\ 7\ 2\ 5)$$

because $q(p(0)) = 3, q(p(3)) = 6, \ldots, q(p(5)) = 0$. That is, p maps 0 to 1 and q maps 1 to 3, so pq maps 0 to 3; p maps 3 to 4 and q maps 4 to 6, so pq maps 3 to 6; . . . ; and p maps 5 to 6 and q maps 6 to 0, so pq maps 5 to 0, closing the cycle. The permutation pq is defined by $q(p(i)) = (i + 1) + 2 = i + 3$ modulo 8. Physically, this means that pq first moves data from PE i to PE $i + 1$ modulo 8 (with interconnection function p) and then from PE $i + 1$ to PE $i + 3$ modulo 8 (with interconnection function q), $0 \le i < 8$.

The product of the permutations p and q in the preceding example is commutative; that is, $pq = qp$. However, in general, the product of two permutations is not necessarily commutative. For example, if:

$$g = (0\ 1)(2\ 3) \text{ and } h = (0\ 1\ 2\ 3)$$

then:

$$gh = (0\ 2)(1)(3)$$

However,

$$hg = (1\ 3)(0)(2) \ne gh$$

When a permutation is expressed by more than one cycle, as is the case for q and g in the previous example, it is said to be represented by a product of cycles. Every permutation can be represented by a unique product of disjoint cycles (Herstein 1964). The *cycle structure* of an interconnection function is its unique disjoint-cycles representation (Siegel 1977). When using the cycle-structure description, cycles of length one (that is, $f(j_i) = j_i$) are

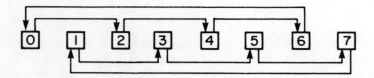

Figure 4–1. Physical Connections of the Interconnection Function $q(i) = i + 2$ Modulo 8, $0 \le i < 8$

typically not included. For example, the cycle structure of gh defined above is:

$$gh = (\,0\ 2\,)(\,1\,)(\,3\,) = (\,0\ 2\,)$$

This terminology is used to define the cycle structure of the cube, Illiac, PM2I, and shuffle-exchange interconnection networks. The definitions and permutation properties discussed in this section will then be used to analyze partitionability later in the chapter.

Cube Network Cycle Structure

Each $cube_i$ function, $0 \le i < m,$ of the cube interconnection network can be described in terms of permutations. The $cube_i$ interconnection function can be expressed uniquely as a product of $N/2$ disjoint cycles of length two by:

$$\prod_{\substack{j=0 \\ i\text{th bit of } j = 0}}^{N-1} (\,j\ \ cube_i(j)\,)$$

This product of cycles will produce a different set of $N/2$ disjoint cycles for each value of $i,\ 0 \le i < m.$ For example, for $N = 8$:

$$cube_2 = (\,0\ 4\,)(\,1\ 5\,)(\,2\ 6\,)(\,3\ 7\,)$$

To relate this to the physical cube interconnections, see figure 2–13.

As stated previously, all active PEs execute the same interconnection function (instruction) at the same time. For a data transfer to be representable as a permutation (bijection), if one PE in a cycle is inactive, the other

PEs in that cycle must also be inactive. For example, consider cube$_2$ for $N = 8$. If PEs 0 and 4 are inactive they keep their own data, so the (0 4) cycle is removed, and the cube$_2$ permutation becomes cube$_2'$, where:

$$\text{cube}_2' = (\,0\,)\,(\,4\,)\,(\,1\;5\,)\,(\,2\;6\,)\,(\,3\;7\,) = (\,1\;5\,)\,(\,2\;6\,)\,(\,3\;7\,)$$

since cube$_2'(0) = 0$ and cube$_2'(4) = 4$. If only PE 0 was inactive in the preceding example, then:

1. PE 0 would keep its own data $(0 \rightarrow 0)$ and PE 4 would send its data $(4 \rightarrow 0)$, a two-to-one, not one-to-one, transfer; and
2. PE 4 would not receive any data, so the transfer would not be onto.

Thus, in general, for each cycle in a permutation, either all PEs in the cycle must be active or all PEs in the cycle must be inactive for the resulting data transfer to be representable as a permutation (Siegel 1977). If the transfer is not representable as a permutation, DTR data will be destroyed (as is PE 0's original DTR data in the preceding example).

Here, only data tranfers that are representable as permutations will be considered. Therefore, when the function cube$_i$ is executed, the way in which data is permuted is:

$$\prod_{j=0}^{N-1} (\ j\ \text{cube}_i(j)\ ),$$

where the ith bit of $j = 0$ and where the cycle containing j is included only if PE j and PE cube$_i(j)$ are active. Furthermore, if a cycle containing k is not included, then PE k and PE cube$_i(k)$ must be inactive.

Illiac Network Cycle Structure

The four Illiac network interconnection functions can be expressed as permutations. The permutation-cycle structure of the Illiac$_{+1}$ and Illiac$_{-1}$ functions each consists of a single cycle of length N. The cycle structure of the Illiac$_{+n}$ and Illiac$_{-n}$ functions each consists of n cycles of length n. In particular:

$$\text{Illiac}_{+1} = (\,0\ 1\ 2\ \ldots\ N-1\,)$$

$$\text{Illiac}_{-1} = (\,N-1\ \ldots\ 2\ 1\ 0\,)$$

$$\text{Illiac}_{+n} = \prod_{j=0}^{n-1} (\; j \quad j+n \quad j+2n \quad \ldots \quad j+N-n \;)$$

$$\text{Illiac}_{-n} = \prod_{j=0}^{n-1} (\; j+N-n \quad \ldots \quad j+2n \quad j+n \quad j \;)$$

The permutation equations for $\text{Illiac}_{\pm n}$ include a cycle for each value of j, $0 \le j < n$. For example, for $N = 16$, $j = 0, 1, 2$, and 3, so Illiac_{+n} is:

$$(0\ 4\ 8\ 12)\ (1\ 5\ 9\ 13)\ (2\ 6\ 10\ 14)\ (3\ 7\ 11\ 15)$$

and Illiac_{-n} is:

$$(12\ 8\ 4\ 0)\ (13\ 9\ 5\ 1)\ (14\ 10\ 6\ 2)\ (15\ 11\ 7\ 3)$$

This result can be related to the physical structure of the network by observing figure 2–9.

As with the cube network, if one PE in a cycle is inactive, the other PEs in that cycle must also be inactive if that data transfer is to be representable as a permutation. For example, for $N = 16$, if the even-numbered PEs are inactive, the Illiac_{+n} permutation becomes:

$$(1\ 5\ 9\ 13)\ (3\ 7\ 11\ 15)$$

and the Illiac_{-n} permutation becomes:

$$(13\ 9\ 5\ 1)\ (15\ 11\ 7\ 3)$$

In general, when either the Illiac_{+1} or Illiac_{-1} interconnection function is executed, data are permuted as described only if all PEs are active. When the interconnection function Illiac_{+n} is executed, the way in which the data is permuted is:

$$\prod_{j=0}^{n-1} (\; j \quad j+n \quad j+2n \quad \ldots \quad j+N-n \;)$$

and when the interconnection function Illiac_{-n} is executed, the way in which the data are permuted is:

$$\prod_{j=0}^{n-1} (\; j+N-n \quad \ldots \quad j+2n \quad j+n \quad j \;)$$

where the cycle containing j is included only if PEs $j + k * n, 0 \leq k < n,$ are all active. Furthermore, if a cycle containing i is not included, then PEs $i + k * n$ modulo $N, 0 \leq k < n,$ must all be inactive.

PM2I Network Cycle Structure

The $2m$ functions of the PM2I interconnection network can each be represented as permutations. The PM2$_{+i}$ interconnection function can be expressed uniquely as a product of 2^i disjoint cycles of length 2^{m-i} by:

$$\prod_{j=0}^{2^i-1} (\, j \quad j+2^i \quad j+2*2^i \quad j+3*2^i \quad \ldots \quad j+N-2^i \,)$$

This product of cycles will produce a different set of 2^i disjoint cycles of length $2^{m-i} (= N/2^i)$ for each value of $i,\ 0 \leq i < m.$ The equation for a given value of i includes a cycle for each value of $j,\ 0 \leq j < 2^i.$ For example, for $N = 8$ and $i = 1, j$ can be 0 or 1, and so PM2$_{+1}$ is:

$$(\, 0 \; 2 \; 4 \; 6 \,) (\, 1 \; 3 \; 5 \; 7 \,)$$

This result can be compared to the PM2I network structure shown in figure 2-10. Similarly, the PM2$_{-i}$ interconnection function can be expressed uniquely as a product of 2^i disjoint cycles of length 2^{m-i} by:

$$\prod_{j=0}^{2^i-1} (\, j+N-2^i \quad \ldots \quad j+3*2^i \quad j+2*2^i \quad j+2^i \quad j \,)$$

For example, for $N = 8$, PM2$_{-1}$ is:

$$(\, 6 \; 4 \; 2 \; 0 \,) (\, 7 \; 5 \; 3 \; 1 \,)$$

As with the other networks, if one PE in a cycle is inactive, the other PEs in that cycle must also be inactive if the data transfer is to be representable as a permutation. For example, consider PM2$_{+1}$ for $N = 8$. If PEs 0, 2, 4 and 6 are inactive, their cycle is removed and the permutation becomes:

$$(\, 1 \; 3 \; 5 \; 7 \,)$$

In general, when the interconnection function PM2$_{+i}$ is executed, $0 \leq i < m,$ the way in which the data are permuted is:

$$\prod_{j=0}^{2^i-1} (\; j \quad j+2^i \quad j+2*2^i \quad j+3*2^i \; \ldots \; j+N-2^i \;)$$

and when the interconnection function PM2$_{-i}$ is executed, $0 \le i < m$, the way in which the data are permuted is:

$$\prod_{j=0}^{2^i-1} (\; j+N-2^i \; \ldots \; j+3*2^i \quad j+2*2^i \quad j+2^i \quad j \;)$$

where the cycle containing j is included only if PEs $j + k * 2^i$, $0 \le k < 2^{m-i}$, are all active. Furthermore, if a cycle containing h is not included, PEs $h + k * 2^i$ modulo N, $0 \le k < 2^{m-i}$, must all be inactive.

Shuffle-Exchange Network Cycle Structure

The shuffle and exchange functions of the shuffle-exchange interconnection can also be described as permutations. The cycle structure of the exchange is defined first. Then the shuffle's cycle structure is defined.

The exchange interconnection function can be expressed uniquely as a product of $N/2$ disjoint cycles of length two by:

$$\prod_{\substack{j=0 \\ j \text{ even}}}^{N-2} (\; j \quad j+1 \;)$$

This is the same as the cycle structure for cube$_0$. For example, for $N = 8$ the exchange is:

$$(0 \; 1)(2 \; 3)(4 \; 5)(6 \; 7)$$

Now consider the shuffle function. Recall that shuffle^i means apply the shuffle function i times. Then, in terms of a permutation, the shuffle interconnection function can be expressed uniquely as a product of disjoint cycles by:

$$\prod_{\substack{j=0 \\ j \text{ not in a} \\ \text{previous cycle}}}^{N-1} (\; j \quad \text{shuffle}(j) \quad \text{shuffle}^2(j) \; \ldots \;)$$

For example, for $N = 8$, $j = 0$ generates the cycle (0), $j = 1$ generates the cycle (1 2 4), $j = 3$ generates the cycle (3 6 5), and $j = 7$ generates the cycle (7), so the shuffle is:

$$(0) (1\ 2\ 4) (3\ 6\ 5) (7) = (1\ 2\ 4) (3\ 6\ 5)$$

This cycle structure can be seen by examining the physical connections of the shuffle shown in figure 2-12. PEs 1, 2, and 4 form a loop (cycle). Similarly, PEs 3, 6, and 5 form a loop (cycle). PE 0 and PE 7 each form a loop (cycle) of length one. In general, for a shuffle based on N elements, the lengths of the cycles in the product of disjoint cycles representation of the shuffle will vary. However, the largest a cycle can be is m because shuffle$^m(k) = k$, $0 \le k < N$. For example, for $N = 16$, the cycle structure of the shuffle is:

$$(0) (1\ 2\ 4\ 8) (3\ 6\ 12\ 9) (5\ 10) (7\ 14\ 13\ 11) (15)$$

Recall that if one PE in a cycle is inactive, the other PEs in that cycle must also be inactive if the data transfer is to be representable as a permutation. For example, consider the shuffle function for $N = 8$. If PEs 1, 2, and 4 are inactive, the (1 2 4) cycle is removed and the permutation becomes:

$$(3\ 6\ 5)$$

In general, when the shuffle interconnection function is executed, the way in which data is permuted is:

$$\prod_{j=0}^{N-1} (\ j \ \text{shuffle}(j) \ \text{shuffle}^2(j) \ \dots\ )$$

where the cycle containing j is included only if j has not appeared in a previous cycle and PEs shuffle$^i(j)$, $0 \le i < m$, are all active. Furthermore, if a cycle containing k is not included, then PEs shuffle$^i(k)$, $0 \le i < m$, must all be inactive. The permutation analysis for the exchange interconnection function of the shuffle-exchange network when some PEs may be inactive is the same as the analysis presented for cube$_0$.

Partitioning Results

The set of PEs in a system are *physically* numbered (addressed) from 0 to $N - 1$. When the PEs are partitioned into independent groups, each group will have its own logical numbering. For example, for $N = 8$, divide the PEs into two groups: GE—those with even physical numbers (0, 2, 4, and 6), and GO—those with odd physical numbers (1, 3, 5, and 7). Within each group, the PEs will be *logically* numbered from 0 to 3. Let logically numbered PEs 0, 1, 2, and 3 in GE be the physical PEs 0, 2, 4, and 6, respectively. Similarly, let logical PEs 0, 1, 2, and 3 of GO be the physical PEs 1, 3, 5, and 7, respectively. Consider what happens if the PEs are connected using the cube network as shown in figure 2–13. If the cube$_0$ function is not used, the two groups are independent and cannot communicate because all PEs in GE have a 0 in the lower-order physical address-bit position and all PEs in GO have 1 in that position. The only way for a PE in GE to communicate with a PE in GO is by using the cube$_0$ connection. Using the logical numbering of the PEs, the physical cube$_1$ connections act as logical cube$_0$ connections and the physical cube$_2$ connections act as logical cube$_1$ connection as shown in figure 4–2.

In this section, the ideas in this example are formalized and used to evaluate the partitionability of single-stage interconnection networks. To analyze formally the partitioning of interconnection networks, the following definitions are introduced:

A. $P = \{0, 1, 2, \ldots, N - 1\}$, the set of physical PE addresses (the physical-address space).

B. $\ell_i = \{\ell_{i/0}, \ell_{i/1}, \ell_{i/2}, \ldots \ell_{i/(\sigma_i - 1)}\}$, the set of logical PE addresses in the ith partition, where $\ell_{i/j}$ is the PE in partition ℓ_i with the logical address j.

C. σ_i is the size of ℓ_i (that is, $|\ell_i| = \sigma_i$), where $0 < \sigma_i \leq N$ and σ_i is a power of two.

D. ν is the number of partitions, where $0 < \nu \leq N$.

E. $L = \ell_0 \cup \ell_1 \cup \ell_2 \ldots \cup \ell_{(\nu - 1)} = \overset{\nu - 1}{\underset{j=0}{\cup}} \ell_j$, the set of logical PE addresses for all partitions (the logical-address space), where

$$|L| = \sum_{i=0}^{\nu - 1} \sigma_i = N$$

F. t is a transformation (bijection) from P to L (that is, $t: P \rightarrow L$), such that if $t(p_k) = \ell_{i/j}$ then $t^{-1}(\ell_{i/j}) = p_k$, where $p_k \in P$, $\ell_{i/j} \in L$, and t^{-1} is the inverse of t (where ϵ means "is a member of").

The physical interconnection network of a system is defined in terms of P. The transformation t establishes a correspondence between the physical PE addresses and the logical PE addresses; that is, t assigns each physical PE number to a partition and a logical number within that partition.

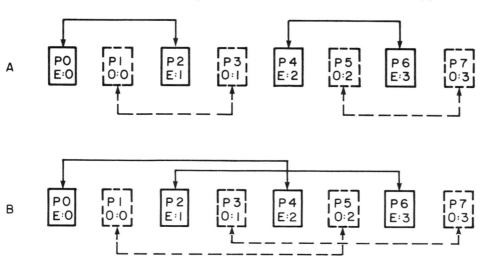

Note: Eight PEs are divided into two groups, based on even and odd physical numbers. P indicates physical numbers; E: and O: indicate even- and odd-group logical numbers, respectively. Solid lines show the even group and dashed lines show the odd group. A. Physical cube$_1$ (logical cube$_0$). B. Physical cube$_2$ (logical cube$_1$).

Figure 4–2. Partitioning a Size-Eight Cube Network

Partitioning the Cube Network

An example of partitioning a size-eight cube network into two subnetworks of size four was shown in figure 4–2. One subnetwork, shown by the solid lines, establishes an independent partition consisting of only the physically even-numbered PEs. The other subnetwork, shown by the dashed lines, establishes an independent partition consisting of only the physically odd-numbered PEs. Within each partition of size four the PEs are logically numbered from 0 to 3. The physical cube$_1$ interconnection function acts as the logical cube$_0$ function for each partition. Similarly, the physical cube$_2$ function acts as logical cube$_1$. In a multiple-SIMD environment, if the physically even-numbered PEs are connected to one control unit and the physically odd-numbered PEs are connected to a second control unit, the two partitions can operate independently with complete cube networks of size four.

In general, the physical cube$_g$ interconnection function causes the PE whose logical address is w to send its data to the PE whose logical address is y if and only if cube$_g(t^{-1}(w)) = t^{-1}(y)$, $w,y \in \ell_i$. To partition the cube network into independent subnetworks, the transformation t must have certain properties. For $0 \leq i < \nu$, the ith partition, ℓ_i, must be such that $\log_2 \sigma_i$

cube interconnection functions are available for its independent use. These $\log_2 \sigma_i$ cube functions will be referred to as $\text{cube}_{i/0}$, $\text{cube}_{i/1}$, . . . , $\text{cube}_{i/(\log_2\sigma_i - 1)}$, where $\text{cube}_{i/r}$ corresponds to logical connection cube_r for partition ℓ_i, $0 \le r < \log_2\sigma_i$. The transformation t must also obey the following labeling constraints. Each element of ℓ_i, $\ell_{i/j}$, $0 \le j < \sigma_i$, must be connected to each of the $\log_2\sigma_i$ PEs in ℓ_i whose logical addresses differ from j in only one bit position. Furthermore, these are the only PEs with which $\ell_{i/j}$ is allowed to communicate. This restriction guarantees that the subnetwork used by partition ℓ_i has the properties of a cube network of size σ_i and that the subnetwork is independent.

Consider how the single-stage cube network will be partitioned into independent subnetworks in terms of the cycle structures of the cube interconnection functions. For each partition ℓ_i there must be $\log_2\sigma_i$ distinct cube functions, each of which has exactly $\sigma_i/2$ cycles containing only elements of P which are mapped to elements of ℓ_i by t. Because the cycles in the cycle structure are disjoint, if exactly $\sigma_i/2$ of the length two cycles contain only elements of P that are mapped by t to elements of ℓ_i, all of the elements of ℓ_i are included, and only elements of ℓ_i are included. Thus, because the cycles are disjoint, no element which maps to an element of ℓ_i is in a cycle other than one of these $\sigma_i/2$. Therefore, the mapping t must be that the collection of the $\sigma_i/2$ cycles in each of $\log_2\sigma_i$ cube functions constitutes a complete and independent cube network of ℓ_i. In addition, for $0 \le r < \log_2\sigma_i$, if the physical cube function acting as $\text{cube}_{i/r}$ connects PEs with physical addresses $t^{-1}(\ell_{i/j})$ and $t^{-1}(\ell_{i/k})$, then j and k can differ in only the rth bit position for all j and k, $0 \le j,k < \sigma_i$. This result follows from the labeling constraints.

For example, consider the odd group shown in figure 4-2, where $t(1) = \ell_{i/0}$, $t(3) = \ell_{i/1}$, $t(5) = \ell_{i/2}$, $t(7) = \ell_{i/3}$, and $\sigma_i = 4$. Physical cube_1 is $\text{cube}_{i/0}$ and physical cube_2 is $\text{cube}_{i/1}$. The ℓ_i (odd) partition uses the (1 3) and (5 7) cycle of cube_1 to form the ($\ell_{i/0}$ $\ell_{i/1}$) and ($\ell_{i/2}$ $\ell_{i/3}$) cycles of $\text{cube}_{i/0}$, and the (1 5) and (3 7) cycles of cube_2 to form the ($\ell_{i/0}$ $\ell_{i/2}$) and ($\ell_{i/1}$ $\ell_{i/3}$) cycles of $\text{cube}_{i/1}$.

Consider dividing a size N cube network into two independent subnetworks of size $N/2$, which can be accomplished by basing the division on any one of the m bit positions—that is, grouping together the $N/2$ PEs with a 0 in the ith bit position and the $N/2$ PEs with a 1 in the ith bit position for a fixed i, $0 \le i < m$. Each group has $\log_2(N/2) = m - 1$ distinct cube functions to use (cube_j, $0 \le j < m$, $j \ne i$). By using t to map PEs with a 0 in the ith bit position into ℓ_0 and the other PEs into ℓ_1, the $N/2$ disjoint cycles of each cube_j function, $j \ne i$, are divided into two independent groups of $N/4$ cycles, no matter what value of i is chosen. This result occurs because PE addresses that agree in the ith bit position are in the same cycles in every cube_j permutation, $0 \le i < m$, $j \ne i$. (No other mapping can do this, that is, there is no other way to divide the N PEs into two independent groups with complete cube subnetworks.) By disallowing the use of physical cube$_i$ no PE in one group can communicate with a PE in the other group. The physical cube$_i$ connection is the only mechanism by which two PEs that differ in the ith physical address bit can communicate. Because each group of $N/2$ PEs has a complete cube network of size $N/2$, this dividing procedure can be repeated on each group independently, forming smaller subgroups of varying sizes.

For example, for $N = 16$, $\nu = 4$, $\sigma_0 = 8$, $\sigma_1 = 4$, $\sigma_2 = 2$, and $\sigma_3 = 2$, one way the partitioning can be done is as follows. First divide the 16 PEs based on the 0th (low-order) bit position. (Note: any of the $m = 4$ bit positions could be used here.) Partitioning on the 0th bit position creates the group 0, 2, 4, 6, 8, 10, 12, and 14 ($= \ell_0$) and the group 1, 3, 5, 7, 9, 11, 13, and 15. This latter group can be divided into two groups of size four based on the 3rd (high-order) bit position (again, any of the three bit positions in which the PE numbers differ could be used.) This division forms the group 1, 3, 5, and 7 ($= \ell_1$) and the group 9, 11, 13 and 15. All the PEs in this latter group agree in the high- and low-order bit positions. Thus, the group can be partitioned based on either of the middle-bit positions. Partitioning on the 1st bit position yields the groups 9 and 13 ($= \ell_2$) and 11 and 15 ($= \ell_3$). Note that even once a bit position on which to base the partitioning is chosen, there is still a choice as to which partition to subdivide further. For example, the physically odd-numbered PEs could have been chosen for ℓ_0 and the physically even-numbered PEs further subdivided to form ℓ_1, ℓ_2, and ℓ_3.

The labeling constraints require that, for $0 \leq r < \log_2 \sigma_i$ and cube$_{i/r}(\ell_{i/j}) = \ell_{i/k}$, j and k can differ only in the rth bit position, for all j and k, $0 \leq j,k < \sigma_i$. These constraints require the cube$_{i/r}$ interconnection function to connect PEs whose logical addresses differ only in the rth bit position. This establishes a correspondence between the physical cube connections and the logical connections for a partition that maintains the properties of the cube network and the independence of the partition. For the preceding example, where $N = 16$, $\nu = 4$, $\sigma_0 = 8$, $\sigma_1 = 4$, $\sigma_2 = 2$, and $\sigma_3 = 2$, one possible correct choice for t is:

$$t(0) = \ell_{0/0} \quad t(1) = \ell_{1/0} \quad t(2) = \ell_{0/1} \quad t(3) = \ell_{1/1}$$

$$t(4) = \ell_{0/2} \quad t(5) = \ell_{1/2} \quad t(6) = \ell_{0/3} \quad t(7) = \ell_{1/3}$$

$$t(8) = \ell_{0/4} \quad t(9) = \ell_{2/0} \quad t(10) = \ell_{0/5} \quad t(11) = \ell_{3/0}$$

$$t(12) = \ell_{0/6} \quad t(13) = \ell_{2/1} \quad t(14) = \ell_{0/7} \quad t(15) = \ell_{3/1}$$

The transformation t meets the requirements by picking the following sets of cycles:

for ℓ_0: $(\,0\ 2\,)\,(\,4\ 6\,)\,(\,8\ 10\,)\,(\,12\ 14\,)$ from cube$_1$ (for logical cube$_{0/0}$),

  $(\,0\ 4\,)\,(\,2\ 6\,)\,(\,8\ 12\,)\,(\,10\ 14\,)$ from cube$_2$ (for logical cube$_{0/1}$), and

  $(\,0\ 8\,)\,(\,2\ 10\,)\,(\,4\ 12\,)\,(\,6\ 14\,)$ from cube$_3$ (for logical cube$_{0/2}$);

for ℓ_1: $(\,1\ 3\,)\,(\,5\ 7\,)$ from cube$_1$ (for logical cube$_{1/0}$), and

  $(\,1\ 5\,)\,(\,3\ 7\,)$ from cube$_2$ (for logical cube$_{1/1}$);

for ℓ_2: $(\,9\ 13\,)$ from cube$_2$ (for logical cube$_{2/0}$); and

for ℓ_3: $(\,11\ 15\,)$ from cube$_2$ (for logical cube$_{3/0}$).

Thus, in ℓ_0 logical PE address-bit positions 0, 1, and 2 correspond to physical PE address-bit positions 1, 2, and 3, respectively; in ℓ_1 logical PE address-bit positions 0 and 1 correspond to physical PE address-bit positions 1 and 2, respectively; and in both ℓ_2 and ℓ_3, logical PE address-bit position 0 corresponds to physical PE address-bit position 2.

   The transformation t is not the only one that obeys the labeling constraints for ℓ_0, ℓ_1, ℓ_2, and ℓ_3. Another transformation t', which also obeys the labeling constraints and is allowable, is defined as follows. For ℓ_0, ℓ_2, and ℓ_3, let $t' = t$. For ℓ_1, let $t'(1) = \ell_{1/0}$, $t'(3) = \ell_{1/2}$, $t'(5) = \ell_{1/1}$, and $t'(7) = \ell_{1/3}$. For ℓ_1 using transformation t', physical cube$_2$ acts as logical cube$_{1/0}$ and physical cube$_1$ acts as logical cube$_{1/1}$. For t', bit positions 2 and 1 of the physical PE addresses correspond to bit positions 0 and 1 of the logical PE addresses, respectively. Figure 4–3A shows the original t for ℓ_1 and figure 4–3B shows t'. For ℓ_1, the transformation t maps the physical PE number $p_3p_2p_1p_0$ to the logical PE number p_2p_1, while t' maps the physical PE number $p_3p_2p_1p_0$ to the logical number p_1p_2. Thus, within a partition the transformation can associate any of the logical PE address-bit positions to any of the physical PE address-bit positions in which the members of the partition vary.

   There is a second way in which the transformation can be modified within a partition and still obey the labeling constraints. Again consider the partition ℓ_1. The transformation t assigns each logical PE with a 0 in its 0th logical address-bit position to the corresponding physical PE with a 0 in its 1st physical address-bit position; for example, $t(5) = \ell_{1/2}$, where physical-address 5 is 0101 in binary and logical-address 2 is 10 in binary. A new transformation t'' can be formed by assigning, for all members of ℓ_1, the logical PE with a 0 in its 0th logical address-bit position to the corresponding physical PE with a 1 in its 1st physical address-bit position, and those with a 1 in the logical 0th to those with a 0 in the physical 1st. Thus, $t''(1) = \ell_{1/1}$, $t''(3) = \ell_{1/0}$, $t''(5) = \ell_{1/3}$, and $t''(7) = \ell_{1/2}$. For example, $t''(5) = \ell_{1/3}$ because 5 is 0101 in binary and 3 is 11 in binary. This is shown in figure 4–3C. Thus, for ℓ_1, the transformation t'' maps the physical PE number

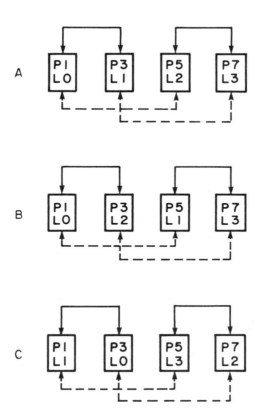

Note: The solid lines show physical cube$_1$ and dashed lines show physical cube$_2$.
A. $t(1) = \ell_{1/0}$, $t(3) = \ell_{1/1}$, $t(5) = \ell_{1/2}$, $t(7) = \ell_{1/3}$.
B. $t'(1) = \ell_{1/0}$, $t'(3) = \ell_{1/2}$, $t'(5) = \ell_{1/1}$, $t'(7) = \ell_{1/3}$.
C. $t''(1) = \ell_{1/1}$, $t''(3) = \ell_{1/0}$, $t''(5) = \ell_{1/3}$, $t''(7) = \ell_{1/2}$.

Figure 4-3. Transformations Between Physical Numbers (P) and Logical
         Numbers (L)

$p_3p_2p_1p_0$ to the logical number $p_2\bar{p}_1$ (in contrast, recall t maps $p_3p_2p_1p_0$
to p_2p_1). Physical cube$_1$ would still act as logical cube$_{1/0}$ and physical cube$_2$
would still act as logical cube$_{1/1}$. This association of 0 to 1 and 1 to 0 instead
of 0 to 0 and 1 to 1 can, in general, be done for any number of address-bit
positions.

An example of a transformation t^* that is not allowed because it does
not obey the labeling constraints for ℓ_1 is: $t^*(1) = \ell_{1/0}$, $t^*(3) = \ell_{1/2}$, $t^*(5) =$
$\ell_{1/3}$, $t^*(7) = \ell_{1/1}$. The labeling constraints do not permit this transformation

for two reasons: first logical PE 0 and logical PE 3 would be connected by physical cube$_2$, and second logical PE 0 and logical PE 1 would not be connected because $(t^*)^{-1}(\ell_{1/0}) = 1$ and $(t^*)^{-1}(\ell_{1/1}) = 7$ differ in two physical address-bit positions.

In summary, there are four allowable ways to vary the transformation t. Two (A and B in the following list) are variations in selecting the members of the partitions, and two (C and D) are variations in selecting the assignment of logical PEs to physical PEs within a partition:

A. The choice of bit positions in which the physical addresses of all PEs in a partition agree can vary.
B. The choice of which partition to subdivide further (assuming that in the final partitioning all partitions are not of the same size) can vary.
C. The choice within each partition of which logical PE address-bit position to associate with each of the physical PE address-bit positions selected in rule A can vary.
D. The choice within each partition of associating either 0 with 1 and 1 with 0, or 0 with 0 and 1 with 1, between the corresponding physical- and logical-bit positions selected in rule C can vary.

In general, the physical addresses of all the PEs in a partition ℓ_i must agree in the $m - \log_2\sigma_i$ bit positions not corresponding to $\log_2\sigma_i$ cube functions the partition will use for communications (Siegel and Smith 1978). Furthermore, within each partition the transformation t must obey the labeling constraints, by following rules C and D.

Consider the model of a multiple-SIMD machine (figure 2–15). To have multiple independent-SIMD machines, multiple controllers must be available. If each PE sets its own input and output selectors, based on the transfer instructions it receives from its controller, each partition can perform cube cycles independently of the other partitions. Subsets of the cycles available to a partition are chosen by disabling the appropriate PEs during the data transfer.

To demonstrate this process using the earlier example, consider the transfers needed to send data from PE $\ell_{0/j}$ to $\ell_{0/(j+2 \bmod 8)}$, for $0 \le j < 8$, based on the cube $\rightarrow$ PM2I algorithm in chapter 3. To do this, use $m = 3$ and $i = 1$ in the algorithm, which produces the following sequence of instructions: cube$_{0/1}$ $[XXX]$, cube$_{0/2}$ $[X0X]$. (The PE address masks correspond to logical addresses.) The first instruction corresponds to the product of cycles:

$$(0\ 4)(2\ 6)(8\ 12)(10\ 14)$$

The second instruction corresponds to:

$$(\, 0 \ 8 \,) \, (\, 2 \ 10 \,)$$

The product of all of these cycles is:

$$(\, 0 \ 4 \,) \, (\, 2 \ 6 \,) \, (\, 8 \ 12 \,) \, (\, 10 \ 14 \,) \, (\, 0 \ 8 \,) \, (\, 2 \ 10 \,) = (\, 0 \ 4 \ 8 \ 12 \,) \, (\, 2 \ 6 \ 10 \ 14)$$

which, by applying t, is:

$$(\, \ell_{0/0} \ \ell_{0/2} \ \ell_{0/4} \ \ell_{0/6} \,) \, (\, \ell_{0/1} \ \ell_{0/3} \ \ell_{0/5} \ \ell_{0/7} \,)$$

These cycles transfer data from PE $\ell_{0/j}$ to $\ell_{0/(j+2 \text{ modulo } 8)}$.

In conclusion, the single-stage cube network can be partitioned into independent subnetworks. Furthermore, each subnetwork of size N' is a complete cube network of size N'.

Partitioning the Illiac Network

The Illiac network cannot be partitioned into independent subnetworks, each of which has the properties of a complete Illiac network. To have a complete Illiac network for a partition of size σ_i, it must first be possible to partition the set P into independent subsets of size σ_i, $0 \leq i < \nu$, such that all PEs whose physical addresses map to logical addresses in ℓ_i can use the four Illiac functions independently of PEs whose physical addresses map to logical addresses not in ℓ_i. However, both the Illiac$_{+1}$ and Illiac$_{-1}$ functions consist of a single cycle including all N PEs. Thus, because they are single-cycle functions neither can be used. For example, if the Illiac$_{+1}$ function is allowed, the PE whose physical number is w can communicate with the PE whose physical number is y using $y - w$ modulo N "$+1$" shifts for any w and y. This situation violates the independent partitions rule. The two remaining Illiac functions cannot act as four distinct functions. Thus the Illiac network cannot be partitioned.

Partitioning the PM2I Network

An example of partitioning a size-eight PM2I network into two subnetworks of size four is shown in figure 4-4. One subnetwork, shown by the solid lines, establishes an independent partition consisting of only the physically even-numbered PEs. The other subnetwork, shown by the dashed lines, establishes an independent partition consisting of only the physically odd-numbered PEs. Within each partition of size four, the PEs are logically numbered from 0 to 3. The physical PM2$_{+1}$ interconnection

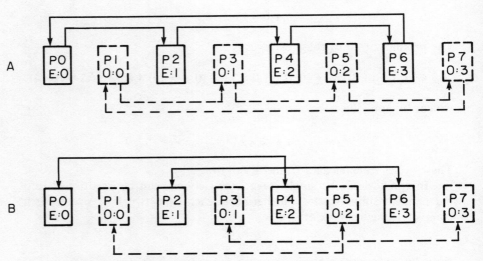

Note: Eight PEs are divided into two groups, based on even and odd physical numbers. *P* indicates physical numbers; *E:* and *O:* indicate even- and odd-group logical numbers, respectively. Solid lines show the even group and dashed lines show the odd group. A. Physical PM2$_{+1}$ (logical PM2$_{+0}$). B. Physical PM2$_{+2}$ = physical PM2$_{-2}$ (logical PM2$_{+1}$ = logical PM2$_{-1}$). For the physical PM2$_{-1}$ (logical PM2$_{-0}$) connections, reverse the direction of the arrows in A.

Figure 4–4. Partitioning a Size-Eight PM2I Network

functions act as the logical PM2$_{\pm0}$ functions for each partition. Similarly, the physical PM2$_{\pm2}$ function acts as the logical PM2$_{\pm1}$. In a multiple-SIMD environment, if the physically even-numbered PEs are connected to one control unit and the physically odd-numbered PEs are connected to a second control unit, the two partitions can operate independently with complete PM2I networks of size four.

Consider how the single-stage PM2I network will be partitioned into independent subnetworks in terms of the cycle structure of the PM2I interconnection functions. For each partition ℓ_i there must be $2\log_2\sigma_i$ PM2I functions, each of which has cycles containing all of the elements of P which are mapped to elements of ℓ_i by t and nothing else. The $2\log_2\sigma_i$ PM2I functions of ℓ_i will be referred to as PM2$_{i/+0}$, PM2$_{i/-0}$, PM2$_{i/+1}$, PM2$_{i/-1}$, ..., where PM2$_{i/\pm r}$ corresponds to logical connection PM2$_{\pm r}$ for partition ℓ_i, $0 \le r < \log_2\sigma_i$. There are also labeling constraints on the transformation t. Each element of ℓ_i, $\ell_{i/j}$, $0 \le j < \sigma_i$, must be connected to the $2\log_2\sigma_i - 1$ PEs in ℓ_i whose logical addresses are $j \pm 2^r$ modulo σ_i, $0 \le r < \log_2\sigma_i$. (There are $2\log_2\sigma_i - 1$ PEs instead of $2\log_2\sigma_i$ because $j + 2^{\log_2\sigma_i - 1} = j - 2^{\log_2\sigma_i - 1}$, modulo σ_i.) As a result, for $0 \le r < \log_2\sigma_i$:

1. If the physical PM2I function acting as $PM2_{i/+r}$ sends data from the PE with physical address $t^{-1}(\ell_{i/j})$ to the PE with physical address $t^{-1}(\ell_{i/k})$, then $k = j + 2^r$ modulo σ_i for all j and k, $0 \le j < \sigma_i$.

2. If the physical PM2I function acting as $PM2_{i/-r}$ sends data from the PE with physical address $t^{-1}(\ell_{i/j})$ to the PE with physical address $t^{-1}(\ell_{i/k})$, then $k = j - 2^r$ modulo ℓ_i for all j and k, $0 \le j,k < \sigma_i$.

As an example, consider the size-four odd-group partition of the PM2I network for $N = 8$ shown in figure 4-4. For this example, $t(1) = \ell_{i/0}$, $t(3) = \ell_{i/1}, t(5) = \ell_{i/2}, t(7) = \ell_{i/3}$, and $\sigma_i = 4$. Physical $PM2_{+1}$ is $PM2_{i/+0}$, physical $PM2_{-1}$ is $PM2_{i/-0}$, and physical $PM2_{\pm2}$ is $PM2_{i/\pm1}$. The ℓ_i (odd) partition uses the (1 3 5 7) cycle of $PM2_{+1}$ to form the ($\ell_{i/0}$ $\ell_{i/1}$ $\ell_{i/2}$ $\ell_{i/3}$) cycle of $PM2_{i/+0}$, the (7 5 3 1) cycle of $PM2_{-1}$ to form the ($\ell_{i/3}$ $\ell_{i/2}$ $\ell_{i/1}$ $\ell_{i/0}$) cycle of $PM2_{i/-0}$, and the (1 5) and (3 7) cycles of $PM2_{\pm2}$ to form the ($\ell_{i/0}$ $\ell_{i/2}$) and ($\ell_{i/1}$ $\ell_{i/3}$) cycles of $PM2_{i/\pm1}$.

The ways in which the PM2I network can be partitioned into independent subnetworks are now considered. Let $\sigma_i = N/2^a = 2^{m-a}$, $j \in P$, and $t(j) \in \ell_i$. The physical PM2I functions $PM2_{+b}$ and $PM2_{-b}$, $0 \le b < a$, cannot be used by j because their cycles are at least of length $N/2^{a-1} = 2^{m-a+1}$ (recall that the cycles of $PM2_{\pm i}$ are all of length 2^{m-i}). If ℓ_i uses a cycle longer than σ_i it will not be independent of some ℓ_k, $0 \le i,k < \nu$, $i \ne k$. This occurs because such a cycle must contain PEs not in ℓ_i. In other words, an element of ℓ_i would share a cycle of $PM2_{\pm b}$ with an element of some ℓ_k $i \ne k$.

By the definition, if a partition is of size σ_i it must have $2\log_2\sigma_i$ PM2I functions to use. Because the $2a = 2(m - \log_2\sigma_i)$ functions $PM2_{\pm b}$, $0 \le b < a$, cannot be used, it leaves the $2\log_2\sigma_i$ functions $PM2_{\pm c}$, $a \le c < m$. It must now be shown that for each of these functions there are cycles that contain all $q \in P$ such that $t(q) \in \ell_i$ and no $w \in P$ such that $t(w) \notin \ell_i$.

Consider the cycle of $PM2_{\pm a}$ that contains PE j, $0 \le j < 2^a$. Assume $t(j) \in \ell_i$. The $PM2_{\pm a}$ cycle containing j will consist of the $2^{m-a} = \sigma_i$ PEs whose physical addresses are of the form $j + k * 2^a$, $0 \le k < 2^{m-a}$. Because $t(j) \in \ell_i$, all PEs in the cycle must be in ℓ_i; that is, ℓ_i will contain all those elements of P whose low-order a bits equal j. For example, if $N = 16$, $a = 1$, and $j = 1$, these elements would be 1, 3, 5, 7, 9, 11, 13, and 15; they are the elements in the cycle of $PM2_{+1}$ that includes $j = 1$. For $a < c < m$, any $PM2_{\pm c}$ cycle containing one element whose low-order a bits are j will contain only elements whose low-order a bits are j. In other words, if a cycle of $PM2_{\pm c}$ contains one element of the cycle of $PM2_{\pm a}$ that contains j, all elements of that cycle of $PM2_{\pm c}$ will be in the cycle of $PM2_{\pm a}$ that contains j, for $a < c < m$ and $0 \le j < 2^a$. To illustrate, consider the following properties of the cycle structures of $PM2_{\pm a}$ and $PM2_{\pm c}$, $a < c < m$:

1. All elements of a cycle of $PM2_{+a}$ agree in their low-order a bits; call them $p_{a-1} \ldots p_1 p_0$. These elements can be represented, using PE address mask notation, as $X^{m-a} p_{a-1} \ldots p_1 p_0$.
2. All elements of a cycle of $PM2_{\pm c}$ agree in their low order c bits; call them $q_{c-1} \ldots q_1 q_0$, where $c > a$. These elements can be represented as $X^{m-c} q_{c-1} \ldots q_1 q_0$.
3. The elements of the cycle of $PM2_{\pm a}$ containing j are $X^{m-a} j_{a-1} \ldots j_1 j_0$, where $0 \le j < 2^a$ and j_k is the kth bit of j.
4. If $w \in X^{m-a} j_{a-1} \ldots j_1 j_0$, the cycle of $PM2_{\pm c}$ containing w must have elements of the form $X^{m-c} q_{c-1} \ldots q_{a+1} q_a j_{a-1} \ldots j_1 j_0$, where $c > a$.
5. The elements $X^{m-c} q_{c-1} \ldots q_{a+1} q_a j_{a-1} \ldots j_1 j_0 \subset X^{m-a} j_{a-1} \ldots j_1 j_0$ (where $\subset$ means "are a proper subset of").

For the previous example with $j = 1$, $PM2_{+2}$ has cycles (1 5 9 13) and (3 7 11 15).

Thus, if $t(j) \in \ell_i$, ℓ_i must consist of the PEs whose physical numbers are $j + k * 2^a$, $0 \le k < 2^{m-a}$. This method is the only way to provide $2\log_2 \sigma_i$ PM2I functions that can be used independently by members of ℓ_i.

In summary, a partition ℓ_i with $\sigma_i = 2^{m-a}$ cannot use $PM2_{\pm b}$, $0 \le b < a$, because it would include cycles whose length was greater than σ_i. This constraint means the $2\log_2 \sigma_i$ connections $PM2_{\pm c}$, $a \le c < m$, must supply the $2\log_2 \sigma_i$ logical functions needed by ℓ_j. $PM2_{\pm a}$, the function with the longest cycle length, consists of 2^a cycles of size $2^{m-a} = \sigma_i$. Thus, there are 2^a choices for ℓ_i (any one of the cycles), which corresponds to the 2^a values of j. Any of these choices is compatible with the cycle structure of $PM2_{\pm c}$, $a < c < m$.

Within a partition, there are two ways to assign physical PM2I interconnection functions to logical PM2I interconnections that obey the labeling constraints: first, use physical $PM2_{+c}$ and $PM2_{-c}$ as logical $PM2_{i/+(c-a)}$ and $PM2_{i/-(c-a)}$, respectively, for all c, $a \le c < m$; second, use physical $PM2_{+c}$ and $PM2_{-c}$ as logical $PM2_{i/-(c-a)}$ and $PM2_{i/+(c-a)}$, respectively, for all c, $a \le c < m$. As an example of the former choice, consider the E partition in figure 4–4, where $N = 8$, $m = 3$, and $a = 1$. Physical $PM2_{+1}$ acts as logical $PM2_{E/+0}$, physical $PM2_{-1}$ acts as a logical $PM2_{E/-0}$ and physical $PM2_{+2} = PM2_{-2}$ acts as logical $PM2_{E/\pm1}$. The second choice of assigning physical PM2I functions to logical PM2I functions for that same partition E is shown in figure 4–5. Here, physical $PM2_{+1}$ acts as logical $PM2_{E/-0}$, physical $PM2_{-1}$ acts as logical $PM2_{E/+0}$, and physical $PM2_{+2} = PM2_{-2}$ acts as logical $PM2_{E/\pm1}$.

Consider dividing a size N PM2I network into two independent subnetworks of size $N/2$. The only way this division can be accomplished is by putting the $N/2$ PEs with a 0 in the low-order bit position of their physical address in one group and putting the other $N/2$ PEs (with a 1 in the low-order bit position) in the other group. Each group has $2\log_2(N/2) = 2(m -$

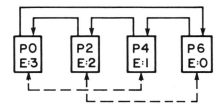

Note: P indicates physical numbers; E: indicates even-group logical numbers. The solid lines show physical $PM2_{-1}$ (logical $PM2_{E/+0}$) and the dashed lines show physical $PM2_{-2}$ = physical $PM2_{+2}$ (logical $PM2_{E/+1}$ = logical $PM2_{E/-1}$). For physical $PM2_{+1}$ (logical $PM2_{E/-0}$) connections, reverse the direction of the arrows of the solid lines.

Figure 4–5. Assigning PM2I Physical Functions to Logical Functions

1) PM2I connections to use; specifically, physical $PM2_{\pm i}$, $0 < i < m$. Physical $PM2_{\pm 0}$ connections are not allowed because they would permit any PE to communicate with any other PE by a sequence of ± 1 transfers, violating the independence of the two groups. This constraint corresponds to the preceding argument that the cycle length of a PM2I function must be equal to or smaller than a partition size if the partition is to be allowed to use it. Furthermore, by not allowing physical $PM2_{\pm 0}$ to be used, independence of the two groups is guaranteed. There is no way for two PEs that differ in the physical low-order bit position of their addresses to communicate without using physical $PM2_{\pm 0}$. Because each group of $N/2$ PEs has a complete PM2I network of size $N/2$, this dividing procedure can be repeated on each group independently (based on the next lowest physical address-bit position), forming smaller subgroups of varying sizes.

For example, for $N = 16$, $\nu = 4$, $\sigma_0 = 8$, $\sigma_1 = 4$, $\sigma_2 = 2$, and $\sigma_3 = 2$, one way to partition the PEs is as follows. First, divide the 16 PEs into the groups 1, 3, 5, 7, 9, 11, 13, and 15 ($= \ell_0$) and 0, 2, 4, 6, 8, 10, 12, and 14. Now divide the latter group to form partitions 2, 6, 10, and 14 ($= \ell_1$) and 0, 4, 8, and 12. This last group can then be partitioned into 0 and 8 ($= \ell_2$) and 4 and 12 ($= \ell_3$). At each step in the partitioning process, either subgroup can be chosen to subdivide further. For example, the physically even-numbered PEs could have been chosen for ℓ_0 and the physically odd-numbered PEs further subdivided to form ℓ_1, ℓ_2, and ℓ_3.

The labeling constraints ensure that t is such that the mathematical properties of the PM2I permutations and independence of partitions are preserved. For the previous example, where $N = 16$, $\nu = 4$, $\sigma_0 = 8$, $\sigma_1 = 4$, $\sigma_2 = 2$, and $\sigma_3 = 2$, one possible correct choice for t is:

$$t(0) = \ell_{2/0} \quad t(1) = \ell_{0/0} \quad t(2) = \ell_{1/0} \quad t(3) = \ell_{0/1}$$

$$t(4) = \ell_{3/0} \quad t(5) = \ell_{0/2} \quad t(6) = \ell_{1/1} \quad t(7) = \ell_{0/3}$$

$$t(8) = \ell_{2/1} \quad t(9) = \ell_{0/4} \quad t(10) = \ell_{1/2} \quad t(11) = \ell_{0/5}$$

$$t(12) = \ell_{3/1} \quad t(13) = \ell_{0/6} \quad t(14) = \ell_{1/3} \quad t(15) = \ell_{0/7}$$

The transformation t meets the requirements by picking the following sets of cycles:

for ℓ_0: (1 3 5 7 9 11 13 15) from PM2$_{+1}$ (for logical PM2$_{0/+0}$)
(15 13 11 9 7 5 3 1) from PM2$_{-1}$ (for logical PM2$_{0/-0}$)
(1 5 9 13) (3 7 11 15) from PM2$_{+2}$ (for logical PM2$_{0/+1}$)
(13 9 5 1) (15 11 7 3) from PM2$_{-2}$ (for logical PM2$_{0/-1}$)
(1 9) (5 13) (3 11) (7 15) from PM2$_{+3}$ = PM2$_{-3}$ (for logical PM2$_{0/\pm2}$)

for ℓ_1: (2 6 10 14) from PM2$_{+2}$ (for logical PM2$_{1/+0}$)
(14 10 6 2) from PM2$_{-2}$ (for logical PM2$_{1/-0}$)
(2 10) (6 14) from PM2$_{+3}$ = PM2$_{-3}$ (for logical PM2$_{1/\pm1}$)

for ℓ_2: (0 8) from PM2$_{+3}$ = PM2$_{-3}$ (for logical PM2$_{2/\pm0}$)

for ℓ_3: (4 12) from PM2$_{+3}$ = from PM2$_{-3}$ (for logical PM2$_{3/\pm0}$)

Thus, in ℓ_0 logical PE address-bit positions 0, 1, and 2 correspond to physical PE address-bit positions 1, 2, and 3, respectively; in ℓ_1 logical PE address-bit positions 0 and 1 correspond to physical PE address-bit positions 2 and 3, respectively; and in both ℓ_2 and ℓ_3, logical PE address-bit position 0 corresponds to physical PE address-bit position 3. The transformation t is such that if physical PE number $p_{m-1} \ldots p_1 p_0$ is assigned to partition ℓ_i, it is associated with the logical PE whose number is $p_{m-1} \ldots p_{(m-\log_2\sigma i)+1} p_{m-\log_2\sigma i}$, $0 \le i < \nu$. For example in ℓ_1, where $\sigma_1 = 4$ and $\log_2\sigma_1 = 2$, $t(14) = \ell_{1/3}$ because physical address 14 is $\underline{11}10$ in binary and logical address 3 is 11 in binary (that is, the PE with physical number $p_3 p_2 p_1 p_0$ is associated with the PE with logical number $p_3 p_2$).

On the basis of the earlier discussion, the transformation t can be modified by associating the positive physical PM2I interconnection functions with the negative logical PM2I functions, and vice versa, within any or all of the partitions. For example, in partition ℓ_1, by using physical PM2$_{+2}$ as logical PM2$_{1/-0}$, physical PM2$_{-2}$ as logical PM2$_{1/+0}$, and physical PM2$_{+3}$ = PM2$_{-3}$ as logical PM2$_{1/\pm1}$, a new transformation t' is formed. Specifically, $t'(2) = \ell_{1/3}$, $t'(6) = \ell_{1/2}$, $t'(10) = \ell_{1/1}$, and $t'(14) = \ell_{1/0}$. In figures 4–6A and 4–6B the transformations t and t', respectively, are shown for ℓ_1. The transformation t' is such that if physical PE number $p_3 p_2 p_1 p_0$

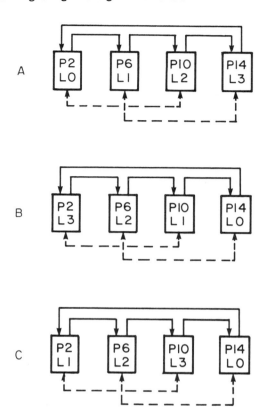

Note: The solid lines show physical $PM2_{+2}$ and dashed lines show physical $PM2_{+3}$.
A. $t(2) = \ell_{1/0}$, $t(6) = \ell_{1/1}$, $t(10) = \ell_{1/2}$, and $t(14) = \ell_{1/3}$.
B. $t'(2) = \ell_{1/3}$, $t'(6) = \ell_{1/2}$, $t'(10) = \ell_{1/1}$, and $t'(14) = \ell_{1/0}$.
C. $t''(2) = \ell_{1/1}$, $t''(6) = \ell_{1/2}$, $t''(10) = \ell_{1/3}$, and $t''(14) = \ell_{1/0}$.

Figure 4-6. Transformations Between Physical Numbers (P) and Logical Numbers (L)

is assigned to partition ℓ_1, it is associated with the logical PE whose number is $\bar{p}_3 \bar{p}_2$. For example, $t'(14) = \ell_{1/0}$ since 14 is $\underline{11}10$ in binary and 0 is $\overline{11} = 00$ in binary. This complementing of the address bits is valid because of the mathematical property that if $y + 2^r = z$, then $\bar{y} - 2^r = \bar{z}$, and if $y - 2^r = z$, then $\bar{y} + 2^r = \bar{z}$, $0 \leq r < \log_2 \sigma_i$, arithmetic modulo σ_i.

Once the physcial PEs in a partition of size 2^{m-a} have been selected and the association of $PM2_{+c}$ to $PM2_{i/+(c-a)}$ or $PM2_{i/-(c-a)}$ (and the corresponding association of $PM2_{-c}$) has been made, another technique may be used to vary t. Because of the cyclic nature of the cycles of each PM2I function, any element of the cycle of $PM2_{+a}$ being used as $PM2_{i/+0}$ (or $PM2_{i/-0}$) may be $\ell_{i/0}$, and each subsequent element of the cycle labeled in consecutive order. This process is called *cyclic relabeling*. For example, in ℓ_1 above, the cycle (2 6 10 14) of $PM2_{+2}$ is mapped to ($\ell_{1/0} \ell_{1/1} \ell_{1/2} \ell_{1/3}$) = $PM2_{i/+0}$ by $t(2) = 0$, $t(6) = 1$, $t(10) = 2$, and $t(14) = 3$. Another valid transformation t'' is $t''(14) = \ell_{1/0}$, $t''(2) = \ell_{1/1}$, $t''(6) = \ell_{1/2}$, and $t''(10) = \ell_{1/3}$, making the cycle ($\ell_{1/1} \ell_{1/2} \ell_{1/3} \ell_{1/0}$), which is equivalent to ($\ell_{1/0} \ell_{1/1} \ell_{1/2} \ell_{1/3}$). Because the distance between $t''^{-1}(\ell_{1/j})$ and $t''^{-1}(\ell_{1/(j+1) \text{ modulo } 4})$ is still four (as was $t^{-1}(\ell_{1/j})$ and $t^{-1}(\ell_{1/(j+1) \text{ modulo } 4})$) the transformation t'' is valid for the other PM2I functions. For this example, ($\ell_{1/0} \ell_{1/2}$) is still a cycle of $PM2_{1/\pm1}$, since ($t''^{-1}(\ell_{1/0})$ $t''^{-1}(\ell_{1/2})$) = (14 6) is a cycle of $PM2_{\pm3}$. In figures 4–6A and 4–6C the transformations t and t'', respectively, are shown for ℓ_1. This labeling method is valid in general because the distance between $\ell_{i/j}$ and $\ell_{i/(j+1) \text{ modulo } \sigma_i}$ is unchanged by the cyclic relabeling. Thus, cyclic relabeling obeys the labeling constraints.

An example of a transformation t^* that is not allowed because it does not obey the labeling constraints for ℓ_0 includes $t^*(1) = \ell_{0/0}$, $t^*(7) = \ell_{0/2}$, and $t^*(3) = \ell_{0/3}$. The labeling constraint does not permit this transformation for two reasons: first, because logical PE 0 and logical PE 3 would be connected by physical $PM2_{+1}$, and second, logical PE 0 and logical PE 2 would not be connected because $(t^*)^{-1}(\ell_{0/0}) = 1$ and $(t^*)^{-1}(\ell_{0/2}) = 7$ do not differ by a power of two, modulo $N = 16$.

In summary, there are three allowable ways to vary the transformation t. First, the selection of the members of the partitions can be varied by the choice of which partition to subdivide further (assuming that in the final partitioning all partitions are not of the same size). Second, there is the choice of assigning physical PM2I functions to logical PM2I functions of the same sign or opposite sign (within each partition). Finally, cyclic relabeling can be used.

In general, the physical addresses of all of the PEs in a partition ℓ_i must agree in their low-order $m - \log_2\sigma_i$ bit positions (Siegel and Smith 1978). The physical $PM2_{\pm r}$ connections, $m - \log_2\sigma_i \le r < m$. are used by the partition. Within each partition, the transformation can be such that either each physical PE $p_{m-1} \ldots p_1 p_0$ which is assigned to partition ℓ_i is associated with the logical PE whose number is $p_{m-1} \ldots p_{(m-\log_2\sigma_i)+1} p_{m-\log_2\sigma_i}$, or each physical PE $p_{m-1} \ldots p_1 p_0$ is associated with the logical PE whose number is $\bar{p}_{m-1} \ldots \bar{p}_{(m-\log_2\sigma_i)+1} \bar{p}_{(m-\log_2\sigma_i)}$. Furthermore, cyclic relabeling can be applied.

Consider the model of a multiple-SIMD machine (figure 2–15). To have multiple-independent SIMD machines, multiple controllers must be available. If each PE sets its own input and output selectors based on the transfer instructions it receives from its controller, each partition can perform PM2I cycles independently of the other partitions. Subsets of the cycles available to a partition are chosen by disabling PEs during the data transfer.

To demonstrate this process using the earlier example, consider the transfer needed to pass data between the PE pairs $\ell_{0/j}$ and $\ell_{0/k}$, where j and k differ only in the low-order bit position, based on the PM2I $\rightarrow$ cube algorithm for cube_0 in chapter 3. Use $m = 3$ and $i = 0$ in the algorithm, which produces the following sequence of instructions: $\text{PM2}_{0/+0}$ [XXX], $\text{PM2}_{0/-1}$ [$XX0$]. (The PE address masks correspond to the logical addresses.) The first instruction corresponds to the cycle:

$$(1\ 3\ 5\ 7\ 9\ 11\ 13\ 15)$$

The second instruction corresponds to:

$$(13\ 9\ 5\ 1)$$

The product of these cycles is:

$$(1\ 3\ 5\ 7\ 9\ 11\ 13\ 15)(13\ 9\ 5\ 1) = (1\ 3)(5\ 7)(9\ 11)(13\ 15)$$

which, by applying t, is:

$$(\ell_{0/0}\ \ell_{0/1})(\ell_{0/2}\ \ell_{0/3})(\ell_{0/4}\ \ell_{0/5})(\ell_{0/6}\ \ell_{0/7})$$

These cycles transfer data between $\ell_{0/j}$ and $\ell_{0/k}$, where j and k differ only in the low-order bit position.

In conclusion, the single-stage PM2I network can be partitioned into independent subnetworks. Furthermore, each subnetwork of size N' is a complete PM2I network of size N'.

Partitioning the Shuffle-Exchange Network

A single-stage shuffle-exchange network cannot be used to partition the set of PEs into independent groups whose sizes σ_i, $0 \le i < \nu$, are powers of two. To have a complete single-stage shuffle-exchange network for a partition of size σ_i, it must first be possible to partition the set P into subsets of size σ_i, $0 \le i < \nu$, such that all PEs whose physical addresses map to logical addresses in ℓ_i have a shuffle interconnection based on σ_i elements. In general, this situation is not possible. Consider the PE whose physical address is 1. It must be in some partition. Let $t(1) \in \ell_i$ for some i, $0 \le i < \nu$, where $0 < \sigma_i \le N$ and σ_i is a power of two. Based on the definition of the shuffle interconnection function, the length of the largest cycle of a shuffle function based on σ_i elements is $\log_2 \sigma_i$, where $0 \le \log_2 \sigma_i \le m$. However, physical PE 1 will be in a cycle of length m. In particular, 1 will be a cycle containing the PEs whose physical addresses are $00 \ldots 01, 00 \ldots 010, 00 \ldots 0100, 10 \ldots 00$. Because PE 1 is in a cycle of length m it must be the case that $\log_2 \sigma_i = m$, which implies that $\sigma_i = N$. Thus, if $t(1) \in \ell_i$, then σ_i must be N and ℓ_i must be P. Therefore, the single-stage shuffle-exchange network cannot be partitioned.

Conclusions

A formal approach to studying the partitionability of permutation networks was presented in this chapter. This approach was used to examine the partitionability of cube, Illiac, PM2I, and shuffle-exchange single-stage SIMD networks. It was shown which of these networks can be partitioned and how to select partitions when they are possible. In particular, it was shown that the cube can be partitioned with the requirement that the addresses of all PEs in a partition of size 2^i agree in any $m - i$ of their bit positions; the PM2I can be partitioned with the restriction that the addresses of all PEs in a partition of size 2^i agree in their low-order $m - i$ bit positions; and the Illiac and shuffle-exchange networks cannot be partitioned. Considering the two partitionable networks, the cube allows more choices for partitions than the PM2I, and the PM2I choices are a subset of those of the cube. The analytic techniques presented in this chapter could also be used to evaluate other single-stage networks.

In the introduction to this chapter, the applicability of network partitioning to multiple-SIMD, MIMD, and partitionable-SIMD/MIMD systems was mentioned. In an SIMD system, information about partitioning can be used in two ways. First, it can be used as an extention to the algorithms presented in chapter 3. Consider, for example, the situation where the cube network is implemented in a size $N = 64$ SIMD machine, and the computational task to be performed requires the PEs to transfer data using a $+ 1$ shift among groups of 16 PEs; that is, $0 \rightarrow 1, 1 \rightarrow 2, \ldots, 14 \rightarrow 15, 15 \rightarrow 0; 16 \rightarrow 17, 17 \rightarrow 18, \ldots, 30 \rightarrow 31, 31 \rightarrow 16; 32 \rightarrow 33, 33 \rightarrow 34, \ldots, 46 \rightarrow 47, 47 \rightarrow 32;$ and $48 \rightarrow 49, 49 \rightarrow 50, \ldots, 62 \rightarrow 63, 63 \rightarrow 48$. By combining the partitioning results in this chapter with the cube $\rightarrow$ PM2I algorithm in chapter 3, a method to transfer data in this way can be devised. Specifically, the cube network can be partitioned into the following groups: PEs 0 to 15, PEs 16 to 31, PEs 32 to 47, and PEs 48 to 63. Within each partition, the logical cube functions could use the cube $\rightarrow$ PM2I algorithm to simulate $PM2_{+0}$ ($+1$ shifts). Because this machine is an SIMD system, all four partitions follow the same instruction stream. The cube $\rightarrow$ PM2I algorithm from chapter 3 can be used by setting $i = 0, m = 4$ (because the partition size is 16), and padding the high-order $\log_2 64 - \log_2 16 =$ positions of the PE address masks with Xs (because no PEs should be disabled based on the two high-order bits of their addresses). The modified algorithm is:

$$\text{for } j = 3 \text{ step } -1 \text{ until } 0 \text{ do}$$

$$\text{cube}_j \ [X^{6-j}1^j]$$

For example, the data from PE 15 is sent to PE 7 when $j = 3$, from PE 7 to PE 3 when $j = 2$, from PE 3 to PE 1 when $j = 1$, and from PE 1 to PE 0 when $J = 0$. Thus, the algorithms of chapter 3 can be combined with the partitioning results to generate SIMD algorithms that perform transfers within partitions.

A second way that the partitioning properties of interconnection networks can be used in an SIMD environment is to improve processing efficiency. In some cases a smaller-size SIMD machine will utilize its PEs more efficiently than a larger-size SIMD machine when both are performing the same task (Siegel, Siegel, and Swain 1982). Consider the image-smoothing example in chapter 2, where $N = 1024$, the image contained 512-by-512 pixels, and each PE processed a 16-by-16 subimage. The number of smoothing operations was reduced by a factor of 1024 ($=N$) compared to a serial (uniprocessor) implementation (from 512^2 to 16^2). There was an additional overhead cost of 68 inter-PE data transfers for smoothing the subimage-edge pixels. The *efficiency* of a parallel algorithm is defined to be the uniprocessor execution time divided by N times the N-PE SIMD machine-execution time (Kuck 1977; Siegel, Siegel, and Swain 1982). For simplicity, assume that one inter-PE data transfer requires the same amount of time as one smoothing operation. Then, in this case, the efficiency is:

$$[512^2 \ / \ (1024 * (16^2 + 68))] = 79\%$$

Assume there are four images to be smoothed, each consisting of 512-by-512 pixels. Consider smoothing all four images simultaneously, one on PEs 0 to 255, one on PEs 256 to 511, one on PEs 512 to 767, and one on PEs 768 to 1023. The case for PEs 256 to 511 is shown in figure 4–7A. Each PE will smooth a 32-by-32 subimage, performing 32^2 smoothing operations and $(4 * 32) + 4 = 132$ parallel inter-PE data transfers (see figure 4–7B). All four images will be smoothed in $32^2 + 132$ smoothing-operation time steps, each image being processed in a different quadrant. Recall that all four images are smoothed simultaneously (which can be done with a single instruction stream). This process requires $4 * 512^2$ smoothing-operation time steps on a uniprocessor system. Thus, the efficiency for smoothing four images in parallel in an SIMD machine in this way is:

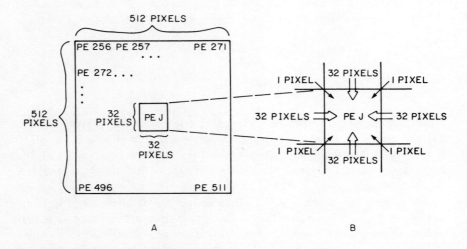

A   B

Note: A. Data allocation for smoothing of 512-by-512 image using the 256 PEs numbered from 256 to 511. B. Data transfers needed to smooth edge pixels in each PE.

Figure 4–7. Partitioning for Efficiency in an SIMD Environment

$$[(4 * 512^2) / (1024 * (32^2 + 132))] = 89\%$$

Intuitively, the efficiency has improved because the larger subimage size (32-by-32 versus 16-by-16) reduces the percentage of time spent doing inter-PE transfers ($132 / (32^2 + 132) = 11$ percent versus $68 / (16^2 + 68) = 21$ percent). Thus, this example shows how partitioning can be used to improve the processing efficiency of an SIMD machine if the same program is to be executed on multiple data sets.

In conclusion, the partitioning properties of single-stage networks are important in SIMD, multiple-SIMD, MIMD, and partitionable-SIMD/ MIMD environments. In chapters 5 and 6, the partitionability of multistage networks is examined. These analyses are based on the concepts developed in this chapter.

5 Multistage Cube/Shuffle-Exchange Networks

This chapter presents the class of multistage interconnection networks known as the generalized cube. These networks are based on the cube and shuffle-exchange interconnection functions defined in chapter 2. The generalized-cube network is, in effect, a wired series of these functions. This type of multistage network has been proposed for use in many future supersystems, including PASM (Siegel and others 1981), PUMPS (Briggs and others 1982), the Ballistic Missile Defense Agency distributed-processing test bed (McDonald and Williams 1978; Siegel and McMillen 1981b), Ultracomputer (Gottlieb and others 1983), Burrough's proposed Flow Model Processor for the Numerical Aerodynamic Simulator (Barnes and Lundstrom 1981), and data-flow machines (Dennis, Boughton, and Leung 1980).

The generalized-cube network topology is used as the basis for many networks, including the omega network (Lawrie 1975), the STARAN flip network (Batcher 1976), and the indirect binary n-cube (Pease 1977). It is a member of the set of networks called SW-banyans; in particular, it is an SW-banyan with spread = 2, fanout = 2, and level = m (Lipovski and Tripathi 1980; Wu and Feng 1980). The baseline network topology is a generalized-cube network topology with a different labeling of input lines (Wu and Feng 1980). Delta networks are a class of networks that include the generalized-cube network (Patel 1981). Various properties of generalized-cube type networks have been examined (for example, Abidi and Agrawal 1980; Batcher 1977a; Barnes and Lundstrom 1981; Bauer 1974; Dias and Jump 1981; Feng and Wu 1981; McMillen and Siegel 1980, 1982b; McDonald and Williams 1980; Pradhan and Kodandapani 1980; Siegel and McMillen 1981b, 1981c; Smith and Siegel 1978; Wah and Hicks 1982; and Wen 1976).

The generalized-cube network represents this class of network in this chapter. The name generalized cube has its origin in the relationship between the generalized-cube network and the cube network described in chapter 2. The generalized-cube network can operate in the SIMD, multiple-SIMD, MIMD, and partitionable-SIMD/MIMD modes of parallelism. The properties of the generalized-cube network discussed in this chapter are applicable to its operation in any of these modes. First, the topology of the generalized-cube network is described, followed by a presentation of routing-tag schemes for establishing paths through this network. The relationship between the generalized-cube network and some other multistage cube-type networks discussed in the literature is examined next, as well as the ways in which the generalized-cube network can be partitioned into independent subnetworks. Also, the number of distinct data permutations performable by the generalized-cube network is explored. Finally, a fault-tolerant variation of the generalized-cube network, called the extra-stage cube, is presented.

Generalized-Cube Network Structure and Properties

Network Definition

The *generalized-cube network* is a multistage cube-type network topology that was introduced in Siegel and Smith (1978). As is shown later, this topology is equivalent to that used by the omega (Lawrie 1975), indirect binary n-cube (Pease 1977), STARAN (Batcher 1976), and SW-banyan ($F = S = 2$) (Goke and Lipovski 1973) networks. In this section, the overall structure of the generalized-cube network is described.

The generalized-cube network topology is shown in figure 5–1. Assume the network has N inputs and N outputs. In figure 5–1, $N = 8$. The generalized-cube topology has $m = \log_2 N$ stages, where each stage consists of a set of N lines (*links*) connected to $N/2$ interchange boxes. Each *interchange box* is a two-input, two-output device. The labels of the links entering the

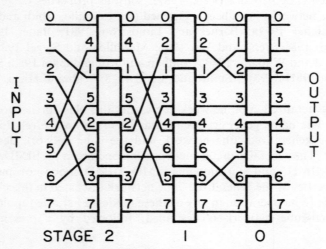

Figure 5–1. Generalized-Cube Network Topology for $N = 8$

upper and lower inputs of an interchange box are used as the labels for the upper and lower outputs, respectively. The labels are the integers from 0 to $N - 1$.

The connections in this network are based on the cube interconnection functions defined in chapter 2. Let $P = p_{m-1} \ldots p_1 p_0$ be the binary representation of an arbitrary link label. Then the m cube interconnection functions can be defined as:

$$\text{cube}_i(p_{m-1} \ldots p_1 p_0) = p_{m-1} \ldots p_{i+1} \bar{p}_i p_{i-1} \ldots p_1 p_0$$

where $0 \le i < m$, $0 \le P < N$, and $\bar{p}_i$ denotes the complement of p_i. That is, the cube_i interconnection function connects link P to link $\text{cube}_i(P)$, where $\text{cube}_i(P)$ is the link whose label differs from P in just the ith bit position. Stage i of the generalized-cube network topology contains the cube_i interconnection function; that is, it pairs links that differ in the ith bit position.

Each interchange box can be set to one of four legitimate states. Let the upper input and output links be labeled J and the lower input and output links be labeled K. The four legitimate states are: (1) *straight*—input J to output J, input K to output K; (2) *swap*—input J to output K, input K to output J; (3) *lower broadcast*—input K to outputs J and K; and (4) *upper broadcast*—input J to outputs J and K (Lawrie 1975), as shown in figure 5–2. The straight and swap settings produce a one-to-one connection at the box, while the lower and upper broadcasts produce a one-to-two connection at the box. A *two-function* interchange box can be in either the straight or swap state and a *four-function* interchange box can be in any of the four states (Siegel and Smith 1978). Note that the swap setting is usually referred

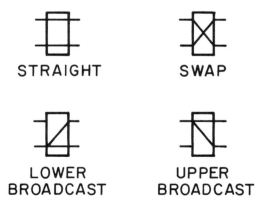

STRAIGHT   SWAP

LOWER   UPPER
BROADCAST   BROADCAST

Figure 5–2. Four Legitimate States of an Interchange Box

to as the "exchange" setting (Lawrie 1975). The term "swap" is used in this book to distinguish the box setting from the "exchange" interconnection function defined in chapter 2.

The name *generalized-cube network* is used here to refer to the network consisting of the generalized-cube topology and four-function interchange boxes. Furthermore, each interchange box is controlled independently through the use of routing tags, as discussed later in this chapter.

One-to-One Connections

One-to-one connections in the generalized-cube network involve just the straight- and swap-box settings. Recall that the two input/output links to an interchange box in stage i differ only in the ith bit position; that is, J and K in the box description in the previous subsection differ only in the ith bit position. Therefore, when an interchange box in stage i is set to swap, it is implementing the cube$_i$ interconnection function. For example, consider the path from source $S = 2$ to destination $D = 4$ in the generalized-cube network for $N = 8$ shown in figure 5–3. Stages 2 and 1 are set to swap and stage 0 is set to straight. This setting corresponds to applying cube$_2$ (in stage 2) and cube$_1$ (in stage 1). Because stage 0 is set to straight cube$_0$ is not applied. Thus, the path followed is from input 2 to cube$_2(2) = 6$ through stage 2, 6 to cube$_1(6) = 4$ through stage 1, and 4 to 4 through stage 0 (no change). In terms of cube functions, cube$_1$(cube$_2(2)) = 4$. This demonstrates the relation between stage i of the generalized-cube network and the cube$_i$ interconnection function.

Consider this path in terms of a mathematical mapping (as defined in chapter 2). To map $S = 2 = 010$ (in binary) to $D = 4 = 100$ (in binary), bit positions 2 and 1 of 010 must be complemented and bit position 0 of 010 left unchanged, since $\bar{0}\bar{1}0 = 100$. Using cube functions, cube$_2$ and cube$_1$ must be applied by setting the interchange boxes through which the data from source 2 travels to swap in stages 2 and 1, and straight in stage 0. In general, to go from a source $S = s_{m-1} \ldots s_1 s_0$ to a destination $D = d_{m-1} \ldots d_1 d_0$, the stage i box in the path from S to D must be set to swap (cube$_i$) if $s_i \neq d_i$ and to straight if $s_i = d_i$. For this example, $s_2 s_1 s_0 = 010$ and $d_2 d_1 d_0 = 100$, so $s_2 \neq d_2$, $s_1 \neq d_1$, and $s_0 = d_0$. Thus, stage i determines d_i; it is $\bar{s}_i$ if the box is set to swap and it is s_i if the box is set to straight.

Because stage i corresponds to cube$_i$, the order in which the cube functions can be applied in a path is determined by the fixed order of the stages. Thus, the order in which cube functions may be applied is cube$_{m-1}$, cube$_{m-2}$, . . . , cube$_1$, and finally cube$_0$, as shown in figure 5–3 for $N = 8$ ($m = 3$). Because stage i determines the value of d_i (that is, if it will be $\bar{s}_i$ or

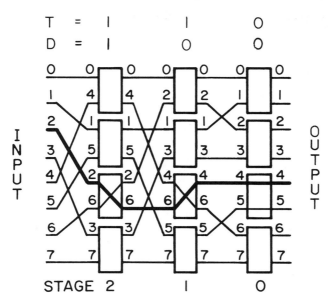

Note: D and T are two routing tags.

Figure 5-3. Path from Input 2 to Output 4 in the Generalized-Cube
Network for $N = 8$

s_i), d_{m-1} is first determined, then d_{m-2}, then d_{m-3}, and so on. The link a message from S to D travels on is therefore $s_{m-1} \ldots s_1 s_0$ before stage $m-1$, $d_{m-1} s_{m-2} \ldots s_1 s_0$ after stage $m-1$, $d_{m-1} d_{m-2} s_{m-3} \ldots s_1 s_0$ after stage $m-2, \ldots, d_{m-1} \ldots d_{i+1} d_i s_{i-1} \ldots s_1 s_0$ after stage $i, \ldots,$ and finally $d_{m-1} \ldots d_1 d_0$ after stage 0. For the example in figure 5-3, where $N = 8$ ($m = 3$), $S = 2$, and $D = 4$, the links traversed are $s_2 s_1 s_0 = 010$ at the input, $d_2 s_1 s_0 = 110$ after stage 2, $d_2 d_1 s_0 = 100$ after stage 1, and $d_2 d_1 d_0 = 100$ after stage 0. In general, the stage i output link used in the path from S to D is $d_{m-1} \ldots d_{i+1} d_i s_{i-1} \ldots s_1 s_0$.

A property of the generalized-cube network that follows from this discussion is that there is only one path from a given source to a given destination. For example, there is only one way to go from input 2 to output 4 in figure 5-3. Only stage i can change the ith bit of the link label in the path from S to D. After stage 0 this link label must be D. Therefore, a message from S must take the output link $d_{m-1} s_{m-2} \ldots s_1 s_0$ at stage $m-1$, the output link $d_{m-1} d_{m-2} s_{m-3} \ldots s_1 s_0$ at stage $m-2$, and so on. This path is the only one available from S to D. Routing tags for finding this path are described later in this chapter.

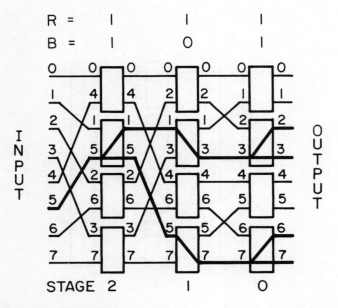

Figure 5-4. Broadcast Path from Input 5 to Outputs 2, 3, 6, and 7 in the Generalized-Cube Network for $N = 8$

Broadcast Connections

When the lower or upper broadcast states of interchange boxes or both are used in a path, a broadcast (one-to-many) connection is performed (for example, see figure 5-4, where input 5 broadcasts to outputs 2, 3, 6, and 7). The path from S to a set of destinations D^* is the combination of the paths from S to each destination D in D^*.

Assume the lower input link to a stage i box is labeled $d_{m-1} \ldots d_{i+2}d_{i+1} s_i \ldots s_1s_0$. This assumption implies that the lower output link is also labeled $d_{m-1} \ldots d_{i+2}d_{i+1}s_i \ldots s_1s_0 = d_{m-1} \ldots d_{i+1}d_is_{i-1} \ldots s_1s_0$ (that is, $d_i = s_i$), by definition of the labeling scheme. Furthermore, the upper output link, which differs from the lower link label in only the ith bit position by definition, is labeled $d_{m-1} \ldots d_{i+2}d_{i+1}\bar{s}_i \ldots s_1s_0 = d_{m-1} \ldots d_{i+1}d_i s_{i-1} \ldots s_1s_0$ (that is, $d_i = \bar{s}_i$). For example, a stage 0 box in the path in figure 5-4 has a lower-input link label of $d_2d_1s_0 = 011$, a lower-output link label of $d_2^1d_1^1d_0^1 = d_2d_1s_0 = 011$, and an upper-output link label of $d_2^2d_1^2d_0^2 = d_2d_1\bar{s}_0 = 010$, where $D^1 = d_2^1d_1^1d_0^1$ and $D^2 = d_2^2d_1^2d_0^2$ are two of the desired destinations. Thus, in general, if the lower-input link label to a stage i box set to lower broadcast is $d_{m-1} \ldots d_{i+2}d_{i+1}s_i \ldots s_1s_0$, the lower- and upper-output links of that box receive the message and their labels are $d^1_{m-1} \ldots d^1_{i+1}d^1_i s_{i-1} \ldots s_1s_0$ and $d^2_{m-1} \ldots d^2_{i+1}d^2_i s_{i-1} \ldots s_1s_0$, respectively, where $d^1_{m-1} \ldots d^1_{i+2}d^1_{i+1} = d^2_{m-1} \ldots d^2_{i+2}d^2_{i+1} = d_{m-1} \ldots d_{i+2}d_{i+1}$, $d^1_i = s_i$, and $d^2_i = \bar{s}_i$. The situation for an upper broadcast is analogous.

The physical structure of the generalized-cube network is such that any source can broadcast to any set of destinations by appropriately setting the interchange boxes. Routing tags for specifying broadcast paths are discussed later in this chapter.

Permutations

Permutation connections, where each input is connected to a single distinct output, are also possible. Because each connection in a permutation is one-to-one, only the straight and swap box settings are used. An example of the generalized-cube network set to connect input j to output $j + 1$ modulo N, $0 \le j < N$, for $N = 8$ is shown in figure 5-5.

The properties of the path from each source to its destination are the same as those for one-to-one connections discussed earlier. Because there is only one path from any given source to its destination, there is at most one way to perform any given permutation. Not all permutations are per-

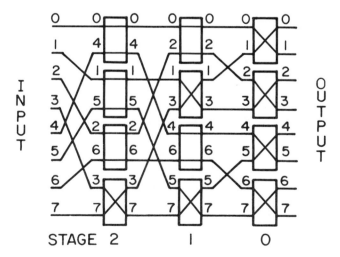

Figure 5-5. The Generalized-Cube Network for $N = 8$ Set To Do the Permutation Input j to Output $j + 1$ Modulo N, $0 \le j < N$

formable. For example, the shuffle (defined in chapter 2) cannot be done. Recall that, for $N = 8$, shuffle(2) $= 4$ and shuffle(6) $= 5$. Consider the generalized-cube network stage 2 box with links 2 and 6. To connect $2 = S^1$ to $4 = D^1$, the output link from that box that must be taken is $d_2^1 s_1^1 s_0 = 110$. To connect $6 = S^2$ to $5 = D^2$, the output link that must be taken from that same box is $d_2^2 s_1^2 s_0^2 = 110$. Therefore, there is a *conflict;* two box inputs want to connect to the same box output, which is not permissible. The permuting capabilities of the generalized-cube network are discussed further later in this chapter.

Summary

The generalized-cube network can perform any one-to-one connection and any broadcast connection. It is limited in the ways it can permute data. It has the property that there is only a single path from a given source to a given destination.

Distributed-Control Schemes

A routing-tag scheme can be used for controlling the generalized-cube network. Using tags allows network control to be distributed among the processors. The routing tags for one-to-one data transfers (not involving broadcasting) consist of m bits. If broadcast capabilities are to be included, then $2m$ bits are used. When a message is to be transmitted through the network, a routing tag is added as the first item in the message—that is, the header. Each interchange box that the message enters examines the routing tag to determine how it should be set and then sets itself. The data portion of the message follows the routing-tag portion through the network.

The use of routing tags is appropriate for operating the network in either the circuit-switched mode or the packet-switched mode. In the *circuit-switched mode,* once a path is established by the routing tag, the interchange boxes in the path remain in their specified state until the path is released. Thus, there is a complete circuit established from input port to output port for that path. The data are then sent directly from the source to the destination over this circuit. In the *packet-switched mode,* the routing tag and data to be transmitted are collected together into a packet. As in the circuit-switched case, the routing tag sets the state of the interchange box. However, a complete path (circuit) from the source to the destination is not established. Instead, the packet makes its way from stage to stage releasing links and interchange boxes immediately after using them. In this way, only one interchange box is used at a time for each message, unlike circuit-switching, where m boxes, one from each stage, are used simultaneously for the entire duration of the message transition. Circuit-switching must be used in networks constructed from combinational logic where there are no buffers in the interchange boxes for storing data. Packet switching uses data buffers in each interchange box to store packets as they move through the network. Details of the communications protocol and interchange box physical implementation are discussed in McMillen, Adams, and Siegel (1981); McMillen and Siegel (1980, 1983); and Siegel and McMillen (1981c).

Routing-tag schemes for performing one-to-one connections and permutations are presented in the next subsection, followed by a discussion of routing tags for broadcasting data. The material in this section is based on Siegel and McMillen (1981b, 1981c) and was done as part of R.J. McMillen's Ph.D. dissertation research.

Routing-Tag Schemes for One-to-One Connections and Permutations

Exclusive-Or Tags. For one-to-one (nonbroadcast) connections, an m-bit routing tag can be computed from the input-port number and desired output-port number. Let $S = s_{m-1} \ldots s_1 s_0$ be the source network address (input-port number) and $D = d_{m-1} \ldots d_1 d_0$ to be the destination network address (output-port number). Then the routine tag $T = t_{m-1} \ldots t_1 t_0 = S \oplus D$, where $\oplus$ means bitwise "exclusive-or" (Siegel and McMillen 1981c). This is called the *exclusive-or* routing-tag scheme. An interchange box in the network at stage i need only examine t_i. If $t_i = 1$, a swap is performed (that is, cube$_i$ is performed). If $t_i = 0$, the straight connection is used. If $N = 8$, $S = 2 = 010$, and $D = 4 = 100$, then $T = 110$. The corresponding stage settings are swap, swap, and straight, as shown in figure 5-3.

Because the exclusive-or operation is commutative (that is, $S \oplus D = D \oplus S$), the incoming routing tag is the same as the return tag. In other words, the same tag used to route data from S to D can be used to route data from D to S. It can be used to "handshake" (that is, to confirm receipt of the data). For the previous example, the tag $T = 110$ used to route data from 2 to 4 is the same tag that is used to route data from 4 to 2.

If each network destination D knows its own address (output-port number), then from the tag it can compute the source address S (input-port number) that sent it data. Specifically, $T \oplus D = S$. For the previous example, where $T = 110$, $D = 100$, and $S = 010$, $T \oplus D = 110 \oplus 100 = 010 = S$.

The reason why this exclusive-or tag scheme works follows directly from the structure of the generalized-cube network and the definition of the cube interconnection functions. If S and D differ in the ith bit position (that is, $s_i \oplus d_i = 1 = t_i$), the cube$_i$ function must be applied to connect (map) the source S to destination D. Using the swap setting in stage i implements this process. If S and D agree in the ith bit position ($s_i \oplus d_i = 0 = t_i$), the cube$_i$ function should not be applied. Using the straight setting in stage i accomplishes this task.

Recall from the discussion in the last section that there is only one path from a given source to a given destination. The tag corresponds to this path. Thus, any one-to-one path can be generated by the appropriate tag.

In the generalized-cube network, any permutation physically performable by the network (see the earlier discussion in this chapter) can be generated by routing tags. Consider the permutation of input j to output $j + 1$ modulo N, $0 \le j < N$, shown for $N = 8$ in figure 5–5. For example, the path from $S = 000$ to $D = 001$ is generated by $T = S \oplus D = 001$ (straight, straight, swap), and the path from $S = 001$ to $D = 010$ is generated by $T = S \oplus D = 011$ (straight, swap, swap). Thus, exclusive-or routing tags can be used for permutations as well as one-to-one connections.

Because each source generates its own tag, it is possible that a conflict can occur in the network; for example, the tag on the upper-input link of a box indicates that the box should be set to swap while the tag on the lower input indicates it should be set to straight. In such situations, one message must wait until the other has completed its transmission. Both requests can not be accommodated simultaneously.

Destination Tags. As an alternative to the exclusive-or routing tag method, destination tags can be used (Lawrie 1975). In the *destination-tag* scheme the destination $D = d_{m-1} \ldots d_1 d_0$ is the tag. An interchange box in the network at stage i need only examine d_i. If $d_i = 0$ the upper output of the box is taken. If $d_i = 1$ the lower output of the box is taken. As an example, consider the path from source 2 to destination $D = 4$ shown in figure 5–3. The lower output of the stage 2 box is taken ($d_2 = 1$), the upper output of the stage 1 box is taken ($d_1 = 0$), and the upper output of the stage 0 box is taken ($d_0 = 0$). This same destination tag ($D = 4$) would be used to route any input to output 4.

This method differs from the exclusive-or method in that the source address is not used in its calculation and that the output link (upper or lower) is explicitly specified, not the box state (straight or swap). If the tag arrives on the upper input of a stage i box, then if $d_i = 0$ the box is set to straight and if $d_i = 1$ it is set to swap. Analogously, if the tag arrives on the lower-input box, then if $d_i = 0$ the box is set to swap and if $d_i = 1$ the box is set to straight.

The destination-tag scheme works because the upper-output link of a stage i box always has a 0 in the ith bit position of its label, while the lower-output link has a 1. Thus, taking the upper-output link means that the ith bit of the network output reached will be a 0, while taking the lower-output link means it will be a 1.

This scheme has an advantage over the exclusive-or method in that a destination can compare the destination tag that arrives with its own address to determine if the message arrived at the correct network output (if it did not, the network must be faulty). It has the disadvantage that it cannot be used to determine the source, as the exclusive-or scheme can. By using m additional bits, both methods can have both the capability to determine whether the data arrived at the proper destination and to identify its source. This ability can be added by sending the source address along with the destination tag or sending the destination address along with the exclusive-or tag.

Obviously, because there is only one path from a given source to a given destination, an exclusive-or tag and a destination tag generate the same path. Just as with exclusive-or tags, destination tags can represent any one-to-one connection. Furthermore, like exclusive-or tags, destination tags can be used for permuting data and can generate any permutation of which the generalized-cube network is capable. In addition, it is possible to generate network conflicts, as with the exclusive-or scheme.

Routing-Tag Scheme for Broadcasting

Routing tags that can be used for broadcasting data are an extension of the exlusive-or routing-tag scheme. First, broadcasting to two destinations is considered. Then, broadcasting to a power of two destinations is discussed.

To broadcast data from one input to any two outputs, the Hamming distance between the outputs addresses must be equal to 1 (the *Hamming distance* is defined to be the number of bit positions that differ between two numbers (Lin 1970)). Let S be the source-processor address and E and F be the destination-processor addresses. Then the individual routing tags are $T_E = S \oplus E$ and $T_F = S \oplus F$. For example, if $S = 101$, $E = 100$, and $F = 110$, then $T_E = 001$ and $T_F = 011$. The routing tags agree in all but the second bit (t_1). Corresponding to that, the paths in the network are identical in stage 2, branch (upper broadcast) in stage 1, and are parallel (that is, the same interchange box settings are used) in stage 0, as shown in figure 5–6. To construct a broadcast-routing tag, in addition to including bits that contain information on routing before and after the branch, the branching point must be specified.

Let the *broadcast-routing tag* be specified by $\{R,B\}$, where $R = r_{m-1} \ldots r_1 r_0$ contains the routing information and $B = b_{m-1} \ldots b_1 b_0$ contains the broadcast information (Siegel and McMillen 1981c). Because both T_E and T_F contain the same needed routing information, arbitrarily set $R = T_E$. To

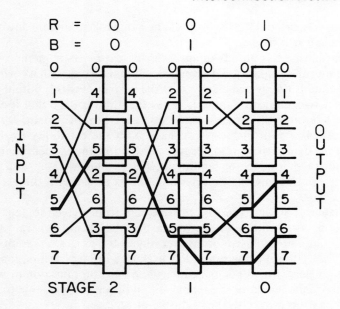

Note: $\{R,B\}$ is the broadcast-routing tag.

Figure 5-6. Broadcast Path from Input 5 to Outputs 4 and 6 in the
Generalized-Cube Network for $N = 8$

specify a broadcast, set b_i to 1 if the interchange box in stage i is to be set to one of the broadcast states, and set b_i to 0 if the interchange box is to interpret R as a normal routing tag. Because the routing tags differ only in the bit position corresponding to the branch point, $B = T_E \oplus T_F$. The computation of B can be simplified by using the fact that $T_E \oplus T_F = E \oplus F$. The tag for the example in figure 5-6 is $\{R = T_E = 001, B = E \oplus F = 010\}$.

To interpret the broadcast-routing tag $\{R,B\}$, an interchange box at stage i in the network must examine r_i and b_i. If $b_i = 0$, r_i is interpreted exactly as t_i. If $b_i = 1$, r_i is ignored and the proper upper or lower broadcast is performed depending on the link on which the message arrived. In particular, if a tag where $b_i = 1$ enters the lower input of a stage i box, the box is set to lower broadcast; if it enters the upper input, it is set to upper broadcast.

Broadcasting can be extended to allow a source to send a message to a power of two number of destinations. If there are 2^j destination addresses, then, given this scheme for computing and interpreting the tags, there may be at most j bits that disagree among any pair of the addresses. Thus, there are $m - j$ bit positions in which all these addresses agree, and there is a fixed set of j bit positions in which any two destination addresses may disagree. For example, the set of addresses $\{010, 011, 110, 111\}$ meets this criterion because there are 2^2 addresses and they differ in at most two bit positions, the 0th and 2nd. If the source address is $S = 101$, the set of individual tags is $\{111, 110, 011, 010\}$. To compute the broadcast-routing tag, $R = S \oplus D_i$, where D_i is any one of the desired destination addresses, and $B = D_i \oplus D_k$, where D_i and D_k are any two destinations that differ by j bits. For the example given, $R = 111$ and $B = 101$ as shown in figure 5–4.

The broadcast-routing tag scheme presented here cannot be used to generate all broadcasts of which the generalized-cube network is capable. For example, setting the stage 0 box with link labels 6 and 7 in figure 5–4 to straight state would result in a broadcast from input 5 to the three outputs 2, 3, and 7. This broadcast cannot be done using this routing-tag scheme. It could be accomplished by a series of transfers (for example, input 5 to outputs 2 and 3, and then input 5 to output 7).

So that the routing tag that arrives at each destination can be used as a return tag, each interchange box that performs a broadcast can modify the routing portion of the tag leaving the upper and lower links. If the message arrived on the upper input link, r_i in the tag leaving on the upper output link is set to 0 (because $d_i = s_i$, which implies $r_i = s_i \oplus d_i = 0$) and r_i in the tag leaving on the lower-output link is set to 1 (because $d_i = \bar{s}_i$, which implies $r_i = s_i \oplus d_i = 1$). If the message arrived on the lower input link, the modifications are reversed. For example, in figure 5–4 the upper-output link of the box in stage 2 with link labels 1 and 5 would set r_2 to 1, while the lower-output link would set r_2 to 0.

A similar broadcast-routing tag scheme, for use with destination tags, is presented in Wen (1976). There m extra bits are used in the tag to send the source address, eliminating the need for modifying the routing portion of the tag. This approach could, of course, also be used here.

Summary

The routing-tag and broadcast-routing tag schemes described in this section were developed to allow control of the network to be distributed among the processors. The schemes are amenable to use in the generalized-cube network operated in circuit- or packet-switched environments. They are suitable for use in the SIMD, multiple-SIMD, MIMD, or partitionable SIMD/MIMD modes of parallel/distributed processing.

Comparison of Multistage Cube-Type Networks

In this section the relationship between the generalized-cube network and each of the omega, indirect binary n-cube, STARAN flip, and SW-banyan

($S = F = 2, L = m$) networks is discussed. Using the generalized-cube network topology (figure 5-1) as a standard, the differences and similarities among these multistage cube-type networks will be examined in terms of topology, interchange-box capabilities, and control structure.

The *topology* of a network can be defined as the actual interconnection pattern used to connect a set of N inputs to a set of N outputs. The multistage networks examined in this section have m stages. Conceptually, each stage consists of an interconnection pattern of N links and $N/2$ interchange boxes.

The *interchange box* is used as a basic building block in many multistage networks. Although an interchange box can be implemented in many different ways, it can be viewed conceptually as defined earlier in this chapter; in particular, as a two-input, two-output device that has the four legitimate states shown in figure 5-2. Recall that a two-function interchange box can be in either the straight or swap states, and a four-function interchange box can be in any of the four states.

The *control structure* of a network determines how the states of the interchange boxes will be set. Three distinct types of control structures used in multistage cube-type networks are individual-stage control, partial-stage control, and individual-box control (Siegel 1979a; Siegel and Smith 1978). *Individual-stage control* uses one control signal to set the states of all the interchange boxes in the same stage. Thus, all the boxes within the stage are set in the same way. Each stage has its own signal. *Partial-stage control* uses $i + 1$ control signals to control stage $i, 0 \leq i < m$. Stage i is divided into $i + 1$ sets of boxes, each controlled by a different signal. Within a set, all boxes must be in the same state. *Individual-box control* uses a separate control signal to set the state of each interchange box. Thus, the setting of each box is independent of the settings of the other boxes through the use of routing tags, such as those described earlier in the chapter.

These classifying parameters are used in the rest of this section to compare the generalized-cube network, omega network, indirect binary n-cube network, STARAN flip network, and SW-banyan ($S = F = 2, L = m$) network.

The Omega Network

The relationship between the generalized-cube network and the omega network is discussed in this subsection (Siegel 1979a; Siegel and Smith 1978). The *omega network* (Lawrie 1975) is a multistage implementation of the single-stage shuffle-exchange network defined in chapter 2. A size N omega network consists of m identical stages, where each stage is a shuffle connection followed by a column of $N/2$ interchange boxes. The omega network is shown for $N = 8$ in figure 5-7. In this figure the links are num-

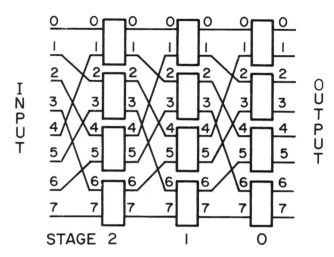

Figure 5-7. The Relationship of the Omega Network for $N = 8$ to the Shuffle Interconnection Function

bered in such a way as to demonstrate the omega network's correspondence to the single-stage shuffle-exchange network. The links are numbered from 0 to $N - 1$ based on their vertical ordering (position). Compare this to the illustration of the shuffle interconnection function shown in figure 2-11. The input links to each stage follow the shuffle connection pattern. For example, in figure 5-7, the link (position) labeled 0 connects to box input (position) labeled shuffle(0) = 0, the link (position) labeled 1 connects to box input (position) labeled shuffle(1) = 2, and so on. In general, the link (position) labeled i connects to the box input (position) labeled shuffle(i), $0 \leq i < N$. Thus, each stage of the omega network consists of the shuffle connection pattern entering $N/2$ interchange boxes.

The omega network is redrawn in figure 5-8 with the same link-labeling convention as used for the generalized-cube network in figure 5-1. In particular, a link labeled j at the input retains this label number, $0 \leq j < N$. (In figures 5-2, 5-7, and 5-8, the lower input and output links of a box are labeled identically, as are the upper input and output links of a box.) Using this labeling it can be seen that stage i of the omega network implements cube$_i$, $0 \leq i < m$; that is, a stage i box set to swap performs the cube$_i$ function. The generalized-cube network is organized in exactly the same way, with the input stage (stage $m - 1$) implementing cube$_{m-1}$, the next stage (stage $m - 2$) implementing cube$_{m-2}$, and so on.

This similarity can be observed by comparing figures 5-8 and 5-9. The interchange boxes of the omega network can be repositioned, as shown in

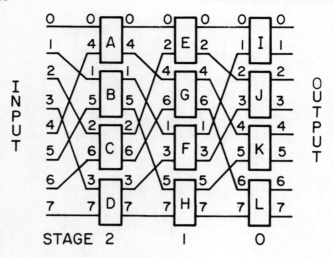

Note: The links labeled using the conventions in figure 5-1.
Figure 5-8. The Omega Network for $N = 8$

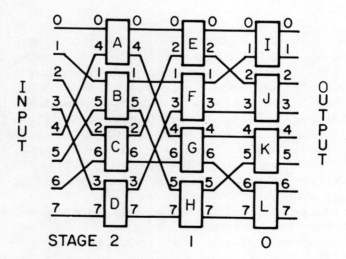

Figure 5-9. The Relationship of the Omega Network for $N = 8$ to the Generalized-Cube Network

figure 5-9, without modifying the interchange-box interconnections. The boxes labeled F and G have been repositioned, but the connections between any two boxes remain the same. For example, in both figures the upper input of box G is connected to the lower output of box A, and the lower input of box G is connected to the lower output of box C. Thus, the networks shown in figures 5-8 and 5-9 are equivalent. Figure 5-9 is identical to figure 5-1, the generalized-cube network.

The correspondence between the generalized-cube network and the omega network can also be shown mathematically using the shuffle-exchange → cube single-stage network simulation algorithm of chapter 3. The algorithm can be summarized as:

$$\text{cube}_j(P) = \text{shuffle}^j(\text{exchange}(\text{shuffle}^{m-j}(P)))$$

$$= p_{m-1} \ldots p_{j+1} \bar{p}_j p_{j-1} \ldots p_0$$

where $P = p_{m-1} \ldots p_1 p_0$, $0 \leq P < N$, and an interchange box set to swap performs the exchange interconnection function. For example, to go from input 1 to output 3 in figure 5-8, where $N = 8$ and $m = 3$, the stage 2 and 0 boxes would be set to straight and the stage 1 box would be set to swap, resulting in:

$$\text{shuffle}(\text{exchange}(\text{shuffle}(\text{shuffle}(1)))) = 3 = \text{cube}_1(1)$$

Note that the data entering a stage j interchange box will have been shuffled $m - j$ times.

If more than one interchange box on a path from a given input to a given output is set to swap, then multiple cube functions are performed. For example, to go from input 1 to output 7 in figure 5-8 the stage 2 and 1 boxes would be set to swap and the stage 0 box would be set to straight. This results in:

$$\text{shuffle}(\text{exchange}(\text{shuffle}(\text{exchange}(\text{shuffle}(1))))) = 7 = \text{cube}_1(\text{cube}_2(1))$$

Thus, the topology of the omega network is the same as that of the generalized-cube network. The omega network has four-function interchange boxes and individual-box control (using the destination-tag scheme described earlier in this chapter) (Lawrie 1975), which makes the omega network equivalent to the generalized-cube network with four-function interchange boxes and individual-box control. Thus, all of the information in this chapter also applies to the omega network.

The Indirect Binary n-Cube Network

The generalized-cube network and indirect binary n-cube network are compared in this subsection (Siegel 1979a; Siegel and Smith 1978). The *indirect binary n-cube network* consists of m stages of $N/2$ two-function interchange boxes under independent-box control (Pease 1977). The structure of the network is defined such that the two input links to a box in stage i differ only in the ith bit position, $0 \leq i < m$. Thus, stage i implements cube_i. The

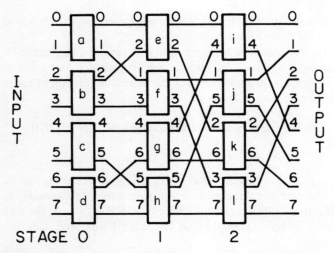

Figure 5-10. The Indirect Binary *n*-Cube Network for $N = 8$

ordering of the stages, from network input to output, is stage 0, stage 1, . . . , stage $m - 1$ (that is, first $cube_0$, then $cube_1$, etc.). The network is shown for $N = 8$ in figure 5-10. It is called an *n*-cube because in Pease (1977) $n = \log_2 N$.

Thus, the indirect binary *n*-cube network topology is the same as that of the generalized-cube network, except the stages are reversed in order. This reversed ordering does not matter for one-to-one connections or broadcasts; that is, the capabilities of the two networks are the same in these two situations. However, the permuting abilities of the networks differ, the reason for which will be explained following an example.

Consider connecting input 0 to output 5 at the same time as connecting input 1 to output 7, for $N = 8$. The indirect binary *n*-cube network cannot do these connections. To map (as defined in chapter 2) 0 to 5, $cube_0$ must be applied, implying that the interchange box in stage 0 to which input 0 is connected must be set to swap. However, to map 1 to 7, $cube_0$ is not used, so the stage 0 box to which input 1 is connected must be set to straight. Thus, it is not possible to connect both 0 to 5 and 1 to 7, because there will be a conflict in the stage 0 box to which both inputs 0 and 1 are connected. The generalized-cube network can connect these source/destination pairs simultaneously. In the generalized-cube network, the path from 0 to 5 and the path from 1 to 7 have no interchange boxes in common (as tracing these paths in the generalized-cube network for $N = 8$ shown in figure 5-1 demonstrates). Analogously, the indirect-binary *n*-cube network can connect 0 to 5 and 4 to 7 simultaneously, while the generalized-cube network cannot.

This difference in permuting capabilities occurs because as data passes through the indirect binary n-cube network and generalized-cube network, the data items that are paired in an interchange box depend on the order of the stages in the network; that is, stage i being encountered as the ith stage or as the $(m - i)$th stage. Consider an arbitrary set of input and output connections that the indirect binary n-cube network can perform. To perform these connections on the generalized-cube network the following address transformation can be used. Conceptually transform the number (address) of each input and output link from $P = p_{m-1} \ldots p_1 p_0$ to $P^* = p_0 p_1 \ldots p_{m-1}$. Use this same *reverse* transformation to specify any desired set of input and output connections. This implies that if the network is used to interconnect N PEs, PE $P = p_{m-1} \ldots p_1 p_0$ must be treated as if it were PE reverse$(P) = p_0 p_1 \ldots p_{m-1}, 0 \le P < N,$ if the generalized-cube network is to act like the indirect binary n-cube network. For example, if this is done for the generalized-cube network for $N = 8$ shown in figure 5-1, the result is the indirect binary n-cube network for $N = 8$ shown in figure 5-10. Thus, using the reverse transformation, any program written for a system using the indirect binary n-cube network can be executed using the generalized-cube network. The reverse transformation can also be used to substitute the indirect binary n-cube network for the generalized-cube network.

For example, consider the 0 to 5 and 4 to 7 connections that the indirect binary n-cube network can perform but the generalized-cube network cannot. It can be done in the generalized-cube network for $N = 8$ if PE 1 acts as PE reverse$(1) = 4$ (note that 0, 5, and 7 equal their respective reverses). The generalized-cube network can connect 0 to 5 and 1 to 7. Similarly, the indirect binary n-cube network can perform the connections 0 to 5 and 1 to 7 if PE 4 acts as PE reverse$(4) = 1$.

This address transformation to substitute the generalized-cube network for the indirect binary n-cube network can be used for any $N = 2^m$ because the renumbering causes the generalized-cube network to first pair data links with new (transformed) labels that differ only in the 0th bit position, then in the 1st bit position, and so on to the final $(m - 1)$st bit position, just the way the indirect binary n-cube network does. The method for substituting the indirect binary n-cube network for the 'generalized-cube network is analogous.

Because of the reversed stage ordering, if the generalized-cube network can perform an interconnection function f, the indirect binary n-cube network can perform f^{-1} (f inverse), and vice versa. (Recall from chapter 3 that $f^{-1}(f(P)) = P, 0 \le P < N.$) To verify this statement, consider the generalized-cube network set to perform f. It will connect input P to output $f(P), 0 \le P < N$. Tracing the N paths from output to input, $f(P)$ is connected to $P, 0 \le P < N$. Setting each box in the indirect binary n-cube network in the same way as the corresponding box in the generalized-cube network is set will result in the same collection of paths because the indirect binary n-cube network is the reverse of the generalized-cube network. (The box corresponding to the stage i box with link labels k and j in the generalized-cube network is the indirect binary n-cube network stage i box with the same labels.) Thus, the relationship between the permutations performable by the generalized-cube network and indirect binary n-cube network can be characterized.

In summary, the indirect binary n-cube network is equivalent to a network with the generalized-cube network topology with the stages in reverse order, two-function interchange boxes, and individual-box control. All the properties (except broadcasting) presented in this chapter for the generalized-cube network also apply to the indirect binary n-cube network.

The STARAN Flip Network

The relationship between the generalized-cube network and STARAN flip network is explored in this subsection (Siegel 1979a; Siegel and Smith 1978). The *STARAN flip network* is the network implemented in the STARAN SIMD machine, where $N = 256$ (Batcher 1976). It is shown in figure 5–11 for $N = 8$. At stage i, input j can be connected to stage i output j or output $cube_i(j)$, $0 \le i < m$, $0 \le j < N$. Thus, stage i of the network implements $cube_i$. The stages are ordered from network input to output as stage 0, stage 1, . . . , stage $m - 1$ (that is, $cube_0$, $cube_1$, . . . , $cube_{m-1}$). Therefore, the connection patterns of the flip network are the same as those of the indirect binary n-cube network.

Using interchange boxes as the basic building block, the flip network is identical to the indirect binary n-cube network shown in figure 5–10. As a result, the discussion in the previous subsection relating the topologies of the indirect binary n-cube network and the generalized-cube network applies here.

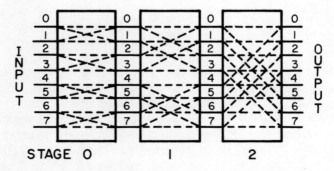

Figure 5–11. STARAN Flip Network for $N = 8$ with Flip Control

The flip network uses two-function interchange boxes. The network has two control mechanisms: flip control and shift control. *Flip control* is a form of individual-stage control, while *shift control* is a form of partial-stage control. An m-bit vector $F = f_{m-1} \ldots f_1 f_0$ is used to implement the flip control. If $f_i = 1$ all interchange boxes in stage i are set to swap, and if $f_i = 0$ all are set to straight. The flip-control scheme is used for "scrambling/unscrambling" data when accessing the STARAN's "multidimensional access memory" (Batcher 1977a).

The shift control allows shifts of data within partitions of size 2^k, $0 \leq k < m$. Assume the network is partitioned into 2^{m-k} groups, where inputs and outputs associated with group g have consecutive physical numbers that have g as their $m - k$ high-order bit positions, for a fixed g, $0 \leq g < 2^{m-k}$. For example, if $N = 8$ ($m = 3$) and $k = 2$, one group is 0, 1, 2, and 3 (the high-order bit is 0), and the other group is 4, 5, 6, and 7 (the high-order bit is 1). Let the inputs and outputs within each partition be logically numbered from 0 to $2^k - 1$. Then, using the logical numbering, the shift control allows shifts of data from input L to output $L + 2^j$ modulo 2^k within each group. This shift occurs for all groups simultaneously. For the preceding example, if $j = 0$, then the physical connections formed are: $0 \rightarrow 1, 1 \rightarrow 2, 2 \rightarrow 3, 3 \rightarrow 0, 4 \rightarrow 5, 5 \rightarrow 6, 6 \rightarrow 7$, and $7 \rightarrow 4$.

The way in which shift-control signals are assigned is shown in figure 5–12 for $N = 8$. Relating this method to figure 5–10, 0A controls boxes *a, b, c,* and *d*; 1A controls *e* and *g*; 1B controls *f* and *h*; 2A controls *i*; 2B controls *j*; and 2C controls *k* and *l*. The values of the controls signals which

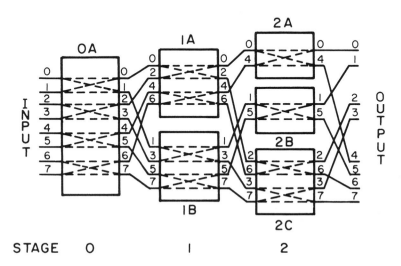

Figure 5–12. STARAN Flip Network for $N = 8$ with Shift Control

Table 5-1
STARAN Network Shift Control

| | | Control Signals | | | | | |
Shift	Group Size	0A	1A	1B	2A	2B	2C
+ 1	8	1	1	0	1	0	0
+ 2	8	0	1	1	1	1	0
+ 4	8	0	0	0	1	1	1
+ 1	4	1	1	0	0	0	0
+ 2	4	0	1	1	0	0	0
+ 1	2	1	0	0	0	0	0

are used for $N = 8$ are shown in table 5-1, where a 1 indicates swap and a 0 indicates straight. (Note that the flip control can be implemented by controlling all the shift-control lines for a given stage by a single signal.)

For example, to do a shift of $+1$ for the entire network ($j = 0$, $k = m = 3$), all boxes controlled by the 0A, 1A, and 2A signals are set to swap, and the rest are set to straight. To do $+1$ shifts in groups of size four ($j = 0$, $k = 2$), all boxes controlled by the 0A and 1A signals are set to swap, and the rest are set to straight.

Each of the shifts can be directly related to the cube $\rightarrow$ PM2I simulation algorithm of chapter 3 in conjunction with the cube partitioning results of chapter 4. First, shifts in a group of size $2^m = N$ ($k = m$) will be considered. Then, shifts in groups of 2^k, $1 \leq k < m$, will be examined.

Each shift of $+2^j$ modulo N is just the PM2I interconnection function $PM2_{+j}$. Because the flip network is a series of cube functions, the cube $\rightarrow$ PM2I simulation algorithm is applicable. The algorithm used in chapter 3 to simulate $PM2_{+j}$ using the single-stage cube network is:

$$\text{for } i = m - 1 \text{ step } -1 \text{ until } j \text{ do cube}_i \, [X^{m-i}1^{i-j}X^j]$$

Because the flip network implements the cube functions in the order cube_0, $\text{cube}_1, \ldots, \text{cube}_{m-1}$, this algorithm, which uses the reverse order, must be modified. The new algorithm is:

$$\text{for } i = j \text{ step } +1 \text{ until } m - 1 \text{ do cube}_i \, [X^{m-i}0^{i-j}X^j]$$

The reasons why this new algorithm correctly performs the $PM2_{+j}$ function is analogous to the reasons discussed in chapter 3 for the original algorithm. The only difference is that, because the ordering is reversed, the 1 in the mask is replaced by a 0. This is because, to do the mapping, bit i should be complemented only if bits j to $i - 1$ are all 0s, indicating they were a string of 1s, which would generate a carry (note $j \leq i$). For example, consider performing $PM2_{+0}(1)$. For $N = 8$ ($m = 3$) and $j = 0$, 1 is mapped to 0 by $cube_0$ $[XXX]$, 0 to 2 by $cube_1$ $[XX0]$, and remains 2 $= PM2_{+0}(1)$ (because 2 does not match $[X00]$).

To see how the shift controls correspond to this algorithm, consider the labels of the links affected by each of the control signals. The 0A signal controls links matching the mask $[XXX]$, 1A controls links matching $[XX0]$, 1B controls links matching $[XX1]$, 2A controls links matching $[X00]$, 2B controls links matching $[X01]$, and 2C controls links matching $[X1X]$. For example, the new cube $\rightarrow$ PM2I algorithm for $N = 8$ ($k = 3$) and $j = 0$ is:

$$cube_0 \quad [XXX] \quad \equiv \quad 0A = 1$$

$$cube_1 \quad [XX0] \quad \equiv \quad 1A = 1$$

$$cube_2 \quad [X00] \quad \equiv \quad 2A = 1$$

where $\equiv$ means "is equivalent to." As another example, the algorithm for $N = 8$ ($k = 3$) and $j = 1$ is:

$$cube_1 \quad [XXX] \quad \equiv \quad 1A = 1B = 1$$

$$cube_2 \quad [X0X] \quad \equiv \quad 2A = 2B = 1$$

where the combination of 1A $=$ 1B $= 1$ indicates those links matching $[XX0]$ or $[XX1]$, which corresponds to $[XXX]$, and the combination of 2A $=$ 2B $= 1$ indicates those links matching $[X00]$ or $[X01]$, which corresponds to $[X0X]$.

Now consider the situation for $k < m$ and the relevance of the partitioning results. When performing shifts, the flip network is divided into 2^{m-k} groups of size 2^k. Because all inputs and outputs in a group of size 2^k agree in their high-order $m - k$ bit positions, a partition is formed by disallowing the use of $cube_i$, $k \leq i < m$. Each group can use $cube_i$, $0 \leq i < k$. Thus, by setting stages k to $m - 1$ of the flip network to straight, each partition of size 2^k can use stages 0 to $k - 1$ as a virtual flip network of size 2^k. The preceding algorithm is still used, but with $k - 1$ replacing $m - 1$ as the loop upper limit because the size of the subnetwork is 2^k. The $m - k$ high-order positions of the masks in the algorithm are Xs because all subnetworks are to perform the algorithm.

For example, consider the algorithm for $k = 2$ and $j = 0$:

$$cube_0 \quad [XXX] \quad \equiv \quad 0A = 1$$

$$cube_1 \quad [XX0] \quad \equiv \quad 1A = 1$$

As an example, let $k = 2$ and $j = 1$:

$$\text{cube}_1 \ [XXX] \quad = \quad 1A = 1B = 1$$

where $1A = 1B = 1$ indicates those links matching $[XX0]$ or $[XX1]$, which corresponds to $[XXX]$.

By examining the new cube $\rightarrow$ PM2I algorithm, the box assignment and settings of the shift controls needed for a flip network for any given N can be derived. Thus, with the new cube $\rightarrow$ PM2I algorithm of chapter 3 and the patitioning theory of chapter 4, one can design the shift controls for the flip network.

In summary, the STARAN flip network is equivalent to a network with the generalized-cube network topology in reverse order, two-function interchange boxes, and partial-stage control. The partial-stage control limits the capabilities of the flip network in comparison to a generalized-cube network with individual-box control.

The SW-Banyan Network

In this subsection, the relationship between the generalized-cube network topology and the SW-banyan network is discussed (Siegel and McMillen 1981b). The classification of different network topologies using banyan networks was proposed in Goke and Lipovski (1973). A banyan is a type of directed graph. One subclass of banyan-network graphs is the *SW-banyan*. To specify a particular SW-banyan network graph, a spread (S), fanout (F), and level (L) must be specified. The constructive definition of SW-banyan network graphs produces the network shown in figure 5–13 for $N = 8$ ($m = 3$), $S = 2$, $F = 2$, and $L = m = 3$. The graph consists of nodes (vertices, dots in the figure) and edges (arcs, lines in the figure). S is the number of edges entering a node from above, F is the number of edges leaving a node from below, and L is the number of levels of edges. The use of an SW-banyan ($S = F = 2$, $L = m$) graph as the topology for a network in a reconfigurable multiprocessor system is discussed in Lipovski and Tripathi (1977).

The network graph in figure 5–13 can be interpreted in different ways. One is to treat each node as a switch and each edge as a link. An implementation based on this interpretation, for an N input/output network, would consist of $m + 1$ stages of N switches, with $2N$ lines between stages. A second interpretation is to treat the nodes as links and the edges as forming interchange boxes. For example, the bold lines in figure 5–13 can be considered to represent the interchange box with inputs 2 and 6 (compare this to

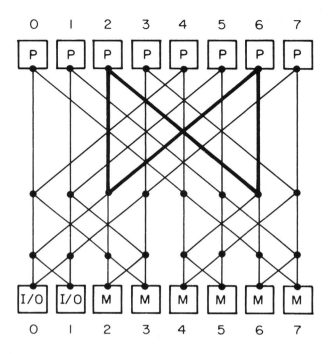

Note: P stands for processor, M for memory, and I/O for input/output device.

Figure 5-13. The SW-Banyan Network Topology ($S = F = 2$, $L = 3$)
for $N = 8$ (Lipovski and Tripathi 1977)

figure 5-1). In this case the SW-banyan network implementation would consist of m stages of $N/2$ two-input, two-output switches, and would have the same structure as the generalized-cube network. The stages of the SW-banyan are ordered in the same way as in the generalized-cube network; that is, from input to output (top to bottom in figure 5-13) the network implements cube_{m-1}, cube_{m-2}, . . . , cube_0.

To summarize, the name SW-banyan refers to a class of network graphs. SW-banyan with $S = F = 2$ and $L = m$ refers to a specific network graph. The graph can be interpreted in different ways, one of which corresponds to the generalized-cube network based on interchange boxes. Because the SW-banyan network is defined as a graph, the type of interchange box and control structure used is unspecified. Its topology is the relevant parameter for use in comparing this network to the generalized-cube network.

Summary

In this section the relationship of the generalized-cube network to each of the omega, indirect binary n-cube, STARAN flip, and SW-banyan networks was described. Using the results of this section, the relationship between any pair of these networks can be determined. The properties of the generalized-cube network presented in this chapter pertain to these networks as well, with restrictions in some cases. Thus, the knowledge of the features of the generalized-cube network can be applied when studying any of these networks.

Partitioning the Generalized-Cube Network

In chapter 4, the partitioning of the cube single-stage network was described. The partitioning of the generalized-cube network is based on these results. The *partitionability* of an interconnection network is the ability to divide the network into independent subnetworks of different sizes (chapter 4). Each subnetwork of size N' must have all of the interconnection capabilities of a complete network of that same type built to be of size N'. A partitionable network can be characterized by any limitations on the way in which it can be subdivided. The partitionability of an interconnection network is an important attribute to consider when choosing a network for a reconfigurable system.

The rules for partitioning the generalized-cube network are from Siegel and Smith (1978) and Smith and Siegel (1978) and were part of the Ph.D. dissertation research of S.D. Smith. The relationship of these rules to the theory developed in chapter 4 is based on Siegel (1980).

The key to partitioning the generalized-cube network so that each subnetwork is independent is the choice of the input/output ports belonging to the subnetworks. The requirement is that the physical addresses of all of the input/output ports in a subnetwork of size 2^s agree (have the same values) in $m - s$ of their bit positions. Furthermore, the interchange boxes used by this subnetwork are set to straight in the $m - s$ stages corresponding to the $m - s$ bit positions in which the addresses agree. The other s stages are used by the subnetwork to form a generalized-cube network of size 2^s. This result follows directly from the relationship of the generalized-cube network to the cube interconnection functions and the cube partitioning results from chapter 4; specifically, the physical addresses of all the PEs in a partition ℓ_i

must agree in the $m-\log_2\sigma_i$ bit positions not corresponding to the $\log_2\sigma_i$ cube functions the partition will use for communications. (Recall σ_i is the number of PEs in partition ℓ_i.)

First consider partitioning a generalized-cube network of size N into two independent subnetworks, each of size $N/2$. There are m ways, with each way being based on a different bit position of the input/output port addresses (that is, a different cube interconnection function). One way is to force all boxes in stage $m-1$ to the straight state (that is, disallow the use of $cube_{m-1}$). This action would form two subnetworks, one consisting of those input/output ports with a 0 in the high-order bit position of their addresses and the other consisting of those ports with a 1 in the high-order bit position. These two groups could communicate with each other only by using the swap setting in stage $m-1$ (that is, the $cube_{m-1}$ function). By forcing this stage to straight, the subnetworks are independent and have full use of the rest of the network (stages $m-2$ to 0, corresponding to $cube_{m-2}$ to $cube_0$).

For example, figure 5–14 shows how a network of size eight can be partitioned into two subnetworks, each of size four. Subnetwork A consists of ports 0 to 3. Subnetwork B consists of ports 4 to 7. All ports in subnetwork A agree in the high-order bit position of their addresses (it is a 0). All ports in subnetwork B agree in the high-order bit position of their addresses (it is a 1). By setting all of the interchange boxes in stage 2 to straight, the two sub-

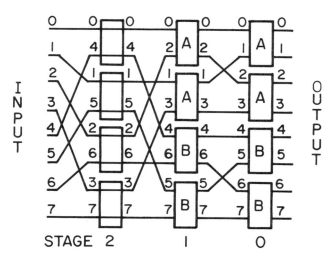

Figure 5–14. Partitioning the Generalized-Cube Network for $N = 8$ into Two Subnetworks of Size Four (A and B) Based on the High-Order Bit Position

networks are isolated because stage 2 is the only stage that allows input/output ports which differ in their high-order bit to communicate. The two other ways of partitioning a size-eight network into two independent networks of four are groupings based on the low-order bit position and groupings based on the middle bit position, as shown in figures 5–15 and 5–16, respectively. In figure 5–15 the input/output ports of the A subnetwork all have a 0 in the low-order bit position of their addresses and the ports in B a 1. In figure 5–16 the A subnetwork ports have a 0 in the middle bit position of their addresses and the B subnetwork ports a 1.

Each subnetwork has the properties of a generalized-cube network. Therefore, each subnetwork can be further subdivided. Thus, a size $N/2$ subnetwork can be divided into two size $N/4$ subnetworks by setting all the stage i boxes in the size $N/2$ subnetwork to straight, for any i, $0 \leq i < m$, as long as stage i was not used to create the size $N/2$ subnetworks (as stage $m - 1$ was earlier). This process of dividing subnetworks into independent halves can be repeated to create any size subnetwork from one to $N/2$. There are only two constraints:

1. The size of each subnetwork must be of power of two.
2. The physical addresses of the input/output ports of a subnetwork of size 2^s must all agree in any fixed set of $m - s$ bit positions.

Again, these restrictions are completely analogous to the situation of partitioning the single-stage cube network, as described in chapter 4.

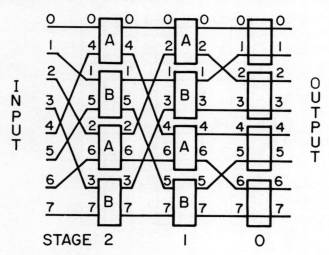

Figure 5–15. Partitioning the Generalized-Cube Network for $N = 8$ into Two Subnetworks of Size Four (A and B) Based on the Low-Order Bit Position

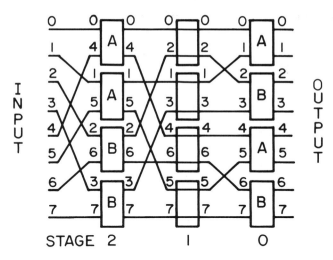

Figure 5-16. Partitioning the Generalized-Cube Network for $N = 8$ into Two Subnetworks of Size Four (A and B) Based on the Middle Bit Position

For example, the B group of figure 5-14 is divided based on the middle bit position in figure 5-17, forming the groups C and D. All input/output ports in C agree in the two high-order bit positions (they are 10). All input/output ports in D agree in the two high-order bit positions (they are 11).

Once a network has been partitioned, the correspondence between a physical-stage number and the logical-stage number for the partition can be established. Very simply, for a partition size of size 2^s, traverse the network from input to output following any link that is a member of the partition. The first stage containing a box not forced to straight acts as logical stage $s - 1$, the next stage containing a box not forced to straight acts as $s - 2$, and so forth. For example, consider the A subnetwork in figure 5-16. By following link number 1 it can be seen that physical stage 2 will act as logical stage 1 and physical stage 0 will act as logical stage 0. In general, if physical stage j is acting as logical stage i for a partition, then the jth bit of the physical address of each input/output port can be the ith bit of that port's logical number within the partition. For the A subnetwork in figure 5-16, the input/output port whose physical number is $p_2 p_1 p_0$ can have the logical number $p_2 p_0$, so 0 becomes 0, 1 becomes 1, 4 becomes 2, and 5 becomes 3.

Thus for the generalized-cube network there are two ways to vary the choice of the physical input/output ports in a subnetwork, just as there were two ways to select the physical PEs for a partition in the single-stage cube case:

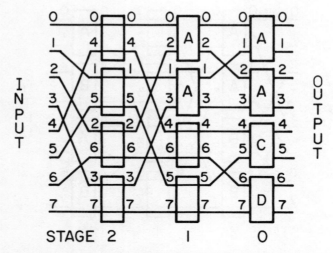

Figure 5-17. Partitioning the Generalized-Cube Network for $N = 8$
into One Subnetwork of Size Four (A) and Two
Subnetworks of Size Two (C and D)

1. The choice of bit position(s) in which the physical addresses of all
    input/output ports in a subnetwork agree (that is, the choice of which
    stages to force to straight).
2. The choice of which subnetwork to subdivide further can vary (unless
    all subnetworks are to be subdivided).

The generalized-cube network is more limited than the single-stage
cube network when it comes to the transformation mapping physical-port
addresses to logical-port addresses within a subnetwork. As stated earlier,
the physical stage acting as logical stage i must come before (be on the input
side of) the physical stage acting as logical stage $i - 1$, and come after (be
on the output side of) the physical stage acting as logical stage $i + 1$. That
is, the subnetwork must have the properties of a generalized-cube network,
so a subnetwork of size 2^s must first use logical stage $s - 1$ (logical cube$_{s-1}$),
then logical stage $s - 2$ (logical cube$_{s-2}$), and so on. Thus, once a partition
is fixed, the association of the physical-stage number (physical cube functions) to the logical-stage numbers (logical cube functions) within the partition is fixed.

As a result of the fixed ordering of the stages, while the single-stage
cube network can vary the way it associates the logical PE address bit positions and physical PE address bit positions, it is fixed for the generalized-
cube network. For example, recall the earlier discussion of the logical num-

bering for figure 5–16. A port's physical address bit position 2 must be associated with the port's logical address bit position 1, and physical address bit position 0 with logical address bit position 0. Both the generalized-cube network and the single-stage cube network can associate a logical bit position with the actual value of the physical bit position or its complement. For the example of figure 5–16, if the physical port numbers are of the form $p_2 p_1 p_0$, the associated logical port numbers could all be $p_2 p_0$, or all be $\bar{p}_2 p_0$, or all be $p_2 \bar{p}_0$, or all be $\bar{p}_2 \bar{p}_0$. For example, using $\bar{p}_2 \bar{p}_0$, physical port 0 would be logical port 3, physical 1 would be logical 2, physical 4 would be logical 1, and physical 5 would be logical 0.

The relationship between the partitioning of the single-stage cube network and multistage generalized-cube network can also be seen by considering the generalized-cube network in terms of the cycle structure of its permutations. For example, if all interchange boxes in the network are set to swap, the way in which the data is permuted is:

$$(\text{cube}_{m-1})(\text{cube}_{m-2}) \ldots (\text{cube}_0) = \prod_{i=m-1}^{0} \left(\prod_{\substack{j=0 \\ i\text{th bit} \\ \text{of } j=0}}^{N-1} (j \ \text{cube}_i(j)) \right)$$

For example, for $N = 4$ ($m = 2$) the permutation is:

$$(0 \ 2)(1 \ 3)(0 \ 1)(2 \ 3)$$

In general, the way in which data are permuted is:

$$\prod_{i=m-1}^{0} \left(\prod_{j=0}^{N-1} (j \ \text{cube}_i(j)) \right)$$

where the ith bit of $j = 0$ and the stage i interchange box whose input/output links are labeled j and $\text{cube}_i(j)$ are set to swap. For example, if in the generalized-cube network for $N = 8$ only the top row of boxes is set to swap and the rest are set to straight, as shown in figure 5–18, the permutation is:

$$(0 \ 4)(0 \ 2)(0 \ 1) = (0 \ 4 \ 2 \ 1)$$

Recall from chapter 4 that if j, $0 \le j < 7$, is not in a cycle it implies it is in a cycle by itself (that is, (j)).

Thus, by setting the interchange box with links j and $\text{cube}_i(j)$ to swap, the cycle $(j \ \text{cube}_i(j))$ is included in the permutation; otherwise it is not. Just as cycles are picked from the physical cube functions to generate logical

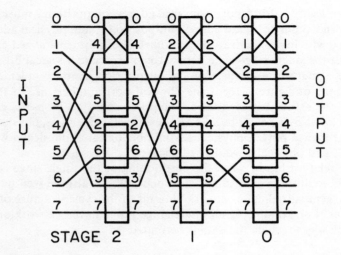

Figure 5-18. The Generalized-Cube Network for N = 8 Set To Do the
      Permutation (0 4 2 1)

cube functions for a partition in chapter 4, cycles (boxes) can be picked
from the physical stages of the network to form the logical stages for a subnetwork.

The ability of the generalized-cube network to be partitioned into
independent subnetworks allows the network to function well in multiple-
SIMD and partitionable SIMD/MIMD environments. It permits the forma-
tion of independent subsystems when operating in MIMD mode. This
ability is also useful with SIMD parallelism, as was discussed in chapter 4.

Counting Generalized-Cube Network Permutations

A size N generalized-cube network has $Nm/2$ interchange boxes. For permuting data, each interchange box can be individually set to one of two
states, either straight or swap (see figure 5-2). Thus, there are $2^{Nm/2}$ different ways to set the $Nm/2$ interchange boxes. It is clear from the structure of
the network that every possible setting will result in a one-to-one mapping
of inputs to outputs—that is, a permutation—because each interchange box
performs a one-to-one connection.

Now consider two distinct network settings. There must be at least one
interchange box that is set to straight in one of the settings and to swap in
the other. Pick a source S that is mapped to its destination D using a path
that goes through this particular interchange box for one of the settings.

There is only one path through the network between any source/destination pair, as discussed earlier in this chapter. Thus, using the other setting does not allow S to map to D, giving a different permutation. Therefore, each distinct setting results in a distinct permutation. Thus, there are $2^{Nm/2}$ distinct possible permutations, each performable in a single pass through the network.

In general, there are $N!$ (N factorial) $= (N) * (N - 1) * (N - 2) \ldots *$ (2) $*$ (1) ways to permute N data elements because the first input can be connected to any of N outputs, the second input to any of the $N - 1$ remaining outputs, and so forth. For $N \geq 4$ the generalized-cube network cannot do all possible $N!$ permutations of data. For example, for $N = 4$, $N! = 24$, while $2^{Nm/2} = 16$, and for $N = 8$, $N! = 40,320$, while $2^{Nm/2} = 4,096$. However, the generalized-cube network can do most permutations found useful in SIMD processing, as discussed in Bauer (1974), Batcher (1976), Lawrie (1975), Lang and Stone (1976), and Pease (1977).

The derivation of the number of different permutations performable in a single pass through cube-type multistage networks is relatively straightforward. It is used in chapter 6 for comparison to the number of permutations performable by the multistage PM2I network called the augmented data manipulator (ADM).

The Extra-Stage Cube Network

The main problem with the generalized-cube network topology is that there is only one path from a given network input to a given output. Thus, if there is a fault on that path no communication is possible between the input and output. This section describes the *extra-stage cube (ESC)* network, a fault-tolerant network derived from the generalized-cube network that is capable of operating in SIMD, multiple-SIMD, MIMD, and partitionable SIMD/MIMD environments. The ESC network consists of a generalized-cube network with one additional stage at the input and hardware to allow the bypass, when desired, of the extra stage or the output stage (stage 0). Thus, the ESC network has a relatively low incremental cost over the generalized-cube network (and its related networks discussed earlier in this chapter). The extra stage provides an additional path from each source to each destination. The known useful attributes of partitionability and distributed control through the use of routing tags are available in the ESC network. Therefore, the ESC network is an answer to the need for reliable communications in parallel/distributed systems.

The ESC network has all of the interconnecting capabilities of the generalized-cube type of networks that have been proposed for many parallel/distributed systems. It is shown in this section that the ESC network provides fault tolerance for any single failure. Further, the network can be controlled even when it has a failure, using a simple modification of a routing-tag scheme proposed for the generalized-cube network. Both one-to-one and broadcast connections under routing-tag control are performable by an ESC network with a single fault. The ability of the ESC network to operate with multiple faults is examined. The ways in which the ESC network can be partitioned and can permute data will also be described. The material in this section is based on Adams and Siegel (1982b), which was done as part of G.B. Adams III's Ph.D. dissertation research.

The ESC network is formed from the generalized-cube network by adding an extra stage along with a number of multiplexers and demultiplexers. Its structure is illustrated in figure 5–19 for $N = 8$. The extra stage, stage m, is placed on the input side of the network and implements the cube_0 interconnection function (defined in chapter 2). Thus, two stages in the ESC network can perform cube_0. In figure 5–19 where $N = 8$ and $m = 3$, both stages 3 and 0 implement cube_0, while stage 2 implements cube_2 and stage 1 implements cube_1.

Stage m and stage 0 can each be enabled or disabled (bypassed). A stage is *enabled* when its interchange boxes can be used to provide cube_0 interconnection capability. It is *disabled* when its interchange boxes are being bypassed. Enabling and disabling of stages m and 0 is accomplished by a demultiplexer at each box input and a multiplexer at each output. Figure 5–20 details an interchange box from stage m or 0. One demultiplexer out-

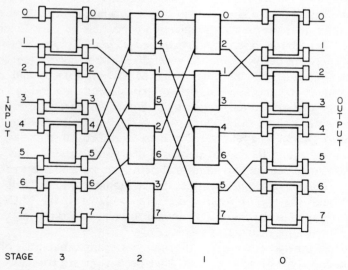

Figure 5–19. The Extra-Stage Cube (ESC) Network for $N = 8$

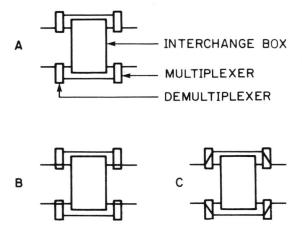

Figure 5-20. Interchange Box for Stage *m* or 0 of the ESC Network.
A. Detail of interchange box with multiplexer and
demultiplexer for enabling and disabling. B. Interchange
box enabled. C. Interchange box disabled

put goes to a box input, the other to an input of its corresponding multiplexer. The remaining multiplexer input is from the matching box output.
The demultiplexer and multiplexer are configured such that they either both
connect to their box (enable) or both bypass it (disable). All demultiplexers
and multiplexers for stage *m* share a common control signal. All demultiplexers and multiplexers for stage 0 also share a common control signal.

The following terminology is used. A *link* is any line connecting two
network interchange boxes. Neither a network input port nor output port is
considered a link. A link has the same label as the box output and input it
joins. A *path* is a set of interchange-box settings and links that forms a connection between a given source and its destintion. A *broadcast path* is a set
of paths that connects a source to two or more destinations (using the lower-
and/or upper-broadcast interchange-box settings—defined previously—as
needed).

Enabling and disabling of stages *m* and 0 is performed by a system-
control unit. Normally, the network will be set so that stage *m* is disabled
(bypassed) and stage 0 is enabled, as shown in the example network setting
for $N = 8$ in figure 5-21. The resulting structure is that of the generalized-
cube network. If after fault-detection and location tests a fault is found, the
network is reconfigured. A fault in stage *m* requires no change in network
configuration; stage *m* remains disabled as shown in figure 5-21. If the

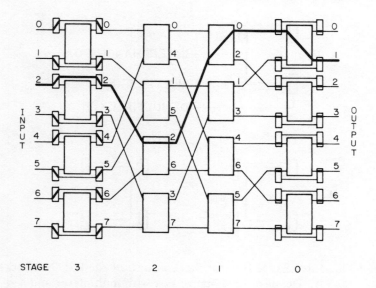

STAGE   3   2   1   0

Figure 5-21. The ESC Network Path from Input 2 to Output 1 for $N = 8$
When Stage 3 Is Disabled and Stage 0 Is Enabled

fault is in stage 0, stage m is enabled and stage 0 is disabled, as is shown in
the example network setting for $N = 8$ in figure 5-22. For a fault in a link
or box in stages $m - 1$ to 1, both stages m and 0 will be enabled. The example network setting for $N = 8$ in figure 5-23 shows both stages $m = 3$ and 0
enabled. If a fault occurs in stages $m - 1$ through 1, in addition to reconfig-
uring the network the system-control units informs each source device of
the fault by sending it a fault identifier.

Intuitively, for both the generalized-cube and ESC networks, stage i,
$1 \le i < m$, determines the ith bit of the address of the output port to which
the data are sent. Consider the route from source $S = s_{m-1} \ldots s_1 s_0$ to destination $D = d_{m-1} \ldots d_1 d_0$. If the route passes through stage i using the
straight connection, the ith bit of the source and destination addresses will
be the same—that is, $d_i = s_i$. If the swap setting (defined earlier in this
chapter) is used, the ith bits will be complementary—that is, $d_i = \bar{s}_i$. In the
generalized-cube network, stage 0 determines the 0th bit position of the
destination in a similar fashion. In the ESC network, however, both stage m
and stage 0 can affect the 0th bit of the output address. Using the straight
connection in stage m performs routings as they occur in the generalized-
cube network. The swap setting makes available an alternative route not
present in the generalized-cube network. In particular, the route enters stage
$m - 1$ at the link labeled $s_{m-1} \ldots s_1 \bar{s}_0$, instead of $s_{m-1} \ldots s_1 s_0$.

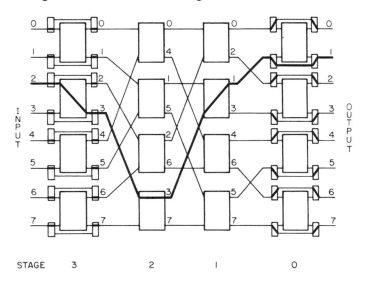

Figure 5–22. The ESC Network Path from Input 2 to Output 1 for $N = 8$ When Stage 3 Is Enabled and Stage 0 Is Disabled

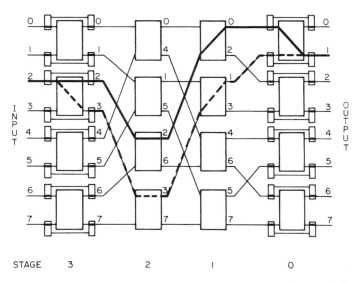

Figure 5–23. The ESC Network Paths from Input 2 to Output 1 for $N = 8$ When Both Stages 3 and 0 Are Enabled

For example, consider the paths from input 2 to output 1 in the ESC network for $N = 8$ shown in figure 5-23. The solid line enters stage $m - 1 = 2$ on link 2 and follows the same path that would be followed in the generalized-cube network. The dashed line enters stage $m - 1 = 2$ on link 3 = $cube_0(2)$ and follows a different path.

In the fault model to be used, failures may occur in network interchange boxes or links. However, the input and output ports and the multiplexers and demultiplexers directly connected to the input/output ports of the ESC network are always assumed to be functional. If the input/output ports or the stage m demultiplexers or the stage 0 multiplexers were faulty, the associated device would have no access to the network. Such a circumstance will not be considered. What is considered is any fault within the network.

Once a fault has been detected and located in the ESC network, the failing portion of the network is considered unusable until the fault is remedied. Specifically, if an interchange box is faulty, data will not be routed through it, nor will data be passed over a faulty link. The extra stage of the ESC network does increase the likelihood of a fault, compared to the generalized-cube network, because of the additional hardware. However, analysis of an independently developed related network shows that for reasonable values of interchange-box reliability there is a significant overall gain in network reliability as a result of an extra stage (Thanawastien 1982). A failure in a stage m multiplexer or stage 0 demultiplexer has the effect of a link fault, which the ESC network can tolerate, as shown in this section.

Techniques such as test patterns (Feng and Wu 1981) or dynamic parity checking (Siegel and McMillen 1981b) for fault detection and location have been described for use in the generalized-cube network topology. Test patterns are used to determine network integrity globally by checking the data arriving at the network outputs as a result of N strings (one per input port) of test inputs. With dynamic parity checking, each interchange box monitors the status of boxes and links connected to its inputs by examining incoming data for correct parity. It is assumed that the ESC network can be tested to determine the existence and location of faults. This section is not concerned with the procedures to accomplish this, but rather with how to recover once a fault is located. Recovery from such a fault is something of which the generalized-cube network and its related networks discussed earlier in this chapter are incapable.

Single-Fault Tolerance

One-to-One Connections. The ESC network gets its fault-tolerant abilities by having redundant paths from any source to any destination. In the ESC network with both stages m and 0 enabled there exist exactly two paths between any source and any destination. Recall that there is exactly one path from a source S to a destination D in the generalized-cube network. Stage m of the ESC network allows access to two distinct stage $m - 1$ inputs, S and $cube_0(S)$. Stages $m - 1$ to 0 of the ESC network form a generalized-cube network topology, so each of the two stage $m - 1$ inputs has a single path to the destination and these paths are distinct as demonstrated for $N = 8$ for the paths from input 2 to output 1 in figure 5–23. The fact that this is true in general is proved in this subsection.

The existence of at least two paths between any source/destination pair is a necessary condition for fault tolerance. Redundant paths allow continued communication between a given source and destination if after a fault occurs at least one path remains fully functional. For the ESC network, the two paths available are sufficient to provide tolerance to single faults for one-to-one connections. The two paths have no links in common and no interchange boxes in stages $m - 1$ to 1 in common.

The two paths between a given source and destination in the ESC network with stages m and 0 enabled have no links in common. A source S can connect to the stage $m - 1$ inputs S or $cube_0(S)$. These two inputs differ in the 0th bit position. Other than stage m, only stage 0 can affect the 0th bit position of the destination address because only stages m and 0 can perform the $cube_0$ function. Therefore, the path from S though stage $m - 1$ input S to the destination D contains only links with labels that agree with S in the low-order bit position. Similarly, the path through stage $m - 1$ input $cube_0(S)$ contains only links with labels agreeing with $cube_0(S)$ in the low-order bit position. Thus, no link is part of both paths.

This proof is demonstrated in figure 5–23 for $N = 8$. Source 2 can enter stage 2 at link 2 or link $cube_0(2) = 3$. The solid line path from 2 to 1 that enters stage 2 in link 2 goes through link 2 (between stages 2 and 1) and link 0 (between stages 1 and 0). Both link labels 2 and 0 agree with $S = 2$ in the 0th bit position (it is 0). The dashed line path from 2 to 1 that enters stage 2 on link $cube_0(2) = 3$ goes through link 3 (between stages 2 and 1) and link 1 (between stages 1 and 0). Both link labels 3 and 1 agree with $cube_0(S) = 3$ in the 0th bit position (it is 1).

The two paths between a given source and destination in the ESC network with stages m and 0 enabled have no interchange boxes from stages $m - 1$ through 1 in common. Because the two paths have the same source and destination, they will pass through the same stage m and 0 interchange boxes. No box in stages $m - 1$ through 1 has input-link labels that differ in the low-order bit position. One path from S to D contains only links with labels agreeing with S in the low-order bit position. The other path has only links with labels that are the complement of S in the low-order bit position. Therefore, no box in stages $m - 1$ through 1 belongs to both paths.

This proof is also demonstrated in figure 5–23 for $N = 8$. The solid line path and dashed line path share the same stage $m = 3$ and stage 0 interchange boxes. However, they go through different stage 2 and 1 boxes. The solid line path goes through boxes whose link labels agree with $S = 2$ in the low-order bit position. The dashed line path goes through boxes whose link labels agree with $cube_0(S) = 3$ in the low-order bit position.

If the faulty box is in stage m or 0, the stage can be disabled. The remaining m stages are sufficient to provide one path between any source and destination (that is, all m cube functions are still available).

This proof is demonstrated for the path from input 2 to output 1 in figures 5–21 and 5–22 for $N = 8$. In figure 5–21, stage $m = 3$ is disabled and stage 0 functions as $cube_0$. Because stages 1 and 0 are set to swap, input 2 is connected to output $cube_0(cube_1(2)) = 1$. In figure 5–22, stage 0 is disabled and stage $m = 3$ functions as $cube_0$. Because stage 3 and stage 1 are set to swap, input 2 is connected to output $cube_1(cube_0(2)) = 1$. Note that for one-to-one connections the order in which the cube functions are applied is irrelevant.

Thus, in general, in the ESC network with a single fault there is at least one fault-free path between any source and destination, no matter which link or box is faulty. Two paths exist when the fault is in neither of the two paths between the source and destination.

Broadcast Connections. The two paths between any source and destination of the ESC network provide fault tolerance for performing broadcasts as well. In the ESC network with both stages m and 0 enabled, there exist exactly two broadcast paths for any broadcast performable on the generalized-cube network.

There is only one broadcast path from a source to its destinations in the generalized-cube network. As stated previously, stage m of the ESC network allows a source S access to two distinct stage $m - 1$ inputs, S and $cube_0(S)$. Any set of destinations to which S can broadcast, $cube_0(S)$ can broadcast, because a one-to-many broadcast is just a collection of one-to-one connections with the same source.

The two broadcast paths between a given source and destinations in the ESC network with stages m and 0 enabled have no links in common because all links in the broadcast path from the stage $m - 1$ input S have labels that agree with S in the low-order bit position, while all links in the broadcast path from the stage $m - 1$ input $cube_0(S)$ are the complement of S in the low-order bit position. Thus, no link is part of both broadcast paths.

For example, consider the broadcast paths from source 0 to destinations 2, 3, 6, and 7 shown in figure 5–24 for $N = 8$. The solid line broadcast path enters stage $m - 1 = 2$ at link $S = 0$. All the links in its broadcast path (0, 2, 4, and 6) agree with 0 in their low-order bit position (it is 0). The

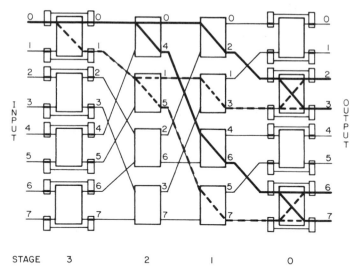

STAGE   3   2   I   0

Figure 5-24. The ESC Network Paths from Input 0 to Outputs 2, 3, 6, and 7 for $N = 8$ When Both Stages 3 and 0 Are Enabled

dashed line broadcast path enters stage $m - 1 = 2$ at link $cube_0(S) = 1$. All the links in its broadcast path (1, 3, 5, and 7) agree with 1 in their low-order bit position (it is 1).

The two broadcast paths between a given source and its destinations in the ESC network with stages m and 0 enabled have no interchange boxes from stages $m - 1$ through 1 in common. Because the two broadcast paths have the same source and destinations, they will pass through the same stage m and 0 interchange boxes. No box in stages $m - 1$ through 1 has input-link labels that differ in the low-order bit position. Because the link labels of the two broadcast paths differ in the low-order bit position, no box in stages $m - 1$ through 1 belongs to both broadcast paths. Thus, a faulty box in stage i, $1 \le i < m$, cannot block both broadcast paths.

In the example in figure 5-24 both broadcast paths share the same stage $m = 3$ and stage 0 boxes, but use different stage 2 and 1 boxes. The solid line broadcast path uses stage 2 and 1 boxes whose links have a 0 in the 0th bit position, as does $S = 0$. The dashed line broadcast path uses stage 2 and 1 boxes whose links have a 1 in the 0th bit position, as does $cube_0(S) = 1$.

Consider the case where the faulty box is in stage 0. Stage 0 is disabled and stage m is enabled. Stages m through 1 of the ESC network provide a complete set of m cube interconnection functions in the order $cube_0$, $cube_{m-1}, \ldots cube_1$. A path exists between any source and destination with stage 0 disabled because all m cube functions are available. This is regard-

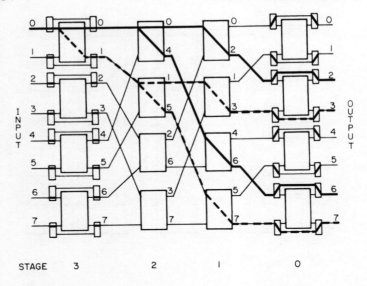

Figure 5-25. The ESC Network Paths from Input 0 to Outputs 2, 3, 6, and 7 for $N = 8$ When Stage 3 Is Enabled and Stage 0 Is Disabled

less of the order of the interconnection functions. Therefore, a set of paths connecting an arbitrary source to any set of destinations exists. As a result, the ESC network with a stage 0 box fault can form any broadcast path that can be formed by the generalized-cube network.

An example of the case where the fault lies in a stage 0 interchange box and so stage 0 is disabled is given in figure 5-25 for an ESC network with $N = 8$. The dashed line paths from input 0 to outputs 3 and 7 correspond to the dashed line paths in figure 5-24. The solid line paths from input 0 to outputs 2 and 6 correspond to the solid line paths in figure 5-24. All paths bypass stage 0 (which is disabled).

Finally, consider the case where the faulty box is in stage m. Stage m is disabled and stage 0 is enabled. This configuration is the same as a fault-free ESC network. The paths followed in stages 2 through 0 are the same as those which would be in the generalized-cube network (as shown by the solid line in figure 5-24).

In summary, in the ESC network with a single fault there exists at least one fault-free broadcast path for any broadcast performable by the generalized-cube network. Assume the fault is in stage 0, then disable stage 0 and enable stage m. Because all cube functions are available, a fault-free broadcast path still exists. Assume the fault is in a link or in a box in stages $m - 1$ to 1. The two broadcast paths will have none of these network elements in common. Therefore, at least one broadcast path will be fault-free, possibly both. Finally, assume the fault is in stage m. Stage m will be disabled (stage 0 will be enabled), and the broadcast capability of the ESC network will be the same as that of the generalized-cube network.

Finding Fault-Free Paths. The ESC network path routing S to D corresponding to the generalized-cube network path from S to D is called the *primary path*. This path must either bypass stage m (stage m is disabled) or use the straight setting in stage m. The other path available to connect S to D is the *secondary path*. It must use the swap setting in stage m (stage m is enabled). For example, see figure 5-23, where the solid line is the primary path and the dashed line is the secondary path.

The concept of primary and secondary paths can be extended for broadcasting. The broadcast path, or set of paths, in the ESC network analogous to that available in the generalized-cube network is called the *primary broadcast path* because each path from the source to one of the destinations is a primary path. If every primary path is replaced by its secondary path the result is the *secondary broadcast path*. This is exemplified in figure 5-24, where the solid lines are the primary broadcast path and the dashed lines are the secondary broadcast path.

Given S and D, the network links and boxes used by the primary or secondary path can be determined. One-to-one connections are considered first, followed by a discussion of broadcasting. For the source/destination pair $S = s_{m-1} \ldots s_1 s_0$ and $D = d_{m-1} \ldots d_1 d_0$, the primary path uses the stage i output labeled $d_{m-1} \ldots d_{i+1} d_i s_{i-1} \ldots s_1 s_0$ and the secondary path uses $d_{m-1} \ldots d_{i+1} d_i s_{i-1} \ldots s_1 \bar{s}_0$, for $0 \le i < m$. This is true because for $0 \le i < m$ in the ESC network only stage i can map (in the sense described in chapter 2) the ith bit of a source address to the ith bit of the destination (that is, determine the ith bit of the destination). Thus, if S is to reach D both ESC network paths must use a stage i output with a label that matches D in the ith bit position. This matching occurs at each stage, so the high-order $m - i$ bits of the output label at stage i will be $d_{m-1} \ldots d_{i+1} d_i$. At the output of stage i, bit positions $i - 1$ to 1 have yet to be affected so they match source address bits $i - 1$ to 1. The low-order bit position is unchanged by stage m for the primary path. The secondary path includes the cube$_0$ connection (swap) in stage m, therefore the low-order bit position is complemented. (The analogous situation for the generalized-cube network was discussed earlier in this chapter).

These connections are demonstrated by the paths from source $S = 2 = 010$ to destination $D = 1 = 001$ in figure 5-23 for an ESC network with $N = 8$. For example, consider the labels of the output links of stage 1. For the primary path (solid line), the link is $d_2 d_1 s_0 = 000 = 0$. For the secondary path (dashed line) the link is $d_2 d_1 \bar{s}_0 = 00\bar{0} = 1$.

When a fault has been detected and located in a link or a stage i interchange box, $1 \leq i < m$, each PE will receive a *fault label* or labels uniquely specifying the fault location. Each fault label consists of two parts: a faulty stage number and a faulty link number. Specifically, if the link between stages i and $i - 1$ from the stage i output j fails, each PE receives the fault label (i,j). If a box in stage i with outputs j and k fails, the pair of fault labels (i,j) and (i,k) is sent to each PE. Because j and k will differ only in the ith bit position, a single faulty link number with an X ("don't care") in the ith position could be used. For a fault in stage 0, no fault label will be given, only notice that a stage 0 fault exists so that stage m can be used instead of stage 0 to implement cube$_0$ if needed because stage 0 will be disabled. Stage m faults require system maintenance but no labels need be issued, as the stage will be disabled, and the network will function as if it is fault-free (stage m disabled, stage 0 enabled).

For one-to-one connections, a source S can check to see if the primary path to its intended destination D contains a faulty link or faulty stage i box, $1 \leq i < m$. If the faulty stage number is i, $1 \leq i < m$, the source forms $d_{m-1} \ldots d_{i+1} d_i s_{i-1} \ldots s_1 s_0$, which is the number of the stage i output it would use to reach its destination. (If there is a faulty stage m output link, $s_{m-1} \ldots s_1 s_0$ is used.) The source then compares this with the faulty link number (or numbers if it is an interchange box that is faulty). If there is a match, the primary path is faulty; if not, it is fault-free. If the primary path is fault-free it will be used. If faulty, the secondary path will be fault-free and thus usable (because only single faults are being considered in this subsection).

For example, in figure 5-23, if the stage 2 box with output links 2 and 6 is faulty the fault label generated would be $(2, X10)$. Source 2 ($S = 2$), which wants to communicate with destination 1 ($D = 1$), would form the address $d_2 s_1 s_0 = 010$. This address matches $X10$, so the secondary path would be used because the primary path is faulty. The paths used for this example when there is a faulty stage m or stage 0 box are demonstrated in figures 5-21 and 5-22, respectively.

Consider a broadcast when there is a faulty link or a faulty stage i box, $1 \leq i < m$. Because a broadcast to many destinations involves many paths from the source to the destinations, checking to see if one of the paths contains a fault may involve more computational effort than is desirable. To decide if the secondary broadcast path should be used, a simpler criterion than checking each path for the fault exists. If the faulty stage number is i, $1 \leq i < m$, compare the low-order i bits of the source address to the faulty link number (note that the faulty link numbers for a faulty interchange box agree in their low-order i bits). The primary broadcast path must use stage i output links and boxes, $1 \leq i < m$, with labels that agree with the source address in the low-order bit i bit positions (as discussed for the generalized-cube network earlier in this chapter). Thus, if the low-order i bits of the faulty link number and the source address agree, the fault *may* lie in the primary broadcast path. (The fault will definitely lie in the primary broadcast path only if the high-order $m - i$ bits of the faulty link number match the high-order $m - i$ address bits of any of the destinations.) Using the secondary broadcast path avoids the possibility of encountering the fault. This method is computationally simpler then exhaustive path fault-checking, but can result in unneeded use of the secondary broadcast path.

To demonstrate, consider the example of broadcasting from input 0 to outputs 2, 3, 6, and 7 shown in figure 5-24 for an ESC network with $N = 8$. If output link 4 in stage 2 is faulty, then compare the low-order two bits of the source 0 (that is, 00) to the low-order two bits of link number 4 (that is, 00). They match, indicating the faulty link may be in the primary path (which it is), so the secondary path would be taken.

If the fault is in a stage 0 box, stage 0 is disabled and stage m is set the way stage 0 would have been to perform the broadcast. The example of broadcasting from source 0 to destinations 2, 3, 6, and 7 for $N = 8$ can be seen by comparing figures 5-24 and 5-25. If the fault is in a stage m box, stage m is disabled, and the ESC network functions in the same way as it would if it were fault-free (the primary broadcast path would be used).

If there is no strong preference to using the primary versus secondary path (or broadcast path), the test to check for a faulty link or faulty stage i box, $1 \leq i < m$, can be reduced to just comparing on a single bit position. If the low-order bit of the source address and faulty link number agree, the primary path (or primary broadcast path) *may* be faulty, so the secondary routing can be used. For example, assume the stage 1 output link 0 is faulty in the sample $N = 8$ ESC network setting in figure 5-23 showing the paths from source 2 to destination 1. Then the low-order bit of link number 0 and source 2 are compared, found to be equal, and so the secondary path is used because the primary path may be blocked (which it is). Because the secondary path uses links whose low-order bit is $\bar{s}_0$ it will be fault-free. This scheme works for faulty links or for faulty boxes in stage i, $1 \leq i < m$, because the faulty link numbers for a box will agree in the low-order bit. This simplified procedure will result in the unnecessary use of secondary paths (one-to-one), and more unnecessary use of secondary broadcast paths. However, in most applications it does not matter whether the primary or secondary path is used, so this method is quite advantageous.

Multiple Fault Tolerance

One-to-One Connections. The previous subsection establishes the capability of the ESC network to tolerate a single fault in the sense that any one-to-one or broadcast connection possible in the fault-free ESC network remains possible. In other words, the ESC network with a single fault retains *fault-free interconnection capability*. For some instances of multiple faults the ESC network also retains fault-free interconnection capability. The necessary and sufficient condition for this is that the primary and secondary paths are not both faulty.

First, consider the situation where there are no faults in stage m or 0 boxes (that is, the multiple faults are the result of faulty links or faulty stage i boxes, $1 \leq i < m$). As faults are detected and located, a system control unit can determine whether fault-free interconnection capability is retained. Let $A = (i, a_{m-1} \ldots a_1 a_0)$ and $B = (j, b_{m-1} \ldots b_1 b_0)$, where $1 \leq j \leq i \leq m$, be two fault labels. If $a_{m-1} \ldots a_{i+1} a_i \neq b_{m-1} \ldots b_{i+1} b_i$, or if $a_{j-1} \ldots a_1 \bar{a}_0 \neq b_{j-1} \ldots b_1 b_0$, there will be at least one fault-free path between any source and destination. This rule is called the *fault-free interconnection capability criterion*. If A corresponds to a faulty stage m output link, the fault-free interconnection capability criterion is $a_{j-1} \ldots a_1 \bar{a}_0 \neq b_{j-1} \ldots b_1 b_0$. The reason the criterion properly determines the state of the network is now considered.

A fault-free path will exist for a source/destination pair S/D if taken together the fault labels A and B do not indicate blockage of both the primary and secondary paths. As shown in the previous subsection, the primary path uses stage i output $d_{m-1} \ldots d_{i+1} d_i s_{i-1} \ldots s_1 s_0$ and the secondary path uses $d_{m-1} \ldots d_{i+1} d_i s_{i-1} \ldots s_1 \bar{s}_0$. The stage j outputs used are $d_{m-1} \ldots d_{j+1} d_j s_{j-1} \ldots s_1 s_0$ and $d_{m-1} \ldots d_{j+1} d_j s_{j-1} \ldots s_1 \bar{s}_0$. Without loss of generality it is assumed that $j \leq i$. Thus, at stages i and j the primary and secondary paths both use outputs with the same bits in positions $m - 1$ through i and positions $j - 1$ through 1, and complementary values in position 0. If $a_{m-1} \ldots a_{i+1} a_i \neq b_{m-1} \ldots b_{i+1} b_i$, at least one of the faults is in neither the primary nor the secondary path, so at least one of the paths is fault-free. Similarly, if $a_{j-1} \ldots a_1 \bar{a}_0 \neq b_{j-1} \ldots b_1 b_0$ at least one fault is in neither path, so at least one path is fault-free. In other words, only if $a_{m-1} \ldots a_{i+1} a_i = b_{m-1} \ldots b_{i+1} b_i$ and $a_{j-1} \ldots a_1 \bar{a}_0 = b_{j-1} \ldots b_1 b_0$ will there be source/destination pairs whose primary and secondary paths are both blocked.

Consider the sample ESC setting from source $S = 2$ to destination $D = 1$ shown in figure 5–23 for $N = 8$. If $A = (2,3)$ and $B = (1,0)$, both paths from 2 to 1 are faulty. In this case (where $m = 3$, $i = 2$, and $j = 1$), $a_2 = b_2 = 0$ and $\bar{a}_0 = b_0 = 0$, so the fault-free interconnection capability criterion is violated. If instead $A = (2,7)$ and $B = (1,0)$, then $a_2 = 1 \neq b_2 = 0$, and the fault-free interconnection capability criterion is satisfied. Therefore, fault-free interconnection capability exists; that is, no source/destination pairs have both their primary and secondary paths blocked.

The source/destination pairs that can no longer communicate when the fault-free interconnection capability criterion is not met due to multiple faults in the links and/or stage i boxes, $1 \leq i < m$, can be determined.

Assume the faults preventing the fault-free interconnection capability are $A = (i, a_{m-1} \ldots a_1 a_0)$ and $B = (j, b_{m-1} \ldots b_1 b_0)$, $1 \le j \le i \le m$. The source/destination pairs S/D that cannot communicate are of the form $s_{i-1} \ldots s_2 s_1 = a_{i-1} \ldots a_2 a_1$; $d_{m-1} \ldots d_{j+1} d_j = b_{m-1} \ldots b_{j+1} b_j$; and $s_{m-1} \ldots s_{i+1} s_i$, s_0, and $d_{j-1} \ldots d_1 d_0$ are arbitrary. The reason for this is as follows.

The primary and secondary paths between a source and destination use stage k outputs that differ only in the low-order bit, $1 \le k \le m$. Assume a path contains the fault denoted by A. Then the stage i output link used is such that $d_{m-1} \ldots d_{i+1} d_i s_{i-1} \ldots s_2 s_1 w = a_{m-1} \ldots a_1 a_0$ and the stage j output link used is $d_{m-1} \ldots d_{j+1} d_j s_{j-1} \ldots s_2 s_1 w$, where w may equal s_0 or $\bar{s}_0$ depending on whether the path is primary or secondary. In this case, $a_{m-1} \ldots a_{i+1} a_i = b_{m-1} \ldots b_{i+1} b_i$ and $a_{j-1} \ldots a_1 \bar{a}_0 = b_{j-1} \ldots b_1 b_0$. Using these equalities, the stage j output link used by the alternate path can be derived: $d_{m-1} \ldots d_{j+1} d_j s_{j-1} \ldots s_2 s_1 \bar{w} = a_{m-1} \ldots a_{i+1} a_i d_{i-1} \ldots$ $d_{j+1} d_j a_{j-1} \ldots a_1 \bar{a}_0 = b_{m-1} \ldots b_{i+1} b_i d_{i-1} \ldots d_{j+1} d_j b_{j-1} \ldots b_1 b_0$. If $d_{i-1} \ldots d_{j+1} d_j = b_{i-1} \ldots b_{j+1} b_j$, the alternate path contains the fault denoted by B. The relationships $d_{m-1} \ldots d_{i+1} d_i s_{i-1} \ldots s_2 s_1 w = a_{m-1} \ldots$ $a_1 a_0$ and $d_{m-1} \ldots d_{j+1} d_j s_{j-1} \ldots s_2 s_1 \bar{w} = b_{m-1} \ldots b_1 b_0$ thus mean that the source and destination addresses of the form $s_{i-1} \ldots s_2 s_1 = a_{i-1} \ldots$ $a_2 a_1$ and $d_{m-1} \ldots d_{j+1} d_j = b_{m-1} \ldots b_{j+1} b_j$ can no longer communicate. The values of $s_{m-1} \ldots s_{i+1} s_i$, s_0, and $d_{j-1} \ldots d_1 d_0$ are unconstrained. Because each of these unconstrained bit positions can contain a 0 or a 1, there are $2^{(m-i)+1+j}$ source/destination pairs that cannot communicate.

As an example, consider an ESC network for $N = 8$ such as shown in figure 5–23. If $A = (2,3)$ and $B = (1,0)$, then $m = 3$, $i = 2$, $j = 1$, $a_2 = b_2 = 0$, and $\bar{a}_0 = b_0 = 0$. Thus, fault-free interconnection capability is lost. The source/destination pairs unable to communicate are those where $s_1 = a_1 = 1$, $d_2 = b_2 = 0$, and $d_1 = b_1 = 0$; specifically, the source/destination pairs 010/000, 011/000, 110/000, 111/000, 010/001, 011/001, 110/001, and 111/001. (Note that this includes the pair 2/1 (010/001) shown in the figure.) There are $2^{(m-i)+1+j} = 8$ such pairs.

When multiple faults are detected and located in the ESC network a system control unit can determine the state of the network. If the multiple faults occur in the links or in stage i boxes or both, $1 \le i < m$, the fault labels of any new faults are compared with all existing fault labels. If each pair of fault labels meets the fault-free interconnection capability criterion, then the network retains its fault-free interconnection capability. (The two fault labels associated with a faulty box do satisfy the fault-free criterion because for stages $m - 1$ through 1 the low-order bit of such labels agree, satisfying $a_{j-1} \ldots a_1 \bar{a}_0 \ne b_{j-1} \ldots b_1 b_0$.) If any pair of fault labels does not meet the criterion, complete fault-free interconnection capability does not exist.

With multiple stage 0 faults only or multiple stage m box faults only, the stage is simply disabled, as for a single fault; fault-free interconnection capability still exists. If faults exist in boxes in both stages m and 0, they are both disabled, and the network is incapable of performing cube_0 (it cannot connect S and D if $s_0 \neq d_0$); thus, fault-free interconnection capability is lost.

If there are faults in either stage m or stage 0 boxes (but not both), and faults in other parts of the network, then fault-free interconnection capability no longer exists because with only one of stages m and 0 enabled there is only one path between any source and any destination. Therefore, any faulty box in stage i, $1 \leq i < m$, or any faulty link will block the only path available for certain source/destination pairs; specifically, pairs S/D such that either $d_{m-1} \ldots d_{i+1}d_i s_{i-1} \ldots s_1 s_0$ matches the faulty link number if the other fault is in stage m, or $d_{m-1} \ldots d_{i+1}d_i s_{i-1} \ldots s_1 d_0$ if the other fault is in stage 0 (because stage m implements the cube_0 function). For example, if the stage 1 link labeled 0 is faulty in the configuration shown in figure 5–21 (where stage $m = 3$ is disabled) $S = 2$ cannot communicate with $D = 1$ because $d_2 d_1 s_0 = 000$. Similarly, if the stage 1 link labeled 1 is faulty in the configuration shown in figure 5–22 (where stage 0 is disabled) $S = 2$ cannot communicate with $D = 1$ because $d_2 d_1 d_0 = 001$.

If fault-free interconnection capability exists, full operation can continue. To continue, the additional fault labels are sent to each source. A source must now check a primary path against a longer list of fault labels to determine whether that path is fault-free. Therefore, system performance may be degraded somewhat, but not at all significantly.

Broadcast Connections. First consider multiple faults in links or stage i boxes $1 \leq i < m$ or both (stage m and 0 boxes are fault-free). Just as with one-to-one connections, the exact conditions under which no fault-free primary and secondary broadcast path exists can be determined and the affected broadcasts characterized. Let $A = (i, a_{m-1} \ldots a_1 a_0)$ and $B = (j, b_{m-1} \ldots b_1 b_0)$, where $1 \leq j \leq i < m$, be any two fault labels. If $a_{j-1} \ldots a_1 \bar{a}_0 = b_{j-1} \ldots b_1 b_0$, there are broadcasts for which no fault-free broadcast path exists. These broadcasts are such that $s_{i-1} s_2 s_1 = a_{i-1} \ldots a_2 a_1$, $d_{m-1}^u \ldots d_{i+1}^u d_i^u = a_{m-1} a_{i+1} a_i$, and $d_{m-1}^v \ldots d_{j+1}^v d_j^v = b_{m-1} \ldots b_{j+1} b_j$, where $S = s_{m-1} \ldots s_1 s_0$ is the source and $D^u = d_{m-1}^u \ldots d_1^u d_0^u$ and $D^v = d_{m-1}^v \ldots d_1^v d_0^v$ are two of the destinations (and are not necessarily distinct), for the following reason.

In general, a broadcast path uses stage i outputs of the form $d_{m-1} \ldots d_{i+1} d_i s_{i-1} \ldots s_2 s_1 w$, where w equals s_0 or $\bar{s}_0$ depending on whether the broadcast path is primary or secondary, and $D = d_{m-1} \ldots d_1 d_0$ represents one of the broadcast destinations. As with one-to-one connections, the primary and secondary broadcast paths from a source to a set of destinations use stage k link outputs whose low-order k bits differ only in the low-order bit, where $1 \le k < m$. Thus, the alternate broadcast path uses stage j link outputs of the form $d_{m-1} \ldots d_{j+1} d_j s_{j-1} \ldots s_2 s_1 \bar{w}$. To determine those broadcasts with faulty primary and secondary paths resulting from faults A and B, consider the following. Let the source S be such that $s_{i-1} \ldots s_2 s_1 = a_{i-1} \ldots a_2 a_1$, and, without loss of generality, let $w = a_0$. Let $D^u = d_{m-1}^u \ldots d_1^u d_0^u$, one of the destinations, be such that $d_{m-1}^u \ldots d_{i+1}^u d_i^u = a_{m-1} \ldots a_{i+1} a_i$. Let $D^v = d_{m-1}^v \ldots d_1^v d_0^v$, another destination (not necessarily distinct from D^u), be such that $d_{m-1}^v \ldots d_{j+1}^v d_j^v = b_{m-1} \ldots b_{j+1} b_j$. Given $a_{j-1} \ldots a_1 \bar{a}_0 = b_{j-1} \ldots b_1 b_0$, the equalities $d_{m-1}^u \ldots d_{i+1}^u d_i^u s_{i-1} \ldots s_2 s_1 w = a_{m-1} \ldots a_1 a_0$ and $d_{m-1}^v \ldots d_{j+1}^v d_j^v s_{j-1} \ldots s_2 s_1 \bar{w} = b_{m-1} \ldots b_1 b_0$ are true. Any broadcast for which the equalities hold does not have a fault-free primary or secondary broadcast path. An easy method for testing for a fault-free primary or secondary broadcast path using broadcast-routing tags is described in the next subsection. (Using a mixture of primary and secondary paths when neither is completely fault-free as a result of this type of multiple-fault situation is not considered here.)

As an example of two faults that prevent fault-free broadcast-connection capability, using either the primary or secondary paths, consider the $N = 8$ ESC network setting for input 0 to broadcast to outputs 2, 3, 6, and 7, shown in figure 5–24. Let $A = (2,4)$ and $B = (1,3)$. In this case $m = 3$, $i = 2, j = 1, \bar{a}_0 = \bar{0} = 1 = b_0, S = 0, D^u = 6, D^v = 2, s_1 = a_1 = 0$, $d_2^u = a_2 = 1$, and $d_2^v d_1^v = b_2 b_1 = 01$ (so $d_2^u s_1 w = a_2 a_1 a_0 = 100$ and $d_2^v d_1^v \bar{w} = b_2 b_1 b_0 = 011$). Note that D^u could be 7, and that D^v could be 3.

Faults in both stage m and stage 0 boxes prevent fault-free broadcast-interconnection capability, as does a fault in a stage m or 0 box and another fault elsewhere in the network for the same reason as for the analogous one-to-one connection situation. For example, a stage 0 fault (disabling stage 0) and a fault in stage 1 output link 3 prevents 0 from being able to broadcast to all of 2, 3, 6, and 7, as can be seen from figure 5–25.

Routing Tags

The use of routing tags to control the generalized-cube network topology has been discussed earlier in this chapter. Routing tags for the ESC network, which take full advantage of its fault-tolerant capabilities, can be derived from the exclusive-or tag scheme for the generalized-cube network. The ESC network uses an $(m + 1)$-bit routing tag $T^* = t_m^* \ldots t_1^* t_0^*$ for one-to-one connections. For one-to-many connections the ESC network uses a $(2m + 2)$-bit broadcast-routing tag $\{R^*, B^*\}$, $R^* = r_m^* \ldots r_1^* r_0^*$ and $B^* = b_m^* \ldots b_1^* b_0^*$. In both cases, the additional bit position (compared to the generalized-cube network tags) controls stage m. Actual tag values depend on whether the ESC network has a fault as well as the source and destination addresses, but are readily computed. Throughout this subsection it is assumed that fault-free interconnection capability exists.

First consider the fault-free case. For both routing and broadcast tags, the mth bit will be ignored because stage m is disabled when there are no faults. The routing tag is given by $T^* = t_m^* t_{m-1} \ldots t_1 t_0$, where $t_{m-1} \ldots t_1 t_0 = T$, the tag used in the generalized-cube network. The bit t_m^* is ignored and so may be set to any convenient value. The bits of T^* are interpreted in the same way as tag bits in the generalized-cube network scheme. The broadcast routing tag is composed of $R^* = r_m^* r_{m-1} \ldots r_1 r_0$ and $B^* = b_m^* b_{m-1} \ldots b_1 b_0$, where $r_{m-1} \ldots r_1 r_0 = R$, $b_{m-1} \ldots b_1 b_0 = B$, $\{R,B\}$ is the broadcast tag used by the generalized-cube network, and r_m^* and b_m^* are arbitrary because they are ignored. Again, the bits of $\{R^*, B^*\}$ have the same meaning as in the generalized-cube network.

Now routing tag and broadcast-routing tag definitions for use in the ESC network with a single fault are described. The primary path in the ESC network is that corresponding to the tag $T^* = 0 t_{m-1} \ldots t_1 t_0$, and the secondary path is that associated with $T^* = 1 t_{m-1} \ldots t_1 \bar{t}_0$. The primary broadcast path is specified by $R^* = 0 r_{m-1} \ldots r_1 r_0$ and $B^* = 0 b_{m-1} \ldots b_1 b_0$, whereas $R^* = 1 r_{m-1} \ldots r_1 \bar{r}_0$ and $B^* = 0 b_{m-1} \ldots b_1 b_0$ denote the secondary broadcast path.

It is assumed that the system has appropriately reconfigured the network and distributed fault labels to all sources as required. With the condition of the primary path known, a routing tag that avoids the network fault can be computed. Specifically, for the ESC network with one fault, any one-to-one connection performable on the generalized-cube network with the routing tag T can be performed using the routing tag T^* obtained from the following rules:

1. If the fault is in stage 0, use $T^* = t_0 t_{m-1} \ldots t_1 t_0^*$ where t_0^* is arbitrary (recall that stage 0 will be disabled).
2. If the fault is in a link or in a box in stages $m-1$ to 1 and the primary path is fault-free, use $T^* = 0 t_{m-1} \ldots t_1 t_0$. If the primary path is faulty, use the secondary path $T^* = 1 t_{m-1} \ldots t_1 \bar{t}_0$.
3. If the fault is in a stage m box, use $T^* = t_m^* t_{m-1} \ldots t_1 t_0$, where t_m^* is arbitrary (recall that stage m will be disabled).

Assume that the fault is in stage 0; that is, stage m will be enabled and stage 0 disabled. Because stage m duplicates stage 0 (both perform cube$_0$), a routing can be accomplished by substituting stage m for stage 0 with the tag $T^* = t_0 t_{m-1} \ldots t_1 t_0^*$, which places a copy of t_0 in the mth bit position. Stage m then performs the cube$_0$ function if it is needed. The low-order bit position of T^*, t_0^*, will be ignored because stage 0 is disabled.

To demonstrate, consider the path from source $S = 2$ to destination $D = 1$ for the ESC network with $N = 8$ shown in figure 5-22. Because $S \oplus D = 011 = T$, $T^* = 1011$ and the path followed is swap in stage $m = 3$, straight in stage 2, and swap in stage 1 (stage 0 is bypassed).

Assume the fault is in a link or in a box in stages $m - 1$ to 1. T specifies the primary path. If this path is fault-free, setting $T^* = 0t_{m-1} \ldots t_1 t_0$ will use this path. The 0 in the mth bit position is necessary because stages m and 0 are both enabled, given the assumed fault location. If the path denoted by T contains the fault, then the secondary path is fault-free and must be used. It is reached by setting the high-order bit of T^* to 1. This setting connects S to the input $cube_0(S)$ of stage $m - 1$. To complete the path to D, bits $m - 1$ to 0 of T^* must be $cube_0(S) \oplus D = t_{m-1} \ldots t_1 \bar{t}_0$. Thus, $T^* = 1 t_{m-1} \ldots t_1 \bar{t}_0$. Another way to explain why stage 0 uses $\bar{t}_0$ instead of t_0 is that stage 0 has to compensate for the swap ($cube_0$) performed by stage m.

To demonstrate, consider the primary and secondary paths from source $S = 2$ to destination $D = 1$ for ESC network with $N = 8$ shown in figure 5-23. Because $S \oplus D = 011 = T$, for the primary path $T^* = 0011$ and for the secondary path $T^* = 1010$. The solid line (primary path) in the figure follows $T^* = 0011$ by using straight (stage $m = 3$), straight (stage 2), swap (stage 1), and swap (stage 0). The dashed line (secondary path) in the figure follows $T^* = 1010$ by using swap (stage $m = 3$), straight (stage 2), swap (stage 1), and straight (stage 0).

Finally, assume the fault is in stage m. Stage m will be disabled, and the routing tag needed will be the same as in the fault-free ESC. This process is demonstrated by the path from source $S = 2$ to destination $D = 1$ for the ESC network with $N = 8$ shown in figure 5-21. Because $S \oplus D = 011 = T$, $T^* = 0011$ (or 1011, since the high-order bit is ignored because stage m is bypassed). This path is straight (stage 2), swap (stage 1), and swap (stage 0).

The rules for formulating routing tags for the ESC network are summarized in table 5-2. In the case of multiple faults where the fault-free connection capability criterion is met (that is, there is at least one fault-free path between any source and destination), the one-to-one routing-tag utility is unchanged. Each source checks the primary path for faults, but against a longer list of fault labels. The routing tag is still formed as in table 5-2. If all faults are in stage 0, rule 1 is used. If all faults are in stage m boxes, then rule 3 is used. In all other cases rule 2 is used.

For an ESC network with one fault, any broadcast performable on the generalized-cube network with the broadcast-routing tag $\{R, B\}$ can be performed using the broadcast-routing tag $\{R^*, B^*\}$ obtained from the following rules:

1. If the fault is in stage 0, use $R^* = r_0 r_{m-1} \ldots r_1 r_0^*$ and $B^* = b_0 b_{m-1} \ldots b_1 b_0^*$, where r_0^* and b_0^* are arbitrary (recall stage 0 is disabled).

Table 5-2
One-to-One Routing Tags for the ESC Network
(X = 0 or 1)

	Fault Location	*Routing Tag T^**
	No fault	$T^* = Xt_{m-1} \ldots t_1 t_0$
Rule 1:	Stage 0	$T^* = t_0 t_{m-1} \ldots t_1 X$
Rule 2:	Stage i box, $1 \le i < m$, or any link	$T^* = 0t_{m-1} \ldots t_1 t_0$ if primary path is fault-free; $T^* = 1t_{m-1} \ldots t_1 \bar{t}_0$ if primary path contains fault
Rule 3:	Stage m box	$T^* = Xt_{m-1} \ldots t_1 t_0$

2. If the fault is in a link or in a box in stages $m - 1$ to 1 and the primary broadcast path is fault-free, use $R^* = 0r_{m-1} \ldots r_1 r_0$ and $B^* = 0b_{m-1} \ldots b_1 b_0$. If the secondary broadcast path has been chosen, use $R^* = 1r_{m-1} \ldots r_1 \bar{r}_0$ and $B^* = 0b_{m-1} \ldots b_1 b_0$.

3. If the fault is in a stage m box, use $R^* = r_m^* r_{m-1} \ldots r_1 r_0$ and $B^* = b_m^* b_{m-1} \ldots b_1 b_0$, where r_m^* and b_m^* are arbitrary (recall stage m disabled).

Assume that the fault is in stage 0. As discussed earlier in this section, any broadcast performable on the generalized-cube network is performable on the ESC network with stage 0 disabled and stage m enabled (that is, with stage 0 faulty). The broadcast-routing tag substitutes stage m for stage 0 by having r_0 and b_0 copied into r_m^* and b_m^*, respectively. This process results in the same broadcast because the order in which the interconnection functions are applied is immaterial for one-to-one routing and broadcasting. Specifically, if $b_i = 0$ and $r_i = 0$, in the set of destination addresses, $d_i = s_i$; if $b_i = 0$ and $r_i = 1$, then $d_i = \bar{s}_i$; and if $b_i = 1$, a broadcast occurs at stage i and d_i can be 1 or 0.

When $b_0 = 0$ (neither stage 0 nor stage m will need to broadcast), if $r_0 = 0$ the primary broadcast path is used, and if $r_0 = 1$ the secondary broadcast path is used. The case for $b_0 = 0$ and $r_0 = 0$ is demonstrated in figure 5-26 for an ESC network with $N = 8$, where the primary path from source 2 to destinations 4 and 6 is used because $2 \oplus 4 = 110 = R$. The case for $b_0 = 0$ and $r_0 = 1$ is demonstrated in figure 5-27 for an ESC network with $N = 8$, where the secondary path from source 3 to destinations 4 and 6 is used because $3 \oplus 4 = 111 = R$.

When $b_0 = 1$, stage m needs to broadcast because stage 0 would broadcast in a fault-free network. Therefore, the stage m interchange box routing

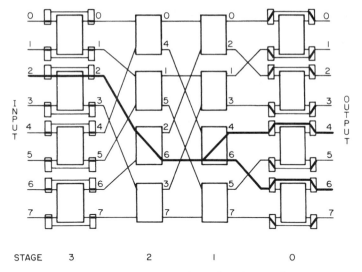

Note: The solid line indicates that this is the primary broadcast path.

Figure 5–26. The ESC Network Paths from Input 2 to Outputs 4 and 6 for $N = 8$ When Stage 3 Is Enabled and Stage 0 Is Disabled

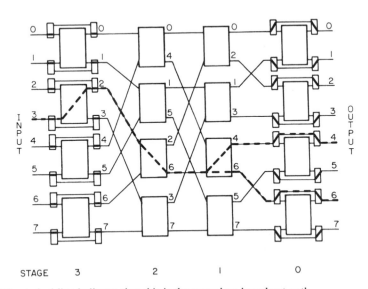

Note: The dashed line indicates that this is the secondary broadcast path.

Figure 5–27. The ESC Network Paths from Input 3 to Outputs 4 and 6 for $N = 8$ When Stage 3 Is Enabled and Stage 0 Is Disabled

the message performs a broadcast, and a combination of primary and secondary paths connect the source to its destinations. Each address bit position is affected individually in mapping the source address to the destination addresses, making the order of stages irrelevant. This effect is demonstrated in figure 5-25 for an ESC network with $N = 8$, where a portion of both the primary (solid lines) and secondary (dashed lines) broadcast paths are used to connect source 0 to destinations 2, 3, 6, and 7 because $B = 2 \oplus 7 = 101$ (so $b_0 = 1$) (in a fault-free network stage 0 would broadcast as shown by the solid lines in figure 5-24).

Assume the fault is in a link or a box in stages $m - 1$ to 1. $\{R, B\}$ corresponds to the primary broadcast path. If it is fault-free, setting $R^* = 0r_{m-1} \ldots r_1 r_0$ and $B^* = 0b_{m-1} \ldots b_1 b_0$ will use this broadcast path. If the primary broadcast path contains the fault then the secondary broadcast path is fault-free, as discussed earlier. Setting $R^* = 1r_{m-1} \ldots r_1 \bar{r}_0$ and $B^* = 0b_{m-1} \ldots b_1 b_0$ causes the broadcast to be performed using the secondary broadcast path. Recall that the procedure for determining whether a primary broadcast is faulty may result in unnecessary use of the secondary broadcast path. However, generating broadcast-routing tags to use the secondary broadcast path incurs negligible additional overhead relative to primary broadcast-path tags.

The primary and secondary broadcast paths from source 0 to destinations 2, 3, 6, and 7 in an ESC network for $N = 8$ shown in figure 5-24 can be used to demonstrate the calculation of $\{R^*, B^*\}$. $R = 0 \oplus 2 = 010$ and $B = 2 \oplus 7 = 101$. If the network is fault-free, $R^* = 0010$ and $B^* = 0101$ and the primary broadcast path (solid lines) uses straight (stage $m = 3$), upper broadcast (stage 2), swap (stage 1), and upper broadcast (stage 0). If the primary broadcast path is blocked, $R^* = 1011$ and $B^* = 0101$ and the secondary broadcast path (dashed lines) uses swap (stage $m = 3$), upper broadcast (stage 2), swap (stage 1), and lower broadcast (stage 0).

Finally, assume the fault is in stage m. Stage m will be disabled, and the broadcast-routing tag needed will be the same as in the fault-free ESC network (the same as used in the generalized-cube network).

The rules for formulating broadcast-routing tags for the ESC network are summarized in table 5-3. A method for detecting a faulty primary broadcast path that sometimes involved the unnecessary use of the secondary broadcast path was described earlier in this section. This unnecessary use of the secondary broadcast path when there is a fault in a link or stage i box, $1 \leq i < m$, can be avoided by using the broadcast-routing tag $\{R, B\}$ to check whether the primary broadcast path is faulty. To check whether a fault in stage i is in the primary broadcast path, the source constructs $L = \ell_{m-1} \ldots \ell_1 \ell_0$ such that for $0 \leq j < i$, $\ell_j = s_j$, and for $i \leq j \leq m - 1$, if $b_j = 1$ then $\ell_j = X$ ("don't care"), otherwise $\ell_j = s_j \oplus r_j$. This process corresponds to using $d_{m-1} \ldots d_{i+1} d_i s_{i-1} \ldots s_1 s_0$ to check for a fault in the pri-

Table 5-3
Broadcast-Routing Tags for the ESC Network
(X = 0 or 1)

	Fault Location	Broadcast Routing Tag $\{R^*, B^*\}$
	No fault	$R^* = Xr_{m-1} \cdots r_1 r_0$ $B^* = Xb_{m-1} \cdots b_1 b_0$
Rule 1:	Stage 0	$R^* = r_0 r_{m-1} \cdots r_1 X$ $B^* = b_0 b_{m-1} \cdots b_1 X$
Rule 2:	Stage i box, $1 \le i < m$, or any link	$R^* = 0 r_{m-1} \cdots r_1 r_0$ $B^* = 0 b_{m-1} \cdots b_1 b_0$ if primary broadcast path is fault-free; $R^* = 1 r_{m-1} \cdots r_1 \bar{r}_0$ $B^* = 0 b_{m-1} \cdots b_1 b_0$ if primary broadcast path contains fault
Rule 3:	Stage m box	$R^* = Xr_{m-1} \cdots r_1 r_0$ $B^* = Xb_{m-1} \cdots b_1 b_0$

mary path of a one-to-one connection. The i low-order bits of L are $s_{i-1} \cdots s_1 s_0$. The $m - 1$ high-order bits of L correspond to the $m - i$ high-order bits of the set of destinations. The reason is that if $b_j = 1$, a broadcast occurs in stage j and the set of destinations will include elements with a 0 in the jth position and elements with a 1 in the jth position, hence the X. Where $b_j = 0$, all destinations must agree in the jth position, because all paths will use the same r_j, setting $d_j = s_j$ if $r_j = 0$ (straight box setting) or $d_j = \bar{s}_j$ if $r_j = 1$ (swap box setting); that is, $d_j = s_j \oplus r_j$ for all destinations. Thus, if L matches the faulty link number (with X matching 0 or 1), the primary path contains a fault. If $\bar{s}_0$ is used in place of s_0, the secondary path can be checked.

The broadcast routing tags for the ESC network can be used in some cases when there are multiple faults but fault-free interconnection capability is retained. If all faults are in stage 0, rule 1 is used. If all faults are in stage m boxes, rule 3 is used. If there are no faults in stage 0 or m boxes, the testing procedure just described can be used to determine whether the primary or the secondary broadcast path is fault-free. If one is fault-free, it can used.

Partitioning

The *partitionability* of a network is the ability to divide the network into independent subnetworks of different sizes (see chapter 4). Each subnetwork of size $N' < N$ must have all the interconnection capabilities of a complete network of that same type built to be of size N'. A partitionable network allows a multiple-SIMD, partitionable SIMD/MIMD, or MIMD machine to be dynamically reconfigured into independent subsystems.

The ways in which the generalized-cube network can be partitioned were discussed earlier in this chapter. The ESC network can be partitioned in a similar manner with the property that each subnetwork has the attributes of the ESC network, including fault tolerance. The only constraint is that the partitioning cannot be based on the 0th bit position of the input/output port addresses because to be able to use either the primary or secondary path and yet remain within a partition, both sources S and $cube_0(S)$ must be in the same partition. Thus, within any given partition the low-order bit of input/output port physical addresses must be allowed to vary.

The ESC network can be partitioned based on any bit positions other than 0; that is, within a given partition of size 2^k the physical addresses of the input/output ports may be fixed in any $m - k$ of the m bits, except for position 0. The cube functions $m - 1$ through 1 each occur once in the ESC network. Setting stage i to all straight, $1 \leq i < m$, separates the network input and output ports into two independent groups. Each group contains ports whose addresses agree in the ith bit position; that is, all addresses have their ith bit equal to 0 in one group and 1 in the other. The other m stages provide the $cube_j$ functions for $0 \leq j < m$ and $j \neq i$, where $cube_0$ appears twice. This comprises an ESC network for the $N/2$ ports of each group. As with the generalized-cube network, each subnetwork can be further subdivided. Because the addresses of the interchange-box outputs and links of a primary path and a secondary path differ only in the 0th bit position, both paths will be in the same partition (that is, they will agree in the bit positions on which the partitioning is based). Thus, the fault-tolerant routing scheme of the ESC network is compatible with network partitioning.

For example, in figure 5–28 the ESC network for $N = 8$ is shown partitioned with respect to stage 2. The two subnetworks are indicated by the labels A and B. Subnetwork A consists of ports 0, 1, 2, and 3. These port addresses agree in the high-order bit position (it is 0). Subnetwork B contains ports 4, 5, 6, and 7, all of which agree in the high-order bit position (it is 1). In figure 5–29 the ESC network for $N = 8$ is shown partitioned with respect to stage 1. In this case, subnetwork A consists of ports 0, 1, 4, and 5 (those with 0 in the middle bit position). Subnetwork B consists of ports 2, 3, 6, and 7 (those with 1 in the middle position). Figure 5–28 and 5–29 can be compared to figure 5–14 and 5–16, respectively, to see the relation to the analogous generalized-cube network partitionings.

If partitioning is attempted on stage m—that is, if all boxes of stage m set to straight—the result will clearly be a generalized-cube network topol-

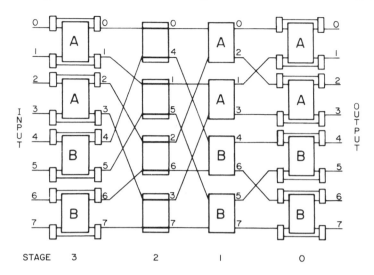

Note: *A* and *B* denote the two subnetworks.

Figure 5-28. The ESC Network for $N = 8$ Partitioned into Two Size-Four Independent Subnetworks Based on the High-Order Bit Position

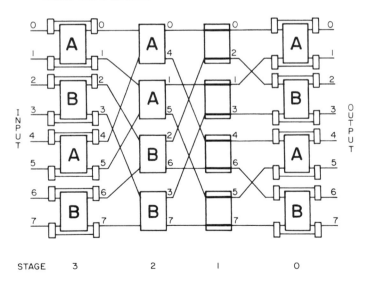

Note: *A* and *B* denote the two subnetworks.

Figure 5-29. The ESC Network for $N = 8$ Partitioned into Two Size-Four Independent Subnetworks Based on the Middle Bit Position

ogy of size *N*, with no fault-tolerant capabilities. Alternatively, attempting to partition on stage 0—that is, with all boxes of stage 0 set to straight—again yields a network of size *N*, in particular a generalized cube with $cube_0$ first, not last. Again, fault-tolerant capabilities are no longer available. In neither case are independent subnetworks formed.

As described earlier for the generalized-cube network, partitioning can be readily accomplished by combining routing tags with masking. By logically ANDing tags with partitioning masks to force to 0 those tag positions corresponding to interchange boxes that should be set to straight, partitions can be established. This process is external to the network and therefore independent of a network fault. Thus, partitioning is unimpeded by a fault (that is, a faulty box is avoided, whether or not it is forced to straight). For example, consider the network configuration shown in figure 5–30. It is desired to connect input 0 to output 1. The stage 2 box with outputs labeled 0 and 4 is on the primary path and is set to straight to enforce the partitioning. If this box is faulty, the secondary path may be used.

As with the generalized-cube network, broadcasting within a partition is allowed. In the ESC network, either the primary or secondary broadcast paths or both may be used if fault-free.

In the PASM system (Siegel and others 1981), partitioning is designed to be based on input/output port addresses within a group agreeing in some

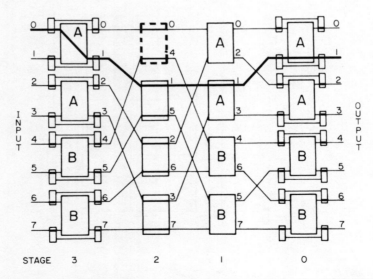

Figure 5–30. The Path from Input 0 to Output 1 in the ESC Network for *N* = 8 When It Is Partitioned Based on the High-Order Bit Position and Has a Faulty Interchange Box

number of low-order bit positions. The ESC network as defined cannot support this type of partition because the low-order bit position must be allowed to vary to have multiple paths. However, a variation of the ESC network can perform low-order bit partitioning. Beginning with a generalized-cube network, an ESC-like network can be constructed by adding an extra stage that implements $cube_{m-1}$ to the output side of the network. Call this new stage -1. Thus, from the input to the output, the stages implement $cube_{m-1}$, $cube_{m-2}$, . . . , $cube_1$, $cube_0$, and $cube_{m-1}$. The same fault-tolerant capabilities are available in this new network, but partitioning may be done on stage 0. Partitioning on the high-order bit is now not available, but low-order bit partitioning is available.

SIMD Operation

Consider permuting data with the ESC network in an SIMD environment. If the ESC network is fault-free it can obviously perform any permutation of which the generalized-cube network is capable. An ESC network with a single fault can perform in two passes through the network any permutation the generalized-cube network can perform in a single pass through the network. The exception is the case where a stage m box is faulty, so stage m is bypassed as in the fault-free situation, and any permutation performable on a generalized-cube network can be done in a single pass through the network.

First, consider the case where the fault is in stage 0. While stages m through 1 provide all m cube functions, it provides them in the order $cube_0$, $cube_{m-1}$, $cube_{m-2}$, . . . , $cube_1$, as opposed to $cube_{m-1}$, $cube_{m-2}$, . . . , $cube_1$, $cube_0$, as in the generalized-cube network. The order in which the cube functions are applied matters when permuting data, as discussed in the section comparing different multistage cube-type networks.

For example, for $N = 8$ the generalized-cube network (shown in figure 5–1) can perform a permutation including the connections 0 to 2 and 1 to 0 by setting the boxes in the path from 0 to 2 straight, swap, and straight, and setting the boxes in the path from 1 to 0 straight, straight, and swap. Using stages $m = 3$ to 1, the ESC network for $N = 8$ cannot perform this permutation. The reason is that to connect 0 to 2 and 1 to 0 the stage 3 output links used by both inputs 0 and 1 are the same (link 0). Thus, there is a conflict.

To perform any generalized-cube network permutation on the ESC network with stage 0 disabled, two passes through the network are used. On the first pass, stage m is set to straight, stage 0 is bypassed, and the remaining stages are set as they would be for the generalized-cube network, implementing $cube_{m-1}$, . . . , $cube_2$, $cube_1$, as needed, in that order. Then, on the second pass, stage m is set as stage 0 would have been, implementing $cube_0$

as needed, with stage 0 disabled and the other stages set to straight. Thus, the order of the application of the cube functions is preserved.

When the fault is in a link or a box in stages $m - 1$ to 1, at the point of the fault there are fewer than N paths through the ESC network. Thus, N paths (a complete permutation) cannot exist simultaneously. The permutation can be completed in two passes in the following way. First, all sources with fault-free primary paths to their destination are routed. One source will not be routed if the failure was in a link; two sources will not be routed if the failure was in a box. With a failed link, the second pass routes the remaining source to its destination using its fault-free secondary path. With a faulty box, the secondary paths of the two remaining sources will route to their destinations without conflict. Recall that paths conflict when they include the same box output. As discussed earlier in this section, if the faulty box is in stage i, then the primary path output labels for these two paths at stage i are $d_{m-1}^1 \ldots d_{i+1}^1 d_i^1 s_{i-1}^1 \ldots s_1^1 s_0^1$ and $d_{m-1}^2 \ldots d_{i+1}^2 d_i^2 s_{i-1}^2 \ldots s_1^2 s_0^2$, $0 \le i < m$, where the superscripts distinguish the two paths. Note that $d_i^1 = \overline{d_i^2}$. Thus, the stage i output labels of the two primary paths are distinct. The secondary-path stage i output labels differ from the primary-path labels only by complementing the 0th bit position. Therefore, the secondary paths are also distinct.

Permutation passing can be extended naturally to the multiple-fault situation. In the ESC network with multiple faults but retaining fault-free interconnection capability, all generalized-cube network permutations can be performed in at most two passes.

Consider multiple faults not involving stage m or 0 boxes. For a performable permutation the primary paths between each source/destination pair are by definition pairwise nonconflicting. From the preceding argument, if two primary paths do not conflict, their two associated secondary paths do not conflict. Thus, there is no conflict among the secondary paths. Therefore, in the ESC network with multiple faults but retaining fault-free interconnection capability, a permutation can be performed by first passing data over those primary paths which are fault-free and then passing the remaining data using secondary paths.

For multiple faults in stage m, that stage is disabled and permutations are performed in one pass. With multiple faults in stage 0 the same procedure for the case of a single stage 0 fault is used, performing permutations in two passes.

Summary

The reliability of large-scale parallel or distributed systems is a function of system structure and the fault tolerance of system components. Fault-tolerant intercommunication networks can aid in achieving satisfactory reliability.

This section has presented the ESC network, a derivative of the generalized-cube network that is fault-tolerant. The fault-tolerant capabilities of the ESC network topology were shown, as well as the partitioning and permuting abilities of the ESC network. A minor adaptation of the exclusive-or routing tag and broadcast-routing tag schemes designed for the generalized-cube network was described that allows the use of tags to control a faulted as well as a fault-free ESC network. Thus, the ESC network has the capabilities of the generalized-cube network plus fault tolerance for a relatively low additional cost.

Fault-tolerant networks similar in concept to the ESC are discussed in Dias and Jump (1981), Wu, Feng, and Lin (1982), and Thanawastien (1982). Other approaches to fault-tolerance multistage cube-type networks are offered by Ciminiera and Serra (1982), Lilienkamp, Lawrie, and Yew (1982), and Shen and Hayes (1980).

Conclusions

In this chapter various properties and capabilities of the generalized-cube network were studied. First, the topology of the network was introduced as a multistage series of cube interconnection functions implemented by interchange boxes, which also allow data broadcasting. Routing-tag schemes were presented for distributing the control of the network among the devices attached to it (rather than attempting to have a centralized network controller). Then, the generalized-cube network topology was shown to be equivalent to that of the omega (multistage shuffle-exchange), indirect binary n-cube, STARAN flip, and SW-banyan ($S = F = 2$, $L = m$) networks. The control structures proposed for these networks were also discussed. Ways in which the generalized-cube network could be partitioned into independent subnetworks were examined next, followed by an analysis of the number of distinct data permutations the generalized-cube network can perform. Finally, the extra-stage cube (ESC) network, a fault-tolerant variation of the generalized-cube network, was described.

The introduction to this chapter indicated that the generalized-cube network was a representative of a large class of networks based on multistage implementations of the cube/shuffle-exchange interconnection networks of chapter 2. This type of network has been recommended for use in a large number of future supersystems. The features of the generalized-cube network that make it appealing include the fact that simultaneous transfers by N devices are permitted; it can be controlled in a distributed fashion using routing tags; it can be partitioned into independent subnetworks of various sizes under operating-system control or under user control (both through the use of routing tags); one device can broadcast to all or a subset of devices; a fault-tolerant variation (the ESC network) has been developed; and it can function in the SIMD, multiple-SIMD, MIMD, and partitionable SIMD/MIMD modes of parallel processing.

6 Data Manipulator Networks

The class of multistage interconnection networks called data manipulators are based on the PM2I interconnection functions defined in chapter 2. Just as the generalized cube discussed in chapter 5 is, in effect, a wired series of cube interconnection functions, data manipulator networks are a wired series of PM2I interconnection functions. The class of data manipulator networks include the data manipulator (Feng 1974); the augmented data manipulator or ADM (Siegel and Smith 1978); the inverse augmented data manipulator or IADM (Siegel and McMillen 1981a); and the gamma (Parker and Raghavendra 1982) multistage interconnection networks. This chapter focuses on the ADM and IADM networks as representatives of this class. These networks can operate in the SIMD, multiple-SIMD, MIMD, and partitionable-SIMD/MIMD modes of parallelism.

The topology of the ADM and IADM networks is described first, followed by a discussion of routing tag schemes for establishing paths through these networks. The relationship between the generalized-cube network of chapter 5 and the ADM network is analyzed next. The ways in which the ADM and IADM networks can be partitioned into independent subnetworks is then examined, followed by a study of the number of distinct data permutations performable by the ADM and IADM networks. Finally, the capability to reroute messages dynamically in the ADM and IADM networks to avoid busy or faulty switching nodes and links is explored.

Data Manipulator Network Structure and Properties

Network Definition

The model of a parallel processing system used here assumes $N = 2^m$ PEs, addressed from 0 to $N - 1$ (as described in chapter 2). The interconnection network contains N input ports and N output ports. PE i is connected to input port i and output port i of the network, $0 \leq i < N$.

The *data manipulator* network (Feng 1974) is shown in figure 6-1 for $N = 8$. It has m stages. Each stage consists of N switching elements (nodes) and $3N$ output links, three output links per node. There is also an $(m + 1)$st

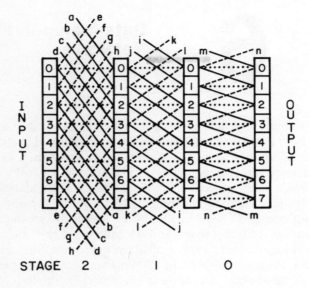

STAGE   2   1   0

Note: Straight connections are shown by the dotted lines, PM2$_{+i}$ by the solid lines, and PM2$_{-i}$ by the dashed lines. The lower-case letters represent end-around connections.

Figure 6-1. The Data Manipulator and Augmented Data Manipulator (ADM) Networks for $N = 8$

column of network output nodes. The stages are ordered from $m - 1$ to 0, where the interconnection functions of stage i are PM2$_{+i}$, PM2$_{-i}$, and the "identity" (straight across). At stage i of the network, $0 \leq i < m$, the first output of node j is connected to node $j - 2^i$ modulo N of stage $i - 1$ (that is, PM2$_{-i}$), the second output to node j of stage $i - 1$ (that is, identity), and the third output to node $j + 2^i$ modulo N of stage $i - 1$ (PM2$_{+i}$). Each node selects one of its input links and connects it either to one of its output links (a one-to-one setting) or to two or three of its output links (a broadcast setting). Because PM2$_{+(m-1)} = $ PM2$_{-(m-1)}$ $(j - 2^{m-1} = j + 2^{m-1}$ modulo N), an actual network implementation may have only two distinct outputs from each node in stage $m - 1$.

The controls of the data manipulator are limited to one pair per stage. At stage i, nodes whose ith bit is 0 respond to one set of controls; nodes whose ith bit is 1 respond to the other set of controls. Specifically, stage i of the network can receive any two of the signals H_1^i, H_2^i, U_1^i, U_2^i, D_1^i, and D_2^i. H (horizontal) corresponds to straight, U (up) to -2^i modulo N, and D (down) to $+2^i$ modulo N. Nodes whose ith address bit is 0 are controlled by the signals with a 1 subscript and those whose ith address bit is 1 are controlled by the signals with a 2 subscript. For example, for $N = 8$ the signals H_1^2, H_2^2, D_1^1, D_2^1, D_1^0, and U_2^0 would set the network as shown in figure 6-2.

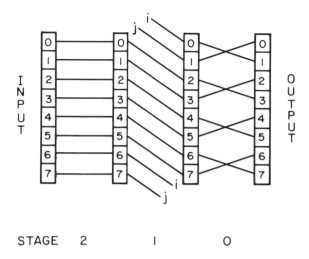

STAGE   2   I   O

Figure 6–2. The Data Manipulator Setting Corresponding to the Control Signals H_1^2, H_2^2, D_1^1, D_2^1, D_1^0, and U_2^0 for $N = 8$

The *augmented data manipulator* (*ADM*) network is a data manipulator network with individual switching-element control—that is, each node can be independently set to straight across, -2^i modulo N, or $+2^i$ modulo N (Siegel and Smith 1978; Siegel and McMillen 1981a). As with the data manipulator network, the data output from node j at stage i becomes the data input to node j' at stage $i - 1$, where $j' \in \{j, (j + 2^i)$ modulo N, $(j - 2^i)$ modulo $N\}$ (see figure 6–1). However, in the ADM network, each node passes data independently of any other node.

If the stages of the ADM network are traversed in reverse order—that is, the interconnection functions of the input stage are $PM2_{\pm 0}$, the interconnection functions of the next stage are $PM2_{\pm 1}$, . . . , and the interconnection functions of the output stage are $PM2_{\pm (m-1)}$—the resulting network is called the *inverse augmented data manipulator* (*IADM*) network (Siegel and McMillen 1981a). The IADM network is shown for $N = 8$ in figure 6–3.

One-to-One Connections

A path from an input (source) S of the ADM network to an output (destination) D is established by using links whose "sum" modulo N is $D - S$ modulo N. For example, in figure 6–4, a path from $S = 1$ to $D = 6$ is shown. The $+2^2$ connection in stage 2 and $+2^0$ connection in stage 0 sum to $5 = D - S$ (the straight connection in stage 1 contributes nothing to the

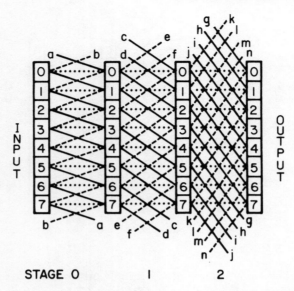

STAGE   0   1   2

Note: Straight connections are shown by the dotted lines, $PM2_{+i}$ by the solid lines, and $PM2_{-i}$ by the dashed lines. The lower-case letters represent end-around connections.

Figure 6-3. The IADM Network for $N = 8$

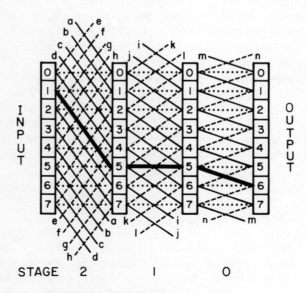

STAGE   2   1   0

Note: The bold line shows one path from input 1 to output 6.

Figure 6-4. A One-to-One Connection in the ADM Network for $N = 8$

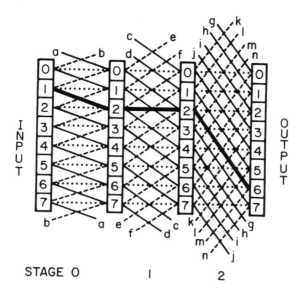

STAGE 0   1   2

Note: The bold line shows one path from input 1 to output 6.
Figure 6–5. A One-to-One Connection in the IADM Network for $N = 8$

sum). Relating this to the single-stage PM2I network, $PM2_{+0}(PM2_{+2}(1)) =$ 6. Other paths between 1 and 6 exist: $+2^2$, $+2^1$, -2^0; and straight, -2^1, -2^0. The only requirement is that the sum of the links in the path equals $D - S$ modulo N. These same stage settings connect input 1 to output 6 in the IADM network. For example, the $+2^0$, straight, and $+2^2$ setting shown for the ADM network in figure 6–4 is shown for the IADM network in figure 6–5. They are equivalent because $PM2_{+0}(PM2_{+2}(1)) = PM2_{+2}(PM2_{+0}(1))$. In general, a given one-to-one connection will be performed by the same setting of switches in both the ADM and IADM networks. That is, for one-to-one connections (as opposed to permutations) the order in which the PM2I functions are executed is irrelevant; modulo N addition and subtraction is commutative. Both the ADM and IADM networks can connect any single source to any single destination.

Recall that in the generalized-cube network there is only one path from a given source to a given destination (chapter 5). In the ADM and IADM networks, there are multiple paths between most source/destination pairs. This property gives the ADM and IADM networks flexibility that the generalized cube does not have. The multiple path feature of the ADM/IADM network differs from that of the extra-stage cube (ESC) network (chapter 5). The ESC, with both stages m and 0 enabled, has exactly two paths between any source and any destination. The ADM/IADM network has only one path between a source S and destination D when $S = D$ and has more than two paths between some source/destination pairs (such as 1 and 6 in the preceding example).

One-to-one connections in the ADM/IADM network are discussed further in the next section. The multiple-path property is exploited to allow dynamic rerouting of connections to avoid busy or faulty nodes, as described later.

Broadcast Connections

When a node in the ADM/IADM network selects one of its inputs and connects it to two or three of its outputs, a broadcast (one-to-many) connection is performed. One or more nodes in a path may be set to broadcast. For example, in the ADM network for $N = 8$, input 0 can be connected to outputs 4, 5, 6, and 7 using the node settings shown in figure 6-6. Broadcasting from input 0 to outputs 4, 5, 6, and 7 in an IADM network of size $N = 8$ is shown in figure 6-7. The physical structure of the ADM/IADM network allows the broadcasting of data from any source to any arbitrary set of destinations (just overlay the one-to-one paths from the source to each destination). In some cases there are multiple paths for broadcasts as there are for one-to-one connections. Broadcasting is discussed further in the next section. The rerouting of broadcasts is considered later.

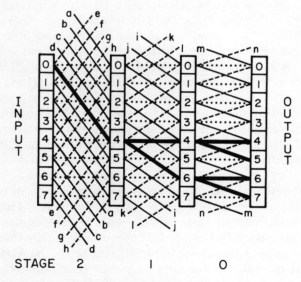

Note: Input 0 is connected to outputs 4, 5, 6, and 7.

Figure 6-6. Broadcasting in the ADM Network for $N = 8$

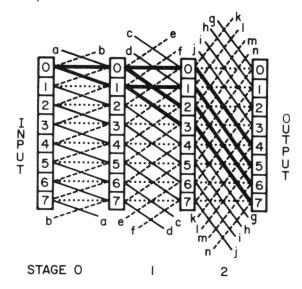

STAGE 0 1 2

Note: Input 0 is connected to outputs 4, 5, 6, and 7.

Figure 6-7. Broadcasting in the IADM Network for $N = 8$

Permutations

Permutation connections, where each input is connected to a single differ-ent output, are also possible. For example, connecting input i to output $i + 3$ modulo N, $0 \leq i < N$, in the ADM network for $N = 8$ is shown in figure 6-8 and for the IADM for $N = 8$ in figure 6-9. For both networks, all stage 2 nodes are set to straight, stage 1 nodes to $+2^1$, and stage 0 nodes to $+2^0$. The sum of the links in all paths is $+3$. Other settings to perform this permutation exist in both networks. For example, for $N = 8$, set stage 2 to -2^2, stage 1 to straight, and set stage 0 to -2^0, for a sum of $-5 = +3$ modulo 8, as shown for the ADM for $N = 8$ in figure 6-10. The relation-ship of these two ADM network settings to alternative methods of perform-ing this permutation using the single-stage PM2I can be seen by considering the fact the $PM2_{+0}(PM2_{+1}(i)) = PM2_{-0}(PM2_{-2}(i))$, $0 \leq i < N$.

In general, there are many permutations that have multiple network settings. Examples include the cube interconnection functions (defined in chapter 2) and uniform shifts (that is, connecting input i to output $i + A$ modulo N, $0 < A < N$, for all i, $0 \leq i < N$, and a fixed A, $0 \leq A < N$ (Smith and others 1980). Thus, permutations can also make use of the mul-tiple paths, as discussed later in this chapter.

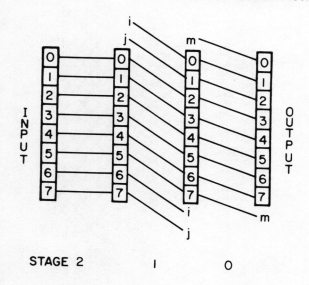

STAGE 2   1   0

Note: Input i is connected to output $i + 3$ modulo N.

Figure 6-8. A Permutation in the ADM Network for $N = 8$

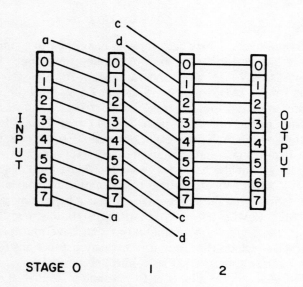

STAGE 0   1   2

Note: Input i is connected to output $i + 3$ modulo N.

Figure 6-9. A Permutation in the IADM Network for $N = 8$

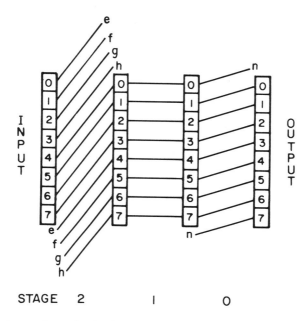

Figure 6-10. Second Method of Performing the Permutation Input i to Output $i + 3$ Modulo N for the ADM Network for $N = 8$

In chapter 5, where the generalized-cube network topology was compared to the topologies of other cube-type networks, it was shown that the ordering of the stages of the network (that is, the ordering in which the m cube interconnection functions were applied) affects which permutations are possible. The same is true in the case of the ADM and IADM networks. Furthermore, as in the case of the generalized-cube network and indirect binary n-cube network, if the ADM network can perform a permutation function f, the IADM network can perform f^{-1}, where $f(f^{-1}(a)) = f^{-1}(f(a)) = a$, $0 \leq a < N$. For example, the ADM network can perform the shuffle (defined in chapter 2), as shown for $N = 8$ in figure 6-11 (Smith and others 1980). Using the same settings in the IADM network, the inverse shuffle (shuffle^{-1}) will be performed, where shuffle$^{-1}(p_{m-1} \ldots p_1 p_0) = p_0 p_{m-1} \ldots p_2 p_1$. This can be visualized by considering figure 6-11 with the input and output sides reversed. Conceptually, following the ADM network set to the shuffle with the IADM network set to the inverse shuffle (that is, putting the networks in sequence) results in the identity permutation, where the identity permutation maps a to a, $0 \leq a < N$. For example, 5 connects to 5 in stage 2 of the ADM network, then to 3 in stage 1, then to 3 in stage 0, then to 3 in stage 0 of the IADM network, then to 5 in stage 1, then to 5 in

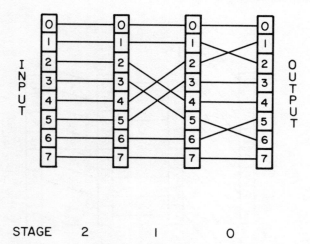

STAGE   2   I   0

Figure 6–11. The ADM Network Set to Perform the Shuffle
Interconnection Function for $N = 8$

stage 2. In general, if the ADM network can perform interconnection function f, input a is connected to output $f(a)$, $0 \le a < N$. In the IADM net-
work, using the same settings, input $f(a)$ will be connected to output a, $0 \le a < N$ (that is, input $f(a)$ will be connected to output $f^{-1}(f(a)) = a$, $0 \le a < N$). Therefore, if the ADM network can perform f, the IADM network
can perform f^{-1} and vice versa—the origin of the name *inverse* ADM.

Some interconnection functions can be performed by the ADM network and not by the IADM network, and vice versa. For example, the
IADM network cannot perform the shuffle (Smith and others 1980). Con-
sider performing the shuffle on the IADM network for $N = 16$. Input $2 = 0010$ must connect to output shuffle(2) $= 4 = 0100$. Because when mapping
2 to 4 (in the sense described in chapter 2) the low-order bit must be un-
changed, node 2 in stage 0 must connect to node 2 in stage 1 (only stage 0
($PM2_{\pm 0}$) can affect the low-order bit). Similarly, input $4 = 0100$ must connect to output shuffle(4) $= 8 = 1000$. Again, the low-order bit must remain
unchanged, requiring node 4 in stage 0 to connect to node 4 in stage 1. However, input $3 = 0011$ must connect to output shuffle(3) $= 6 = 0110$. The
only way to map the 1 in the low-order bit position to a 0 is by connecting
node 3 in stage 0 to node 4 (using $+1$) or node 2 (using -1) in stage 1.
Either of these connections would cause a conflict in the network (two stage
0 nodes cannot connect to the same stage 1 node). Analogously, the ADM
network cannot perform the inverse shuffle. Thus, the permutations that
each network can perform are limited and the sets of permutations performable by the ADM and IADM networks are not the same.

Later in this chapter, the data-permuting capability of the ADM/ IADM network is compared to that of the generalized-cube network. The number of distinct data permutations performable by the ADM/IADM network is also examined.

Summary

Both the ADM and IADM network can perform one-to-one, broadcast, and permutation connections. Any one-to-one or broadcast connection is physically possible in both networks. Neither network can perform all possible data permutations. However, if the ADM network can perform an interconnection function f, the IADM network can perform f^{-1}, and vice versa.

Distributed-Control Schemes

The ADM (and IADM) network contains Nm switching elements, each of which can be in one of three states for one-to-one connections and one of seven states if broadcasting is included. For large N, any type of centralized network controller would create a bottleneck. Distributed control is established by having each PE associate a routing tag with the data it is to transmit. Each switching element in the network derives its control signals from certain bits in the routing tag. The same concept was described for the generalized-cube network in chapter 5.

Routing tag schemes for performing one-to-one connections in the ADM and IADM networks are presented in this section, as well as routing tags for broadcasting data in these networks, and performing permutations in an SIMD environment. The schemes discussed and terminology used are from McMillen and Siegel (1982c) and Siegel and McMillen (1981a), which were done as part of R.J. McMillen's Ph.D. dissertation research. The notation $w_{a/b}$ is used to indicate bits $w_a w_{a-1} \ldots w_b$ of W, $a \geq b$.

Routing Tag Schemes for One-to-One Connections

Full Routing Tags. To be able to specify any arbitrary path in the ADM (or IADM) network, at least $\lceil \log_2(3^{m-1} \cdot 2) \rceil$ bits are required, because in stages 0 to $m - 2$ there are three choices of node outputs and at stage $m - 1$ there are two choices (if the $+2^{m-1}$ and -2^{m-1} connections are not implemented separately). This is a theoretical lower bound. *Full routing tags* use $2m$ bits to represent arbitrary paths in an easily decoded fashion. A full routing tag has the form $F = f_{2m-1/0}$. The m low-order bits represent the magnitudes of the route and the m high-order bits represent the signs corresponding to the magnitudes. In stage i, a given switching elements examines bits i and $m + i$ of the full tag. If $f_i = 0$, the straight link is used regardless of the value of f_{m+i}. If $f_i = 1$, the corresponding sign bit is examined. If $f_{m+i} = 0$, the $+2^i$ link is used. If $f_{m+i} = 1$, the -2^i link is used. Each PE generates its own routing tag. For example, in the ADM network, for $N = 16$, if the source is 3 and the destination is 10, one possible value for F is 00101011. The path traversed is $+2^3$, straight, -2^1, $+2^0$.

Given a source (input port) S and a full routing tag F, the destination (output port) D can be calculated as:

$$D = \left[S + \sum_{i=0}^{m-1} (-1)^{f_{m+i}} * f_i * 2^i \right] \text{ modulo } N$$

For example, for $N = 16$ if a message at source 5 has tag 00110110 it will be routed straight at stage 3, $+2^2$ at stage 2, -2^1 at stage 1, and straight at stage 0. The destination which will receive the message is:

$$5 + [(-1)^0 * 0 * 2^3 + (-1)^0 * 1 * 2^2 + (-1)^1 * 1 * 2^1$$
$$+ (-1)^1 * 0 * 2^0] = 5 + [0 + 2^2 - 2^1 + 0] = 7$$

Methods for automatically calculating a full-routing tag given a source and a destination are discussed later.

This routing tag scheme uses a relative-addressing approach in which the information contained in the tag is the modulo N additive distance from the source to the destination. This approach is analogous to the exclusive-or tag scheme for the generalized-cube network based on the Hamming distance between the source and destination (described in chapter 5). It differs from the destination address scheme proposed by Lawrie (1975) for the omega network, also discussed in chapter 5.

Natural Routing Tags. If all the sign bits in a full tag are the same, the information contained in those bits can be represented by one bit that is the sign bit for the whole tag. The high-order bit will be used for this purpose. For example, for $N = 16$, 00001011 can be collapsed into 01011 because all the sign bits are 0. Thus the new tag requires only $m + 1$ bits. However, because this more compact tag requires that all the sign bits be equal, paths that use both positive links (of the form $+2^i$) and negative links (of the form -2^i) cannot be represented. Although all possible paths cannot be represented, a tag can be found to route a message between any source/

destination pair because there is more than one route between all source/ destination pairs (source $\neq$ destination). For example, for $N = 16$ to connect source 5 to destination 7 the full routing tag 00000010 can be used instead of the tag 00110110 specified previously. This tag, which routes the data $+2^1$ at stage 1 and straight at all other stages, can be collapsed to 00010. The availability of multiple paths is not wasted if this compact tag is used because dynamic rerouting can be performed, as discussed later.

Let S denote the source address and D denote the destination address. An $m + 1$ bit routing tag is formed by computing the *signed magnitude* difference between the destination and the source: $T = t_{m/0} = D - S$. The *sign bit* is t_m, where $t_m = 0$ indicates positive or zero (that is, $D \geq S$), and $t_m = 1$ indicates negative (that is, $D < S$). Bits $t_{m-1/0}$ equal the absolute value of $D - S$, the *magnitude* of the difference. For example, if $N = 16$, $S = 13$, and $D = 6$, then $T = -7 = 10111$. A routing tag formed in this manner is called a *natural routing tag*. It consists of a single sign bit and m magnitude bits. Each PE can generate its own natural tag, based on the knowledge of its own address (PE number) and the address of the PE to receive the data. To form a routing tag for a return or handshaking message, simply complement the sign bit of an incoming tag. For the preceding example, with $S = 13$, $D = 6$, and $T = 10111$, the return tag from 6 to 13 is $\overline{1}0111 = 00111 = +7$.

To route a message through either the ADM or IADM network, stage i need examine only bits t_m and t_i in the routing tag. If $t_i = 0$, the straight connection is used regardless of the value of t_m. If $t_i = 1$, the sign bit t_m is examined. If $t_m = 0$, the $+2^i$ link is used. If $t_m = 1$, the -2^i link is used. In the previous example, with $T = 10111$, when a message enters the ADM network at stage 3, the sequence of connections traversed from port 13 to 6 is straight, -2^2, -2^1, -2^0. When a message with tag T enters the IADM network at stage 0, the sequence of connections from 13 to 6 is -2^0, -2^1, -2^2, straight. A route consisting of only straight or $+2^i$ connections is called *positive dominant* and a route consisting of only straight or -2^i connections is called *negative dominant*. Given a source address S and a natural routing tag $T = t_{m/0}$, the value of the destination address D is calculated as:

$$D = \left[S + (-1)^{t_m} \sum_{i=1}^{m-1} (t_i * 2^i) \right] \text{ modulo } N$$

The $\sum_{i=0}^{m-1} (t_i * 2^i)$ factor is the magnitude—that is, the absolute distance between S and D. The $(-1)^{t_m}$ factor determines the direction (positive or negative) in which to move the data to go from S to D.

Two tags T_1 and T_2 are *equivalent* (denoted $T_1 \simeq T_2$) if and only if they route a message from the same source address to the same destination address; that is, given $T_1(S) \rightarrow D_1$ and $T_2(S) \rightarrow D_2$, $T_1 \simeq T_2$ if and only if $D_1 = D_2$. A characteristic of the routing tag scheme is that for any arbitrary natural tag an equivalent routing tag can be computed that uses links of the opposite sign. For example, for $N = 16$, consider the positive dominant tag $T_1 = 00010 = +2$. T_1 is equivalent to the negative dominant tag $T_2 = 11110 = -14$ because -14 modulo $16 = +2$. That is, $T_1 \simeq T_2$ because $T_1(S) = T_2(S) = S + 2$ modulo 16. In general, the following property holds.

Two's Complement Property: If T' is the two's complement of T, $T \neq 0$, then $T' \simeq T$. To show this, let T_M denote the magnitude bits of T; that is, $T_M = t_{m-1/0}$. For $T = t_m T_M$, $T \neq 0$, $T' = \bar{t}_m T'_M$; that is, $t'_m = \bar{t}_m$. (Recall the two's complement of a j bit number T is evaluated by subtracting T from 2^j.) Assume arithmetic is modulo N.

$$T'(S) = S + (-1)^{t'_m} T'_M = S - (-1)^{t_m}(2^m - T_M)$$

$$= S + (-1)^{t_m} T_M = T(S)$$

For example, for $N = 16$, if $S = 3$, and $D = 8$, then $T = 00101$. The equivalent tag T' is 11011. In the ADM network, the first route is straight, $+2^2$, straight, $+2^0$ (which establishes the positive dominant route of $+5$). The equivalent route is -2^3, straight, -2^1, -2^0 (which establishes the negative dominant route of $-11 = +5$ modulo 16).

Thus, the two's complement property allows conversion from a positive dominant tag to a negative dominant tag and vice versa. Also, the return tag generated from complementing just the sign bit of T is equivalent to the return tag generated from complementing just the sign bit of T'.

Consider the difference in the paths T and T', $T \neq 0$, in the IADM network. Because the input stage of the IADM network is stage 0, corresponding to t_0 and t'_0, the lowest-order difference in the two tags is of interest. If t_i is the first 1 encountered when scanning the bits of T from low order to high order, $t_{i/0} = t'_{i/0}$ and $t'_{m/i+1} = \bar{t}_{m/i+1}$. For example, if $T = 01100$, then $T' = \overline{01}100, = 10100$. Thus, in general, T and T' follows the same straight paths until stage i, and then diverge (because $t_i = t'_i = 1$ and $t'_m = \bar{t}_m$). Therefore, if the first node of the IADM network where a nonstraight link is requested resides in stage i, the two's complement property is useful if the $+2^i$ link is requested but blocked and the -2^i link is available or vice versa. The equivalent tag can be formed and the message routed on the oppositely signed link.

Consider the difference in the paths T and T', $T \neq 0$, in the ADM network. In this case, the highest-order difference between the two tags is of interest because the input stage of the ADM network is stage $m - 1$, corresponding to t_{m-1} and t'_{m-1}. If there is a $t_i = 1$, $0 \leq i \leq m - 2$, then $t'_{m-1} = \bar{t}_{m-1}$. For example, if $T = 00010$, then $T' = \overline{00}010 = 11110$. For this example T uses the straight link at stage $m - 1$, whereas T' uses the -2^{m-1} link. In general, if there is a $t_i = 1$, $0 \le i \le m - 2$, and T uses a straight link at stage $m - 1$, T' uses a nonstraight link $(+2^{m-1}$ or $-2^{m-1})$ and vice versa. Therefore, in the ADM network, the two's complement property is useful if a straight link is blocked in the input stage and the $\pm 2^{m-1}$ link is available or vice versa.

Natural tags can be used in other ways for rerouting. These are described later in this chapter.

The concept of natural routing tags can be used in a system where the hardware for full routing tags has been implemented. All that is needed is for the sign bit in the natural tag to be expanded (replicated) in bits $2m - 1$ through m of the full tag. This is one way to compute the value for a full routing tag.

Routing Tag Schemes for Broadcasting

Broadcast-Routing Tags. The physical structures of the ADM and IADM networks allow arbitrary broadcasts to be performed. However, a practical requirement imposed on these networks is that they be controllable in a distributed fashion through the use of routing tags. The broadcast-routing tags discussed in this section have the property that a single tag completely specifies the path configuration of a particular broadcast. This property implies that when a network node performs a broadcast, it merely sends identical (or slightly modified) copies of the tag on each output link involved. This property is important because it keeps the node architecture simple. Broadcasting could be implemented by sending a list of tags (one per destination), but the overhead and cost for doing so would be high. The difference between the two approaches is in the flexibility to choose destinations for the broadcast. The latter method allows for arbitrary sets of destinations, while the former method is more limited. The capabilities of the former method are investigated in this subsection. Except where noted, all the schemes to be discussed are applicable to both the ADM and IADM networks. (The above tradeoffs also apply to the generalized cube.)

One way to add a broadcast capability to either the full or natural routing tags is to include an $m + 1$ bit broadcast mask. The broadcast routing tag is denoted by $\{R,B\}$, where R is the routing control and B is the broadcast mask. R corresponds to F if full routing tags are used or to T if natural routing tags are used. A broadcast-routing tag is interpreted by a node in stage i as follows. If the ith bit of B, b_i, is 0, no broadcast is performed in the ith stage and R is treated exactly as F or T would be (interpreted as a one-to-one route). If b_i is 1, R is ignored and a broadcast is performed.

This broadcast-routing tag scheme allows a switching node to send the same message out on two links (it does not include facilities for sending the same message on all three links). Two kinds of broadcasts can be performed. The two types are named for the distance by which the replicated messages are separated after the broadcast is performed. A 2^i-*type broadcast* uses a straight link and one of the remaining nonstraight links. To specify a 2^i-type broadcast, b_m is set to 0. The appropriate sign bit of R (either r_{m+i} for full routing tags or t_m for natural routing tags) determines which nonstraight link is used. A 2^{i+1}-*type broadcast* uses the $+2^i$-link and the -2^i-link. To specify a 2^{i+1}-type broadcast, b_m is set to 1.

For the rest of this subsection, natural routing tags will be assumed for R. The extension to full tags is straightforward. First, broadcasting to a number of destinations that is a power of two is considered. After defining the notion of equivalence among broadcast-routing tags, it is shown that alternative routes exist for certain broadcasts. Finally, a method is described for modifying the broadcast-routing tag to allow an arbitrary number of destinations to receive a broadcast (with restrictions on the destination addresses).

A broadcast tag is interpreted by a node in stage i as follows:

If the ith bit of B, $b_i (0 \le i < m)$, is 0, no broadcast is performed and R is treated exactly as T would be (interpreted as a normal route).

If b_i is a 1, the ith bit of R is ignored and a broadcast is performed.

The sign bit of B, b_m, specifies a 2^i-type broadcast if equal to 0 and a 2^{i+1}-type broadcast if equal to 1.

If a 2^i-type broadcast is specified, the sign bit of R, r_m, specifies which nonstraight link to use.

Various properties of 2^i-type broadcasting are examined in the rest of this subsection. Dynamic rerouting of 2^i-type broadcasts is discussed in a later section. More information about 2^{i+1}-type broadcasts is in McMillen and Siegel (1982c).

Broadcasting to a Power of Two Destinations. Using 2^i-type broadcast-routing tags, 2^j destinations, each separated by a distance of 2^k, can receive a message from any source S. To do this, set bits k through $k + j - 1$ of B to 1 (all others to 0), and set R to $q - S$, where q is one of the desired destinations. As an example, let $N = 32$, $S = 3$, $q = 12$, $k = 1$, and $j = 2$. Then $B = 000110$ and $R = +9 = 001001$. The four destination addresses are 12 (01100), 14 (01110), 16 (10000), and 18 (10010). The broadcast path used by this tag is shown for the ADM network by the solid lines in figure 6–12 and for the IADM network by the solid lines in figure 6–13.

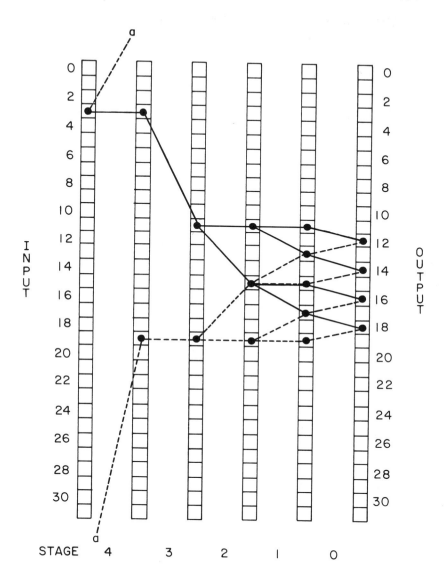

Note: The solid lines show the positive dominant broadcast path for {R = 001001, B = 000110}. The dashed lines show the negative dominant broadcast path for {R' = 110111, B = 000110}.

Figure 6-12. The Paths of Equivalent Broadcast-Routing Tags in an ADM Network for N = 32

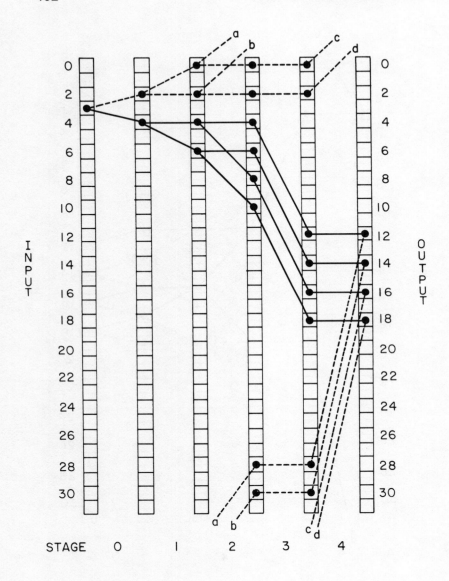

Note: The solid lines show the positive dominant broadcast path for $\{R = 001001, B = 000110\}$. The dashed lines show the negative dominant broadcast path for $\{R' = 110111, B = 000110\}$.

Figure 6–13. The Paths of Equivalent Broadcast-Routing Tags in an IADM
Network for $N = 32$

To see why this broadcast rule works in general, consider the set of destinations reached by S using B and R as described above. Call this set Q. Because 2^i-type broadcasts are being used, $b_m = 0$. Each 1 in B corresponds to a branch point, doubling the number of destinations. There are $(k + j - 1) - k + 1 = j$ 1s in B, indicating 2^j-destinations, as desired. At each of the j branch points, one copy of the message (and broadcast-routing tag) is routed on the straight output link and another on the link with sign $(-1)^{r_m}$. These branches will occur in stages k through $k + j - 1$. It can be shown by induction on j that the 2^j destinations can be described by taking all possible values of a j-bit number g and adding $(-1)^{r_m} * g * 2^k$ to:

$$[S + (-1)^{r_m} r_{m-1/k+j} 2^{k+j} + r_{k-1/0})]$$

where the notation $w_{a/b} 2^c$ represents the $(a - b + 1 + c)$-bit number $w_a w_{a-1} \ldots w_b$ followed by c 0's (for example, $w_{5/3} 2^2 = w_5 w_4 w_3 00$). Thus:

$$Q = \{[S + (-1)^{r_m}(r_{m-1/k+j} 2^{k+j} + g * 2^k + r_{k-1/0})];$$
$$g = 0, 1, 2, \ldots, 2^{j-1}\}$$

The values of $r_{k+j-1/k}$ are irrelevant because $b_{k+j-1/k}$ are all ones.

Now consider the concept of equivalent broadcast-routing tags. Two broadcast-routing tags, $\{R^1, B^1\}$ and $\{R^2, B^2\}$, are equivalent (that is $\{R^1, B^1\} \simeq \{R^2, R^2\}$) if and only if, given the same source, a message routed by either tag arrives at the same set of destinations. Given a broadcast-routing tag $\{R, B\}$, assume bits k to $k + j - 1$ of B are ones (all others are 0). If $r_{k-1/0} \neq 0$, then $\{R', B\} \simeq \{R, B\}$. To demonstrate, consider the previous example for $N = 32$, $k = 1$, $j = 2$, $B = 000110$, and $R = 001001$, which sends data from source 3 to destinations 12, 14, 16, and 18. $R' = 110111$. The broadcast path used by the tag $\{R', B\}$ is shown for the ADM network by the dashed lines in figure 6–12 and for the IADM network by the dashed lines in figure 6–13.

To show that, in general, $\{R', B\} \simeq \{R, B\}$, given $b_{k+j-1/k} = 11\ldots1$ and $r_{k-1/0} \neq 0$, consider the set of destinations Q^* reached by S using $\{R', B\}$. Based on the analysis for Q, Q^* can be computed as:

$$Q^* = \{[S + (-1)^{r_m} r'_{m-1/k+j} 2^{k+j} + g * 2^k + r'_{k-1/0})];$$
$$g = 0, 1, 2, \ldots, 2^{j-1}\}$$

Because $r_{k-1/0} \neq 0$, $r'_{m-1/k+j} = \bar{r}_{m-1/k+j}$. Furthermore, because in general $A' = \bar{A} + 1$, $\bar{r}_{m-1/k+j} = 2^{m-(k+j)} - r_{m-1/k+j} - 1$. Substituting this, $r'_{k-1/0} = 2^k - r_{k-1/0}$, and $r'_m = \bar{r}_m$:

$$Q^* = \{[S + (-1)^{r_m}((2^{m-(k+j)} - r_{m-1/k+j} - 1)2^{k+j}$$
$$+ g * 2^k + 2^k - r_{k-1/0})]; \ g = 0, 1, 2, \ldots 2^{j-1}\}$$

$$= \{[S + (-1^{r_m}(r_{m-1/k+j}2^{k+j} + 2^{k+j} - g * 2^k - 2^k$$
$$+ r_{k-1/0})]; \ g = 0, 1, 2, \ldots 2^{j-1}\}$$

Because g is a j-bit number, $2^{k+j} - g * 2^k - 2^k = (2^j - g - 1)2^k = \bar{g} * 2^k$. Because $g = 0, 1, 2, \ldots, 2^{j-1}, \bar{g} = 2^{j-1}, 2^{j-1} - 1, 2^{j-1} - 2, \ldots, 0$. Thus, both g and $\bar{g}$ can take on any value from 0 to 2^{j-1}. Therefore, substituting $g * 2^k$ for $2^{k+j} - g * 2^k - 2^k$:

$$Q^* = \{[S + (-1)^{r_m}(r_{m-1/k+j}2^{k+j} + g * 2^k + r_{k-1/0})];$$
$$g = 0, 1, 2, \ldots, 2^{j-1}\} = Q$$

Thus, $\{R',B\} \simeq \{R,B\}$.

If $r_m = 0$, the routing control is positive dominant, and $\{R,B\}$ is a *positive dominant broadcast route*. Similarly, if $r_m = 1$, $\{R,B\}$ is a *negative dominant broadcast route*. Thus, $\{R',B\}$ is the equivalent broadcast tag of $\{R,B\}$ of opposite dominance. This equivalence is shown for the example broadcast routes in figures 6–12 and 6–13.

In the discussion thus far, it was assumed that the 1s in B were adjacent. This assumption was for notational convenience and is not a restriction on the broadcast capabilities of this scheme. For example, for $N = 32$, let $S = 3$, $R = 001001$, and $B = 001010$. S sends its data to four destinations because B contains two 1s. The destinations are 4, 6, 12, and 14, as shown for the ADM network by the solid lines in figure 6–14. The equivalent tag is $\{R',B\}$, where $R' = 110111$, and is shown for the ADM network by the dashed lines in figure 6–14.

Broadcasting to an Arbitrary Number of Destinations. Broadcasting to an arbitrary number of destinations (note that the destinations are not arbitrary, but only the number of destinations) is accomplished by reducing the number of destinations in a set of 2^j specified by the broadcast-tag scheme just described. The restrictions on valid destination addresses implied by that scheme still apply. No additional bits have to be added to the broadcast-routing tag. More processing is required of the nodes, however, which increases their complexity.

The scheme detailed here is appropriate for the IADM network only. A similar scheme exists for the ADM network (McMillen and Siegel 1983). For convenience it is again assumed that the 1s in the broadcast mask are adja-

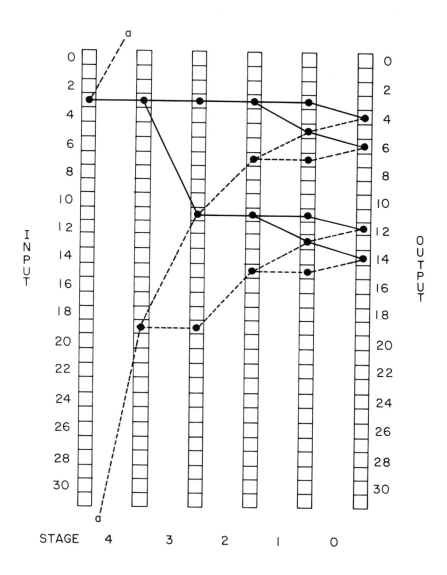

Note: The solid lines show the positive dominant broadcast path for $\{R = 001001, B = 001010\}$. The dashed lines show the negative dominant broadcast path for $\{R' = 110111, B = 000110\}$.

Figure 6–14. The Paths of Equivalent Broadcast-Routing Tags in an ADM Network for $N = 32$ When the 1s in B Are Not Adjacent

cent. If they are not, some extra operations are required when manipulating the routing tags. To see how to modify the general broadcasting scheme, examine the binary tree representing the paths used in a broadcast in the IADM network shown in figure 6–15. One way to reduce the number of destinations is to prune an appropriate number of lower branches (represented by dashed lines) from the tree. A *pruning node* is defined to be any node in the last stage of those stages involved in performing a broadcast. To perform the pruning, a mechanism is needed to instruct the nodes that would route data to those branches not to do so. The method employed is to include a counter with the broadcast-routing tag that is decremented in accordance with the path followed.

Consider first a positive dominant broadcast-routing tag; that is, one where $r_m = 0$. A message routed onto a nonstraight link in stage i has its counter reduced by 2^i. A message routed on a straight link in stage i is left with its counter unaltered. A counter may not become negative, and so is reduced to zero if the amount to be subtracted is larger than the count. It is the zero counter value that instructs a pruning node to abort its broadcast and route a message only on the straight link. To initialize the counter, it should contain the number of pruning nodes that are to participate in the broadcast. The initial value of the counter is calculated by finding the difference between the number of destinations to receive the broadcast and the largest power of two less than that number.

Two observations demonstrate that a counter can be included in the broadcast-routing tag without adding any extra bits. First, recall that where the broadcast mask contains ones, the corresponding bits of the routing control have no significance and are thus unused. If there are $W = 2^w$ destinations, w bits of the routing tag are unused. Second, if Y is the number of destinations to receive a broadcast under the new scheme, a tree with 2^y leaves is to be pruned, where $y = \lceil \log_2 Y \rceil$. There are 2^{y-1} pruning nodes involved in deciding whether to perform a broadcast. If $W = 2^y$, there will always be enough unused bits in the routing tag R to accommodate the counter.

In general, $Y - 2^{y-1}$ is the number of pruning nodes that are to perform the broadcast, and $2^{y-1} - (Y - 2^{y-1}) = 2^y - Y$ pruning nodes send that data straight only. Thus, the total number of destinations is $2 * (Y - 2^{y-1}) + (2^y - Y) = Y$.

For example, to broadcast to 13 PEs the counter should be initialized to $13 - 2^3 = 5$. If $N = 16$, source $S = 0$, $R = 00000$, and $B = 01111$, modify R replacing the bits corresponding to the 1s in B with the counter value 5, making $R = 00101$ as shown in figure 6–15.

Negative broadcast tags, those where $r_m = 1$, are handled slightly differently. A message routed on a straight link in stage i has its counter reduced by 2^i. A message routed on a nonstraight link in stage i is left with

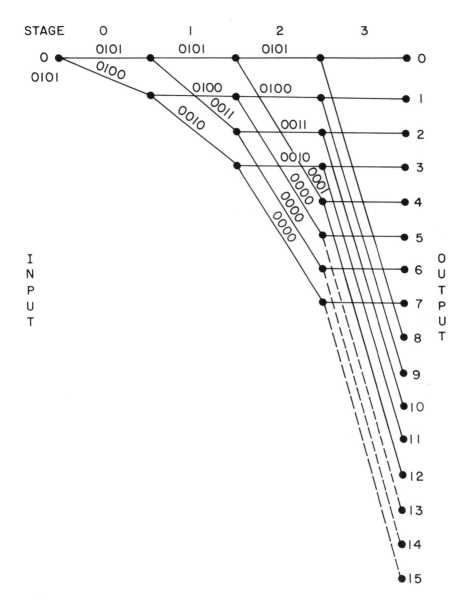

Note: The value of the broadcast counter when it enters each node is shown. A node does not replicate the message on its $+2^i$-link if the counter is 0, as indicated by the dashed lines.

Figure 6-15. A Broadcast to 13 Destinations in an IADM Network. $N = 16$, $S = 0$, $R = 00000$ without the counter, $R = 00101$ with the counter, and $B = 01111$

its counter unaltered. A pruning node receiving a negative broadcast tag whose counter is zero will send the message on the negative link only. The different treatment of negative broadcast tags is required to guarantee that the same set of destinations is generated by equivalent positive and negative dominant broadcast tags.

An example of positive and negative dominant broadcast routes to six destinations for $N = 32$ is shown in figure 6–16 for $\{R = 000101, B = 001110\}$ and $\{R* = 110101, B = 001110\}$. (When using the scheme to broadcast to an arbitrary number of destinations, set the bits of $R*$ corresponding to ones in B to the same value of those bits in R (the counter) and set the other bits to the two's complement of R). For identical sets of destinations to be generated, the pruning nodes in stage 3 of the negative dominant path must eliminate two straight links. If negative dominant broadcast tags were not treated differently, the destination addresses would be 16, 18, 20, 22, 24 and 26.

The algorithm shown in figure 6–17 is to be used by each node to interpret a broadcast-routing tag. If $b_{m/i+1} = 0$, then stage i contains the pruning nodes. If $(R \text{ AND } B) = 0$, then the counter is 0. The algorithm can be compared to figure 6–15, where the value of the counter for a broadcast to 13 destinations is shown at each node as it is received. The broadcast mask bits equal to 1 are assumed to be adjacent in this algorithm. The procedure requires slight modification if this is not the case.

The additional broadcast capability just described for the IADM network increases the complexity of nodes in the network but does not require any extra connections between nodes. If the nodes are implemented as VLSI chips, adding this feature is highly desirable. The functional complexity of the chip is increased without the addition of any pins.

The same technique can be used with the broadcast-routing tags for the generalized-cube network, defined in chapter 5. The method is described in McMillen and Siegel (1983).

Permutations

Full routing tags can represent any data permutation the ADM (or IADM) network is physically capable of performing because any one-to-one path can be described by a full routing tag. Calculation of the tags for any permutation passable by the ADM network so that the N paths specified do not conflict, however, is not a trivial problem. A conflict occurs if two nodes in stage i try to send data to the same node in stage $i - 1$. For a given pair of the N source/destination pairs in the permutation, one may have to choose among many possible paths to complete the individual connection. Assum-

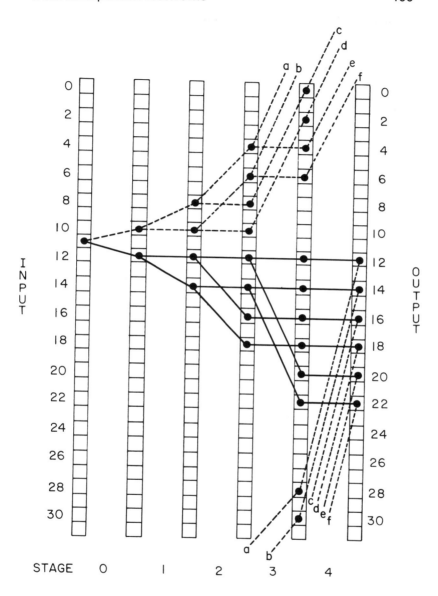

Note: The solid lines show the positive dominant broadcast path for $\{R = 000101, B = 001110\}$. The dashed lines show the negative dominant broadcast path for $\{R^* = 110101, B = 001110\}$.

Figure 6-16. The Paths Traversed to Six Destinations by Equivalent Broadcast-Routing Tags in an IADM Network for $N = 32$

if $b_i = 1$: indicates broadcast in stage i
  then
    if $r_m = 0$
      then   : indicates positive dominant broadcast route
        if $(R$ AND $B) = 0$ *and* $b_{m/i+1} = 0$: counter is 0 and i is
                                                        pruning stage
        then send message straight only
        else subtract 2^i from R AND B setting the counter bits to 0 if the
            result is negative. If not, subtract 2^i from R and send this
            copy $+2^i$. Send an unmodified copy straight.
      else   : indicates negative dominant broadcast route
        if $(R$ AND $B) = 0$ *and* $b_{m/i+1} = 0$: counter is 0 and i is
                                                        pruning stage
        then send message -2^i only
        else subtract 2^i from R AND B setting the counter bits to 0 if
            the result is negative. If not, subtract 2^i from R, then send
            this copy straight. Send an unmodified copy -2^i.

Figure 6–17. Algorithm Used by a Node in Stage i of the IADM Network
to Interpret a 2^i-Type Broadcast Tag That Can Specify an
Arbitrary Number of Destinations

ing the other $N - 1$ paths have been specified properly, there will be only
one path that does not conflict with those already established. If the method
used to calculate tags does not specify that particular path, the routing tag
control scheme will not pass the permutation even though the network is
physically capable of doing so.

One solution to this problem is based on the relationship between the
generalized-cube network and the ADM network. It is shown in the next
section that the ADM network can perform any permutation that the generalized cube can. Also in that section a method to calculate full routing
tags allowing the ADM network to perform all generalized-cube passable
permutations is given. The types of permutations these include are described in papers about cube-type multistage networks. Specifically, for the
STARAN flip network see Batcher (1976) and Bauer (1974); for the shuffle-
exchange multistage network see Lang and Stone (1976); for the omega network see Lawrie (1975); and for the indirect binary n-cube network see
Pease (1977).

It is more difficult to handle permutations that can be performed by the
ADM network but cannot be by the generalized-cube network. If it is
known at compile time that such a permutation of data must be performed
(and the permutation itself is known), the full routing tags can be precom-

puted and the execution of the SIMD algorithm will not be impeded. Between the ability to do all generalized-cube performable permutations and the ability to precompute the full routing tags for other permutations not in this class, but known at compile time, the ADM network can function very well in an SIMD environment.

If, however, it is necessary to perform an arbitrary data-dependent ADM network performable permutation that is not performable by the generalized cube and not known at compile time, the preceding method cannot be used. In this case, the permutation can be treated as N independent data transfers in an MIMD environment. Natural routing tags can be computed for the transfers. If there are conflicts in the network the rerouting schemes presented later in this chapter can be used. The SIMD control unit can query the PEs using an "if-all" type of statement to determine when the transfer is completed. This procedure will take more time than using tags known to perform the connections without conflicts.

Thus, using the generalized-cube-based full routing tags, precomputed full routing tags, or natural tags with rerouting when necessary, the ADM network can use the routing tags described in this section to perform all permutations of which it is physically capable. Permuting on the IADM can be handled similarly.

Summary

In this section routing tag schemes for the ADM and IADM networks were explored. Full routing tags and natural routing tags for one-to-one paths through the network were described and compared. Broadcast-routing tags, which allowed the broadcasting of data to an arbitrary number of destinations, were presented. These routing tag schemes are such that each PE can compute the tag for its own message independently. Thus, network control is distributed, and no centralized controller is needed. The ability of these networks to permute data in an SIMD environment was also discussed.

**Relationship Between the ADM and
Generalized-Cube Networks**

The relationship of the generalized-cube topology to that of other multistage cube-type networks was discussed in chapter 5. In this section the capabilities of a generalized-cube network with four-function interchange boxes (also described in chapter 5) are compared to those of the ADM network. It is shown that the capabilities of the ADM network are a superset of those of the generalized-cube network.

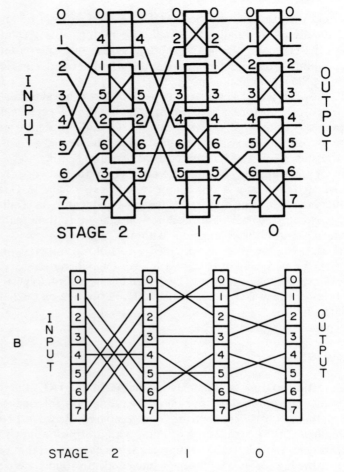

Figure 6–18. Performing the Same Permutation in the ADM and
Generalized-Cube Networks. A. The generalized-cube
network for $N = 8$ set to connect i to $i + 3$ modulo 8,
$0 \le i < 8$. B. The ADM network for $N = 8$ set to connect
i to $i + 3$ modulo 8, $0 \le i < 8$, using the same paths as
the generalized-cube network

Consider simulating the action of a four-function interchange box
using the ADM network. Assume the interchange box is in stage i and the
labels on its input/output links are j and $j + 2^i$. The four states of this
interchange box can be simulated by the ADM network nodes j and $j + 2^i$ in
stage i as follows:

1. For straight state: set both nodes j and $j + 2^i$ to straight.
2. For swap state: set node j to $+ 2^i$ and set node $j + 2^i$ to $- 2^i$.
3. For upper broadcast: set node j to both straight and $+ 2^i$.
4. For lower broadcast: set node $j + 2^i$ to both straight and $- 2^i$.

For example, consider the generalized-cube network set to connect input i to output $i + 3$ modulo 8, as shown in figure 6–18A for $N = 8$. Using these simulation rules, the ADM network can be set to do the same permutation, as shown in figure 6–18B for $N = 8$. As a specific example of the swap state, compare the generalized-cube network interchange box in stage 1 with input/output links 4 and 6 to the ADM network stage 1 nodes 4 and 6. As a specific example of the straight state, compare the generalized-cube network interchange box in stage 1 with input/output links 1 and 3 to the ADM network stage 1 nodes 1 and 3.

Thus, the ADM network has all of the interconnection capabilities of a generalized-cube network with four-function interchange boxes. Furthermore, the ADM network can perform sets of connections that the generalized cube cannot. For example, the ADM network can connect 0 to $N - 1$, $N - 1$ to 0, and i to i, $1 \le i \le N - 2$, whereas the generalized cube cannot. The difference between the number of data permutations performable in a single pass through the network by the generalized-cube and ADM networks is examined later in this chapter.

The relationship between the generalized-cube and ADM networks can be exploited to generate full routing tags (defined in the previous section) that allow the ADM network to perform any generalized-cube-passable-permutations (Siegel and McMillen 1981a), as mentioned earlier. The method used is based on the exclusive-or routing tag scheme presented in chapter 5. Consider the case for the generalized-cube network, where the source $S = s_{m-1/0}$, the destination $D = d_{m-1/0}$, and the tag $T = t_{m-1/0}$. If $s_i = d_i = 0$, $s_i \oplus d_i = 0 = t_i$, so the stage i interchange box receiving this tag should be set to straight. Therefore, if $s_i = d_i = 0$, in order for the ADM network to simulate the generalized cube, f_{m+i} is set to 0 and f_i is set to 0. If $s_i = d_i = 1$, the situation is the same. If $s_i = 0$ and $d_i = 1$, then $t_i = 1$ and the stage i interchange box receiving this tag is set to swap. Because at stage i the upper input label to all interchange boxes has a 0 in the ith bit position (and the lower a 1), this message must be moving from the upper input of the box to the lower output. To simulate this move on the ADM network, set f_{m+i} to 0 and f_i to 1 (that is, the $+ 2^i$ setting, which will transform $s_i = 0$ to $d_i = 1$.) Analogously, if $s_i = 1$ and $d_i = 0$, then f_{m+i} is set to 1 and f_i is set to 1. These settings are summarized in table 6–1.

As this table indicates, an ADM network full routing tag can be set to a generalized-cube performable permutation by having each PE calculate $f_{m-1/0} = S \oplus D$ and $f_{2m-1/m} = S\bar{D}$. For example, the path from 1 to 4 in

Table 6-1
Full Routing-Tag Settings for Generalized-Cube Network
Allowable Permutations on the ADM Network

s_i	d_i	Route	f_{m+i}	f_i
0	0	straight	0	0
0	1	$+2^i$	0	1
1	0	-2^i	1	1
1	1	straight	0	0

the ADM network for $N = 8$ shown in figure 6–18B can be formed using the full routing tag $f_{m-1/0} = 001 \oplus 100$, and $f_{2m-1/m} = (001)(\overline{100})$; that is, $F = 001101$.

In summary, the ADM network can do all of the permutations performable by the generalized-cube network and some it cannot. This result can be used in conjunction with the material presented in the previous chapter to determine the relationship of the ADM network to the other multistage cube-type networks discussed. In addition, the ADM network can be easily set to do any generalized-cube performable permutation using full routing tags.

Partitioning the ADM and IADM Networks

In chapter 4, the partitioning of the PM2I single stage network was described. The partitioning of the ADM and IADM multistage PM2I networks is based on these results. Recall that the *partitionability* of an interconnection network is the ability to divide the network into independent subnetworks of different sizes (chapter 4). Each subnetwork of size N' must have all of the interconnection capabilities of a complete network of that same type built to be of size N'. A partitionable network can be characterized by any limitations on the way in which it can be subdivided. The partitionability of an interconnection network is an important attribute to consider when selecting a network for a reconfigurable system.

The rules for partitioning the ADM and IADM networks are examined in the following subsection. The basic rules for partitioning the ADM network were first described in Siegel and Smith (1978) and Smith and Siegel (1978) and were part of the Ph.D. dissertation research of S.D. Smith. After presenting the rules, their correctness is verified in the next subsection, using the theory developed in chapter 4. Finally, broadcasting within a partition is discussed.

ADM/IADM Network-Partitioning Rules

Consider partitioning an ADM network of size N into two independent sub-networks, each of size $N/2$. The only way to do this is to treat the even-numbered input/output ports as one subnetwork (A) and the odd-numbered ports as the other (B) as shown in figure 6–19 for $N = 8$. By setting all of the stage 0 connections to straight, no PE attached to subnetwork A can communicate with a PE attached to subnetwork B and vice versa. The only way a PE with a 0 in the 0th bit of its address can route data to a PE with a 1 in its 0th bit of its address is by using a $+2^0$ or -2^0 connection at stage 0. Thus, by setting stage 0 to all straight connections, a size N ADM network can be partitioned into two size $N/2$ ADM networks. Each subnetwork has the properties of a complete ADM network of size $N/2$.

In each of the even (A) and odd (B) subnetworks, the input/output ports can be logically numbered from 0 to $(N/2) - 1$, similar to the way in which PEs using subnetworks of a single-stage PM2I network were renumbered logically in chapter 4. For example, the logical number of a port can be the $m - 1$ high-order bits of its physical number. For $N = 8$, for the A subnetwork, 0 becomes 0, 2 becomes 1, 4 becomes 2, and 6 becomes 3; for the B subnetwork, 1 becomes 0, 3 becomes 1, 5 becomes 2, and 7 becomes 3. In conjunction, stage i of the physical network acts as logical stage $i - 1$ for each partition of size $N/2$. For example, physical stage 1, which allows input port 2 to communicate with output port $2 + 2^1 = 4$, becomes logical stage 0, which allows the subnetwork A logical input port 1 to communicate with subnetwork A logical output port $1 + 2^0 = 2$.

Because each subnetwork of size $N/2$ is a complete ADM network of size $N/2$, with all the properties of an ADM network, this process of dividing subnetworks into two independent halves can be repeated to create any size subnetwork from one to $N/2$. The only constraints are:

1. The size of each subnetwork must be a power of two.
2. The physical address of the input/output ports of a subnetwork of size 2^s must agree in their low-order $m - s$ bit positions.

For example, for $N = 8$, ports 0, 2, 4, and 6 can form a subnetwork of size four, ports 1 and 5 can form a subnetwork of size two, and 3 and 7 can form another subnetwork of size two. This partitioning is shown in figure 6–20. Each subnetwork is completely independent of the others. For the 0, 2, 4, and 6 partition, physical stage 2 acts as logical stage 1 and physical stage 1 acts as logical stage 0. For the two size-two partitions, physical stage 2 acts as logical stage 0.

The partitioning of the IADM network is similar to the partitioning of the ADM network. The nodes in stage i that must be set to straight in the

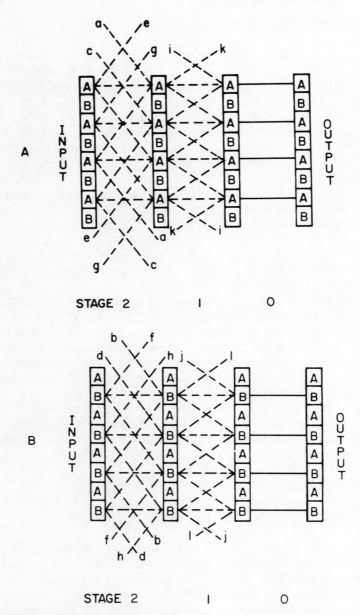

Figure 6-19. Partitioning a Size-Eight ADM Network into Two
Independent Size-Four Networks. A. The *A* subnetwork,
input/output ports 0, 2, 4, and 6. B. The *B* subnetwork,
input/output ports 1, 3, 5, and 7

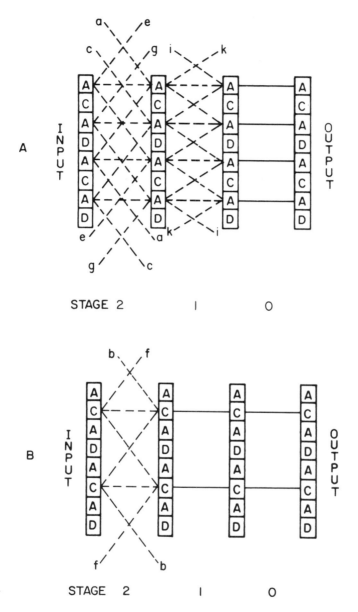

Figure 6–20. Partitioning a Size-Eight ADM Network into Three
Independent Subnetworks: One of Size Four and Two of Size
Two. A. The *A* subnetwork, input/output ports 0, 2, 4, and 6.
B. The *C* subnetwork, input/output ports 1 and 5

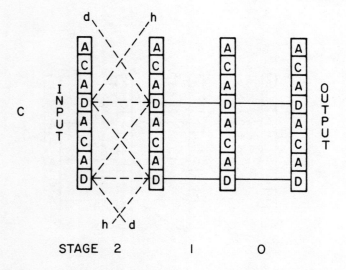

Figure 6–20 (continued). C. The *D* subnetwork, input/output ports 3 and 7.

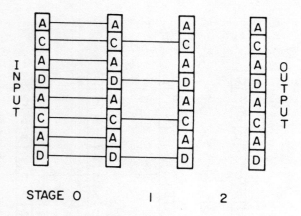

Note: Only the required straight connections are shown.

Figure 6–21. Partitioning a Size-Eight IADM Network into Three Independent Subnetworks: One of Size Four and Two of Size Two

ADM network to guarantee independence must be set to straight in the IADM network. This setting is shown for the IADM network in figure 6–21 for the ADM network-partitioning example given in figure 6–20.

In general, if input/output port j is in a subnetwork (partition) of size 2^s, then switch j in stages $0, 1, \ldots, (m - s) - 1$ must be set to straight. This setting prevents input port j from accessing an output port that differs from it in any of the low-order $m - s$ bit positions of its address. Each input/output port in the subnetwork can be logically numbered by the s high-order bits of its physical address (number). This process corresponds to one of the transformations for the single-stage PM2I network discussed in chapter 4. Furthermore, physical stage i acts as logical stage $i - (m - s)$ for the partition, just as physical PM2$_{\pm i}$ would act as logical PM2$_{\pm (i-(m-s))}$ for the single-stage PM2I network. An example of partitioning the ADM network with $m = 4$ ($N = 16$) and $s = 2$ is given in figure 6-22. One possible logical numbering of the input/ouput ports (PEs) is shown in this figure. Other logical numberings are possible, as discussed in chapter 4.

The partitioning of the ADM/IADM network can be enforced using the routing tag schemes described earlier in this chapter. If full routing tags are used, construct a $2m$-bit partitioning mask whose high-order m-bits are all 1s and whose low-order bits contain a 0 in those bit positions that correspond to stages which should be set to straight and 1s elsewhere. If this partitioning mask is logically ANDed with a tag before it is used, the partitioning will be guaranteed. The $(m + 1)$-bit partitioning mask for natural routing tags is similar, where the high-order bit is set to 1 and the low-order m-bits are set in the same way.

ADM/IADM Network-Partitioning Theory

The ADM/IADM network partitioning rules are now formally related to the network partitioning theory developed in chapter 4 for the ADM network. This analysis is based on material in Siegel (1980). The case for the IADM network is analogous. The partitioning study of the single-stage PM2I network in chapter 4 was based on the permutation-cycle structure of that network. To examine the partitionability of the ADM network, a multistage PM2I network, the cycle structure of the permutations that each stage of the ADM network can perform must first be derived.

Consider the ADM network. To represent the entire data transfer (from the input of the network to the output of the network) as a permutation, no data can be destroyed at any stage. This rule implies that, for $0 \leq i < m$, the transfer of data from the nodes of stage i to the nodes of the next stage must be representable as a permutation; that is, each stage i node must be connected to exactly one node of the next stage. In general, at stage i, the flexible control scheme allows some nodes to execute PM2$_{+i}$, whereas others execute PM2$_{-i}$; still others execute straight. With the single-stage structure such variations were not allowed, that is, either all active PEs exe-

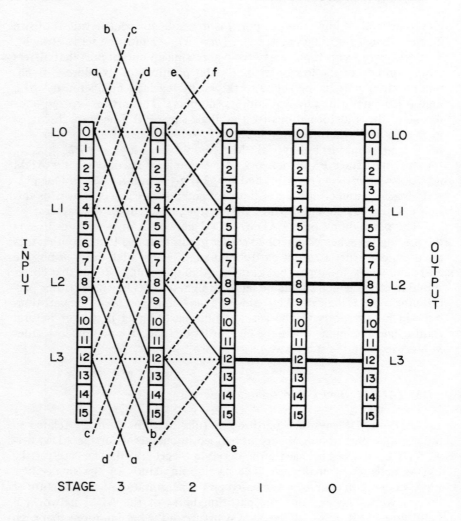

Figure 6–22. Forming a Size-Four Partition in a Size-Sixteen ADM
Network

Note: The partition consists of the physical input/output ports 0, 4, 8, and 12. L indicates the logical number of inputs/outputs in the subnetwork. Physical stage 2 acts as logical stage 0 and physical stage 3 acts as logical stage 1.

cuted $PM2_{+i}$ or all active PEs executed $PM2_{-i}$ (inactive PEs being equivalent to the straight state for the multistage network). This increased flexibility affects the set of permutations performable by the ADM network.

Consider the permutations performable by the ADM network. If all data transfers are representable as permutations, then in the ith stage of the ADM network, $0 \le i < m$, the transfer of data from node j can be represented only as one of the following five cycles:

A. $(\; j \;)$

B. $(\; j \;\; j+2^i \;\; j+2 \; * \; 2^i \;\; j+3 \; * \; 2^i \; ... \; j+N-2^i \;)$

C. $(\; j+N-2^i \; ... \; j+3 \; * \; 2^i \;\; j+2 \; * \; 2^i \;\; j+2^i \;\; j \;)$

D. $(\; j \;\; j+2^i \;)$

E. $(\; j \;\; j-2^i \;)$

where all arithmetic is modulo N. For example, for $N = 8, j = 3$, and $i = 1$, these cycles are: A. (3); B. (3 5 7 1); C. (3 1 7 5); D. (3 5); and E. (3 1), as shown in figure 6–23. As indicated in the figure, for cycle A, node 3 of stage 1 is connected to node 3 of stage 0; for cycle B, node 3 of stage 1 is connected to node 5 of stage 0, node 5 of stage 1 is connected to node 7 of stage 0, node 7 of stage 1 is connected to node 1 of stage 0, and node 1 of stage 1 is connected to node 3 of stage 0; for cycle C, the situation is analogous to cycle B; for cycle D, node 3 of stage 1 is connected to node 5 of stage 0, and node 5 of stage 1 is connected to node 3 of stage 0; and for cycle E node 3 of stage 1 is connected to node 1 of stage 0, and node 1 of stage 1 is connected to node 3 of stage 0.

These five types of cycles are the only ones that can include node j of stage i if the data transfer is to be representable as a permutation. To prove this is true, three cases must be considered for the ith stage: stage i node j connects to stage $i - 1$ node $j, j + 2^i$, or $j - 2^i$. Assume all arithmetic is modulo N.

Case 1: Stage i node j connects to stage $i - 1$ node j, which is form A.

Case 2: Stage i node j connects to stage $i - 1$ node $j + 2^i$. Because the data transfer must be representable as a permutation, stage i node $j + 2^i$ cannot also be connected to stage $i - 1$ node $j + 2^i$, so it must be connected to either stage $i - 1$ node $(j + 2^i) - 2^i = j$ or $(j + 2^i) + 2^i = j + 2 * 2^i$. If $j + 2^i$ is connected to j, it is of form D. If $j + 2^i$ is connected to $j + 2 * 2^i$, it is form B because for $k = 2, 3, 4, \ldots$, (in that order) stage i node $j + k * 2^i$ cannot be connected to either stage $i - 1$ node $j + k * 2^i$ or $j + (k - 1) * 2^i$ because they are already connected to stage i nodes. For example, stage i node $j + 2 * 2^i$ cannot connect to stage $i - 1$ node $j + 2 * 2^i$ or $j + 2^i$ (because they are connected to stage i nodes $j + 2^i$ and j, respectively). Therefore, if $j + 2^i$ is connected to $j + 2 * 2^i$, then

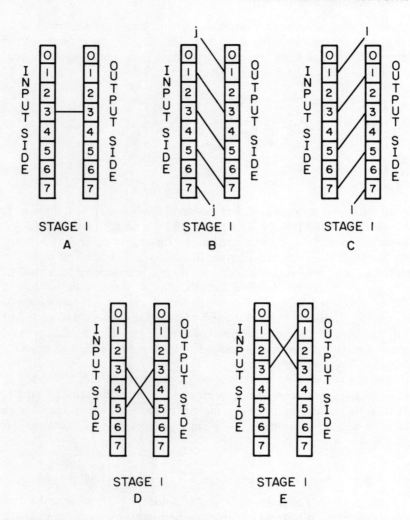

Figure 6–23. The Five Permutation Cycles of Which Node 3 of Stage 1 Can Be a Part in an ADM Network with $N = 8$. A. (3). B. (3 5 7 1). C. (3 1 7 5). D. (3 5). E. (3 1)

stage i node $j + k * 2^i$ must be connected to stage $i - 1$ node $j + (k + 1) * 2^i$, $0 \leq k < 2^{m-i}$.

Case 3: Stage i node j connects to stage $i - 1$ node $j - 2^i$. Using arguments similar to those in case 2, it can be shown that this case must generate a cycle of either form C or E.

For $i = m - 1$, form B, C, D, and E are all the same because $j + 2^{m-1} = j - 2^{m-1}$ modulo N.

Thus, a permutation is performable at stage i if and ony if it can be represented as the product of disjoint cycles of the forms A through E. For example, for $N = 8$, at stage 1, the permutation

$$(0\ 2\ 4\ 6) (1\ 3) (5\ 7)$$

is performable, as shown in figure 6-24. If perm_i represents the permutation performed at stage i of the ADM network, the permutation performed by the entire network is

$$\prod_{i=m-1}^{0} \text{perm}_i$$

Subscript i goes from $m - 1$ to 0 because data travels from stage $m - 1$ to stage $m - 2$ to stage $m - 3$ and so forth. This order would be reversed for the IADM network.

To relate this cycle-structure analysis to the single-stage PM2I analysis in chapter 4, first consider network settings of the forms B and C. The stage i cycles of forms B and C are those of the PM2_{+i} and PM2_{-i} interconnection functions, respectively, for $0 \leq j < 2^i$. The form B and C cycles contain only those nodes whose numbers are $j + k * 2^i$, $0 \leq k < 2^{m-i}$. For stage q, $i < q < m$, this set of nodes compose 2^{q-i} cycles of form B or C. For example, for $N = 16$, $j = 1$, and $i = 1$, this set is 1, 3, 5, 7, 9, 11, 13,

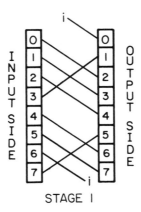

STAGE I

Figure 6-24. The Permutation (0 2 4 6) (1 3) (5 7) Performable by Stage 1 of an ADM Network for $N = 8$

and 15. The stage 1 form B cycle is (1 3 5 7 9 11 13 15). The stage 2 form B cycles are (1 5 9 13) and (3 7 11 15). The stage 3 form B cycles are (1 9), (3 11), (5 13), and (7 15). This structure follows from the single-stage PM2I-partitioning discussion in chapter 4.

From the results in chapter 4, if j is in a partition of size 2^s, only stages $m - 1, m - 2, \ldots, m - s$ can use form B or C settings involving j because the stage i form B or C cycle that j is in will be of size 2^{m-i}, just as the single-stage PM2$_{\pm i}$ cycles are of size 2^{m-i} (see chapter 4). Thus, stages $m - (s + 1), m - (s + 2), \ldots, 0$ cannot use B or C permutations involving this set of nodes (that is, it cannot function as ADM-network stages for nodes in this partition) because the size of the cycles is greater than 2^s and must therefore contain nodes not in the partition. This restriction is analogous to the inability to use the interconnection functions PM2$_{\pm i}$, $0 \le i < m - s$ derived in chapter 4. Therefore, because an ADM network of size 2^s must have s stages, stages $m - 1$ through $m - s$ must all be included in the logical ADM network for this partition. Thus, j must be in the same partition with $j + k * 2^{m-s}$, $0 \le k < 2^s$.

Now consider the ADM network cycles of forms D and E. For stage i, $m - s \le i < m$, node $j + k * 2^{m-s}$ is paired with $(j + k * 2^{m-s}) \pm 2^i$ modulo N, $0 \le k < 2^s$. For i in this range, $(j + k * 2^{m-s}) \pm 2^i$ modulo $N \in \{j + k * 2^{m-s}, 0 \le k < 2^s\}$. For example, for $N = 16$ $(m = 4)$, $s = 2$, $j = 0$, and $i = 3$, $\{j + k * 2^{m-s}, 0 \le k < 2^s\} = \{0, 4, 8, 12\}$; and $\{j + k * 2^{m-s}) \pm 2^i$ modulo N, $0 \le k < 2^s\} = \{8, 12, 0, 4\}$. Thus, settings D and E do not violate the partition.

For stage i, $0 \le i < m - s$, cycles of form D and E pair $j + k * 2^{m-s}$ with $(j + k * 2^{m-s}) \pm 2^i$ modulo N, $0 \le k < 2^s$. For k in this range

$$((j + k * 2^{m-s}) \pm 2^i) \text{ modulo } N \notin \{(j + k * 2^{m-s}), 0 \le k < 2^s\}$$

For the example in the preceding paragraph, if $i = 1$, $\{(j + k * 2^{m-s}) \pm 2^i$ modulo 16, $0 \le k < 2^s\} = \{2, 6, 10, 14\} \ne \{0, 4, 8, 12\}$. Therefore, form D and E settings cannot be allowed in stage i, $0 \le i < m - s$. Thus, for $0 \le i < m - s$, stage i nodes $(j + k * 2^{m-s})$, $0 \le k < 2^s$, cannot use forms B, C, D, or E; they must use form A—that is, they must be set to straight.

In summary, the allowable partitions of size 2^s for the ADM (and IADM) network are the same as those for the single-stage PM2I derived in chapter 4. Specifically, nodes $(j + k * 2^{m-s})$, $0 \le k < 2^s$. This partitioning allows each of stages $m - 1$ through $m - s$ to perform all five forms of permutation of which the ADM network is capable. Within each partition, the logical numbers of the input/output ports can be chosen in the same ways as the logical numbering of PEs in a single-stage PM2I network partition are selected in chapter 4. The labeling constraint there implies that physical stage i, $m - s \le i < m$, acts as logical stage $i - (m - s)$. Nodes $j + k *$

$2^{m-s}, 0 \leq k < 2^s$, must be set to straight in stages $m - (s + 1)$ through 0 because they must be in permutations of form A.

Broadcasting Within Partitions

The rules that have been derived for partitioning the ADM (and IADM) network into independent subnetworks also hold for broadcast communications. A subnetwork of size 2^s is a complete independent ADM network, and each switching node in the subnetwork can use its $+2^i$, -2^i or straight link in physical stage i, $m - s \leq i < m$ (which act as logical stages 0 through $m - s$ for the partition). Thus, a stage i switching node in the subnetwork, $m - s \leq i < m,$ could use any two (or all three) of its links simultaneously to broadcast data to other nodes within its partition.

The partitioning of the ADM/IADM network can be enforced using a partitioning mask, as was described earlier in this chapter for one-to-one connections. In addition to the action specified there, the natural tag partitioning mask must be logically ANDed with B.

Summary

The rules for partitioning the ADM and IADM networks into independent subnetworks were presented in this section. The correctness of the rules was shown by relating them to the partitioning analysis for the single-stage PM2I given in chapter 4. These rules also apply to other multistage PM2I-type networks, such as the gamma network (Parker and Raghavendra 1982). The ability to partition the ADM and IADM networks into independent subnetworks makes these networks suitable for use in multiple-SIMD and partitionable-SIMD/MIMD systems. As discussed in chapter 4, the partitionability of a network can also be exploited in a purely SIMD environment. In a purely MIMD environment, the ability to create independent partitions allows multiple users to execute tasks on a system simultaneously without interfering with one another.

Counting ADM-Performable Permutations

It has been shown earlier in this chapter that the permuting abilities of the ADM network are a superset of those of the generalized-cube network. Straightforward, obvious implementations would indicate that the ADM network is more expensive than the multistage cube, which has been confirmed by detailed analysis (McMillen and Siegel 1982b). To compare the cost-effectiveness of the two approaches accurately, many aspects of the capabilities of the two networks and implementation possibilities must be considered. In this section, one particular measure of ADM network capability is examined—the number of distinct data permutations performable in a single pass through the ADM network. That is, this section explores how many settings of the ADM network there are that produce distinct permutations of the input data. The material in this section is based on Adams and Siegel (1982a), which was done as part of G.B. Adams III's master's dissertation research.

Counting the number of data permutations performable by an ADM network involves the use of both partitioning properties of the network topology and combinatorial mathematical techniques. Thus, the problem is of both theoretical interest (from the mathematical viewpoint) and practical interest (from a network-comparison viewpoint). The results are also valid for the IADM network because it is the mirror image of the ADM network.

Unlike the case of counting generalized-cube network permutations (chapter 5), the problem of determining the number of distinct permutations performable in a single pass by the ADM network does not yield to a straightforward consideration of all possible network states. There are two reasons for this difficulty. First, in the ADM network, unlike the generalized-cube network, an arbitrary network setting may not result in a permutation of network inputs to outputs, as figure 6–25 shows. In the figure, each node is performing an allowable switch setting. However, in stage 1 both nodes 0 and 4 connect to node 2 and in stage 0 node 5 connects to both nodes 4 and 5. If the network setting is f, then $f(0) = f(4) = 2$ and $f(5) = 4$ or 5. Clearly, f is not a permutation (that is, not all of the connections are one-to-one). Second, for certain permutations more than one valid network setting exists, as shown for the permutation $f(i) = i + 3$ modulo N in figures 6–8, 6–10, and 6–18B. As another example of two network settings that are equivalent pairings of network inputs to outputs, consider figure 6–26. With each setting shown, the same permutation of network inputs to outputs is performed—that is, 0 to 3, 1 to 6, 2 to 5, 3 to 2, 4 to 7, 5 to 4, 6 to 1, and 7 to 0.

For $N = 4$, the ADM network can perform all possible $N! = 24$ permutations; that is, it can perform all possible one-to-one pairings of network inputs to outputs, which can be derived by direct enumeration. For $N > 4$, direct enumeration is not a practical alternative for counting the number of permutations.

To count the number of distinct permutations performable by the ADM network, consider conceptually separating stage 0 from the rest of the network, as shown in figure 6–27 for $N = 8$. Stages $m - 1$ through 1 can be partitioned into two independent subnetworks, each with $N/2$ inputs, as was described earlier. All the odd-numbered nodes in stages $m - 1$ through 1 constitute one of the subnetworks—the *odd subnetwork*. All the even-numbered nodes in stages $m - 1$ through 1 constitute the other subnet-

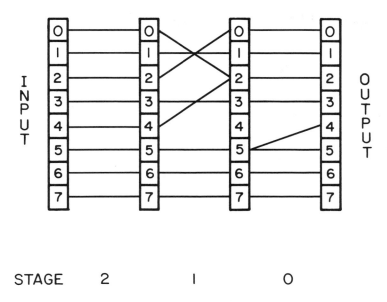

STAGE   2   I   O

Figure 6-25. An ADM Network Setting for $N = 8$ not Corresponding to an Overall Permutation

work—the *even subnetwork*. The relationship of these two subnetworks to the final stage of the N-input ADM network, stage 0, is shown in figure 6-28.

The partitioning described connects all of the outputs of the even subnetwork to even-numbered inputs of stage 0. The outputs of the odd subnetwork are connected to the odd-numbered inputs of stage 0. Partitioning the ADM network allows a size N network to be treated as two size $N/2$ independent ADM networks combined at stage 0 of the size N network. This fact is the basis for the divide-and-conquer approach to be taken in counting the ADM-network-performable permutations.

For the discussion in this section, permutations performable by the complete ADM network are referred to as *overall permutations*. Configurations of stage 0 of the network, which are permutations of stage 0 inputs to outputs, are called *stage 0 permutations*.

In this section, first the number of permutations performable by stage 0 of the ADM network is counted. Then, using partitioning theory, the network is treated as two subnetworks connected to stage 0, and upper and lower bounds on the number of data permutations performable by the entire ADM network are established. Finally, the tightness of these bounds and a comparison of the number of ADM-network-performable permutations to that of the generalized-cube network are given.

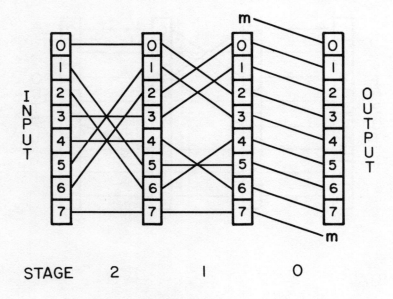

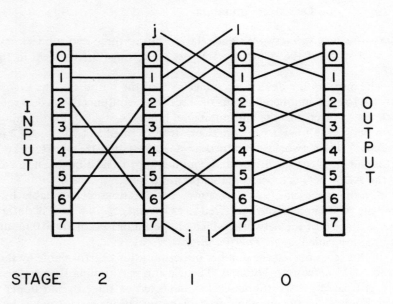

Figure 6-26. Two Distinct Network Settings for an ADM Network
with $N = 8$ Corresponding to the Same Overall
Permutation

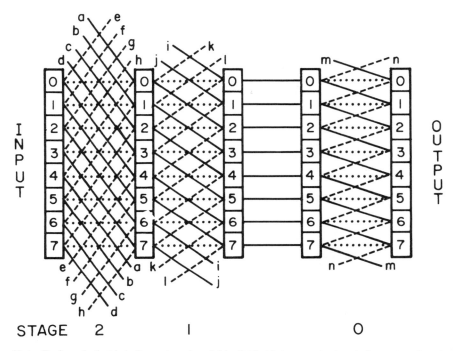

STAGE   2   1   O

Note: Each node that interfaces stage 1 and 0 is divided into an output node from stage 1 and an input node to stage 0.

Figure 6-27. The First Step in the Conceptual Process of Partitioning an ADM Network for $N = 8$ into Two Independent Subnetworks Joined at Stage 0

Stage 0 Permutations

Consider the possible stage 0 permutations. Stage 0 (PM2$_{\pm0}$) is the only stage of the network that can cause a source address to be mapped to a destination address that differs from the source address in the low-order bit position. Let $S = s_{m-1}...s_1s_0$ be a source, and $D = d_{m-1}...d_1d_0$ be its destination. A connection in stage 0 that does not affect the low-order bit of the destination address—that is, $s_0 = d_0$—is called a *straight connection*. A connection, other than all $+2^0$ or all -2^0, that changes the low-order bit, $s_0 = \bar{d}_0$, is called an *exchange*. This is shown in figure 6-29. A *regular exchange* is between stage 0 nodes $p_{m-1}...p_10$ and $(p_{m-1}...p_10 + 2^0)$ modulo N. An *irregular exchange* is between stage 0 nodes $p_{m-1}...p_10$ and $(p_{m-1}...p_10 - 2^0)$ modulo N. Because a permutation is one-to-one, any possible stage 0 permutation, except the all $+2^0$ or all -2^0 configurations, consists of straight and/or exchange connections only (that is, every $+2^0$ or

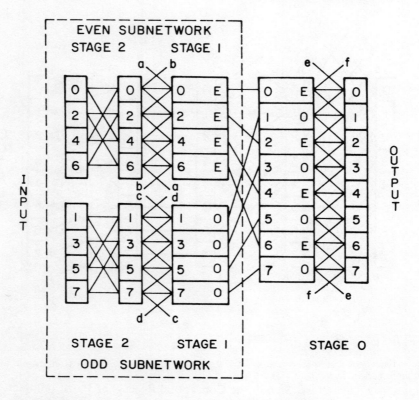

Note: E and O designate the even and odd subnetworks, respectively.

Figure 6–28. Nodes from Stages 2 and 1 of an ADM Network for $N = 8$ Rearranged into Two Independent Subnetworks, Each with $N/2$ Inputs

-2^0 connection is part of an exchange). This result follows directly from the analysis in the partitioning section earlier in this chapter. Specifically, it was shown that if the data transfer is a stage 0 permutation, the transfer of data from stage 0 node j must be of one of the following forms, where all arithmetic is modulo N and $\equiv$ means "is equivalent to":

A. $(\quad j \quad) \equiv$ straight.
B. $(\quad j \quad j+1 \quad j+2 \quad \ldots \quad j+N-1 \quad) \equiv$ all $+2^0$.
C. $(\quad j+N-1 \quad j+N-2 \quad j+N-3 \quad \ldots \quad j \quad) \equiv$ all -2^0.
D. $(\quad j \quad j+1 \quad) \equiv$ regular (j even) or irregular (j odd) exchange.
E. $(\quad j \quad j-1 \quad) \equiv$ regular (j odd) or irregular (j even) exchange.

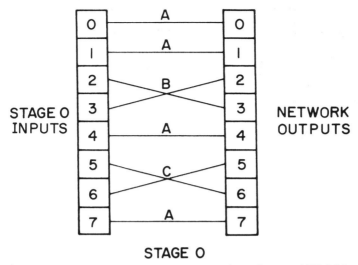

STAGE 0

Figure 6–29. Three Types of Stage 0 Connections for an ADM Network
with $N = 8$. A. Straight connections. B. Regular exchange.
C. Irregular exchange

Consider the stage 0 permutations other than the all $+2^0$ or all -2^0.
To count the stage 0 permutations, the settings of the stage 0 nodes are represented by an N-bit binary number, called the *characteristic binary number*. A binary digit is associated with each adjacent pair of nodes, including
a digit for the wrap-around pairing of the nodes labeled 0 and $N - 1$. If the
adjacent pair of nodes together form an exchange connection, the characteristic binary digit is 1. If not, the digit is 0. An example of this assignment is
shown in figure 6–30. Bit i corresponds to nodes i and $i + 1$.

To use the characteristic binary numbers for counting stage 0 permutations, two kinds of digit adjacency are distinguished. When bits $N - 1$ and
0 of the characteristic binary numbers are not considered adjacent it is *linear
adjacency*. When bits $N - 1$ and 0 are considered adjacent it is *circular adjacency*.

Every stage 0 permutation, except the settings all $+2^0$ or all -2^0, has
a unique characteristic binary number with no circularly adjacent bits that
are both 1s. To show this fact, recall from the partitioning section that
every stage 0 permutation, except the all $+2^0$ and all -2^0 configurations, is
formed from straight and exchange connections. If the characteristic binary
number of a configuration has circularly adjacent ones, there is a node
involved in two exchanges such that

$$p_{m-1}...p_1p_0 \rightarrow (p_{m-1}...p_1p_0 + 2^0) \text{ modulo } N$$

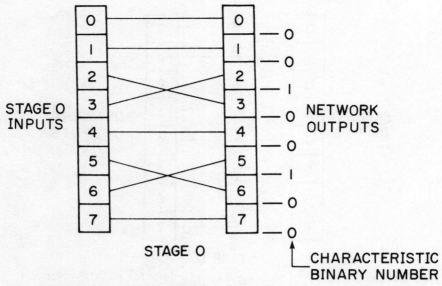

Figure 6–30. A Stage 0 Permutation and Its Characteristic Binary Number
for an ADM Network with $N = 8$

and

$$p_{m-1}...p_1p_0 \rightarrow (p_{m-1}...p_1p_0 - 2^0) \text{ modulo } N$$

This is shown in figure 6–31. This mapping is not one-to-one, hence the configuration is not a permutation. If the associated binary number has no circularly adjacent 1s, every stage 0 input can be involved in at most one exchange. Because every input is involved in either a straight or an exchange connection, the configuration will be one-to-one, and hence a permutation.

The characteristic binary numbers of stage 0 permutations can be used to count the number of these permutations. First, the ways to count the number of N-bit numbers with no linearly or circularly adjacent 1s are shown, based on O'Donnell and Smith (1982). This result is then applied to counting stage 0 permutations.

The number of N-bit binary numbers with no linearly adjacent 1s is:

$$L(N) = L(N - 1) + L(N - 2)$$

where $L(2) = 3$, $L(3) = 5$, and $N \geq 4$, for the following reason. If an N-bit number ends in a 0, then it will have no linearly adjacent 1s if it has no linearly adjacent 1s in the first $N - 1$ bits. The number of all such N-bit numbers is $L(N - 1)$. If an N-bit number ends in 1, then the immediately preceding bit must be a 0 if the number is to have no linearly adjacent 1s. Also, the first $N - 2$ bits of the number must have no linearly adjacent 1s. The number of all such N-bit numbers is $L(N - 2)$. Thus, $L(N) = L(N - 1) + L(N - 2)$. (This recursive relationship is that of Fibonacci numbers; see Hoggatt 1969.) The initial conditions may be derived by enumeration; that is, $L(2) = 3$ (00, 01, 10) and $L(3) = 5$ (000, 100, 010, 001, 101).

The number of N-bit binary numbers with no circular adjacent 1s is:

$$C(N) = L(N) - L(N - 4)$$

where $N \geq 8$. $L(N)$ exceeds $C(N)$ by the number of N-bit numbers with no linearly adjacent 1s that do have circular adjacent 1s. These numbers are all of the form

$$1\,0\,a_1 a_2 \ldots a_{N-4}\,0\,1$$

where the number $a_1 a_2 \ldots a_{N-4}$ is a binary number with no linearly adjacent 1s. There are $L(N - 4)$ such numbers. Thus, $C(N) = L(N) - L(N - 4)$.

Because every stage 0 permutation, except all $+2^0$ and all -2^0, has a

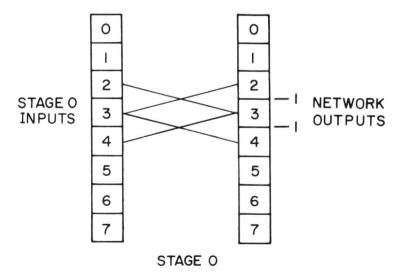

STAGE 0

Figure 6–31. ADM Network Configuration for $N = 8$ Implied by Two Adjacent 1s in the Characteristic Binary Number (Not a Permutation)

unique characteristic binary number with no circularly adjacent 1s, for a size N ADM network, the number of stage 0 permutations is:

$$P_0(N) = C(N) + 2$$

where $N \geq 8$. By enumeration it can be shown that $P_0(2) = 2$ and $P_0(4) = 9$.

Bounds on the Number of Overall Permutations

Now consider an arbitrary destination D of an ADM network. The source for the data arriving at D may have been either the even subnetwork or the odd subnetwork (see figure 6–28), depending on the stage 0 configuration. Call the subnetwork that is the source of D the *source subnetwork*.

The four stage 0 permutations, all regular exchanges, all irregular exchanges, all $+2^0$, and all -2^0 connect all even subnetwork outputs to odd-numbered network outputs and all odd subnetwork outputs to even-numbered network outputs. These four stage 0 permutations are the only ones with this property because each uses $PM2_{\pm 0}$ and so forces $d_0 = \bar{s}_0$ for all source/destination pairs as shown in figure 6–32 for $N = 8$. Any other permutation must have a straight connection. If a network output D is connected to a straight stage 0 link, then $d_0 = s_0$. This case would connect an even subnetwork output to an even-numbered network output port, or an odd subnetwork output to an odd-numbered network output port (for example, see figure 6–28).

Consider the set of all stage 0 permutations except all regular exchanges, all irregular exchanges, all $+2^0$, and all -2^0. Each of the permutations in this set generates a unique pairing of source subnetwork output with network output. For example, see the differences for network outputs 3 and 4 in figure 6–33. To prove this is true, it is shown that if two permutations in this set produce identical pairings, they must be the same permutation (stage 0 setting). What matters is the subnetwork the source is from, not the specific address of the source.

Assume that two stage 0 permutations of this set both link the same source subnetwork to a given network output, and that this is true for every network output. A permutation of the named set must have a straight connection. If an output D is connected to a straight stage 0 link, then $d_0 = s_0$. If it is connected to an exchange, then $d_0 = \bar{s}_0$, and the source subnetwork differs from the previous case. Thus all straight connections of one permutation must be duplicated in the other, and vice versa, if the source subnetworks are to be the same for each output.

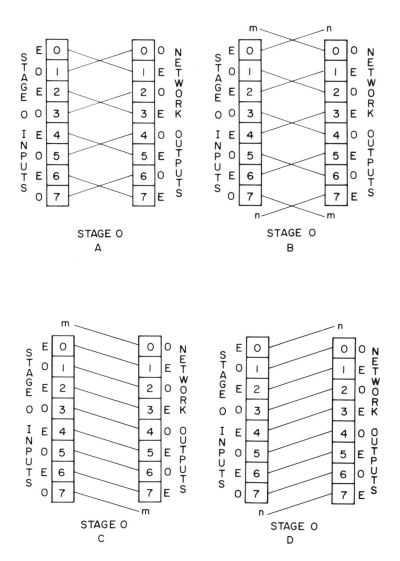

Note: Data from even and odd subnetworks are indicated by *E* and *O*, respectively.

Figure 6-32. The Four Stage 0 Permutations for the ADM Network with $N = 8$ Connecting All Even Subnetwork Outputs to Odd Network Outputs and Odd Subnetwork Outputs to Even Network Outputs. A. All regular exchanges. B. All irregular exchanges. C. All $+2^0$. D. All -2^0

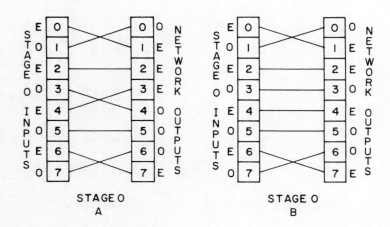

Note: Data from even and odd source subnetworks are indicated by *E* and *O*, respectively.

Figure 6–33. Different Stage 0 Settings for the ADM Network with $N = 8$ Resulting in Different Pairings of Source Subnetwork to Network Output

A circularly adjacent pair of 0s in a characteristic binary number corresponds to a straight connection (see figure 6–30). Specifying all straight connections thus specifies all circularly adjacent 0s in the characteristic binary numbers of both permutations. The remaining bits of the numbers must contain no circularly adjacent 0s. Recall that no circularly adjacent 1s may appear because this is a permutation. Thus, any string of bits between two sets of 0s must be 1010...101, that is, alternating 1 and 0, beginning and ending with a 1. Single unspecified bit positions must become 1s (because all straight links, which are identified by adjacent 0s, have been already specified). Each unspecified bit position is thus assigned a unique value. Therefore, both numbers are identical, and the corresponding permutations must be the same.

The bounds on the number of ADM network permutations can now be determined. Let $P(N)$ be the number of distinct overall permutations performable in a single pass by a size N ADM network. Let $P_L(N)$ and $P_U(N)$ be lower and upper bounds on $P(N)$, respectively. The ADM network can perform at least $P_L(N)$ distinct permutations, but no more than $P_U(N)$. First a lower bound is derived, then an upper.

The number of permutations performable by one of the two independent subnetworks that can be formed by partitioning the ADM network is, by definition, at least $P_L(N/2)$. Call the two subnetwork permutations available at the inputs of stage 0 the *input permutations*. Because the two subnetworks of the partition are independent, the number of distinct input permutations is at least $P_L(N/2)^2$.

Finally, consider an arbitrary overall permutation. Assume that the stage 0 permutation is fixed. Any change in the input permutation will result in a change in the overall permutation. Assume the input permutation and the stage 0 permutation are both allowed to change. Let the set of stage 0 permutations be restricted so that only one of the permutations all regular exchanges, all irregular exchanges, all $+2^0$, or all -2^0 is allowed; there are $P_0(N) - 3$ permutations in this restricted set. From the preceding analysis, any change in the stage 0 permutation will cause at least one network output port to be connected to a different subnetwork (from even to odd, or from odd to even). But because the two subnetworks are independent, no change of the input permutation (the settings of the subnetworks) can result in the connection of an input of one subnetwork to the output of the other. For the example in figure 6–33, originally network output 3 received data from the even subnetwork and network output 4 from the odd subnetwork. After changing the stage 0 permutation, this case is reversed. There is now no way in which network output 3 can receive data from a source in the even subnetwork, and no way in which 4 can receive data from a source in the odd subnetwork. In general, when using one of these $P_0(N) - 3$ stage 0 permutations, because each produces a unique assignment of source subnetworks to network outputs, no other stage 0 permutation can produce the same overall permutation no matter how stage 0 and the subnetworks are manipulated.

Thus, no overall permutation can be duplicated by changing the input permutation and/or changing the stage 0 permutation (provided the stage 0 permutation is not one of the three excluded). Hence, each composition of an input permutation with an allowable stage 0 permutation (that is, not one of the three excluded) results in a unique overall permutation. As a result, the number of input permutations is multiplied by the number of stage 0 permutations, minus the three special cases, to yield a lower bound on the number of performable overall permutations. Formally:

$$P_L(N) = P_L(N/2)^2 * [P_0(N) - 3]$$

where $N \geq 8$ and $P_L(4) = P(4) = 24 = 4!$.

On the basis of this lower-bound analysis, an exact count of the number of performable permutations for $N = 8$ can be derived. As stated, the set of stage 0 permutations all regular exchanges, all irregular exchanges, all $+2^0$, and all -2^0 are the only stage 0 permutations that share a common set of pairings of source subnetwork with network output. Consider a particular overall permutation involving a stage 0 permutation selected from this set of four. The same overall permutation can be maintained after changing stage 0 to another of the given set of four stage 0 permutations if the input permutation can be suitably modified.

For example, figure 6-26 shows a given overall permutation in the upper network that uses the all $+2^0$ setting in stage 0. The lower network shows stage 0 set to all regular exchanges and the necessary changes in the settings of stages 2 and 1 (the input permutation) so that the same overall permutation is performed. Because the choice of source subnetwork remains unchanged for all outputs after resetting stage 0, the necessary changes in the input permutation occurs only within each of the two independent source subnetworks.

For $N = 8$ the sources subnetworks are size-four ADM networks (that can perform any permutation of four items). Therefore, any needed modification of the input permutation can be performed. As a result, the overall permutations performable using any member of the given set of four stage 0 permutations will be exactly the same as those performable using any of the three other stage 0 permutations in this set. Thus,

$$P(8) = P_L(8) = P_L(4)^2 * [P_0(8) - 3] = 26,496$$

(recall $P_L(4) = P(4) = 24$). Because the ADM network with $N = 8$ cannot perform all $N! = 40,320$ permutations, this method does not extend directly to an ADM network of size $N = 16$ or larger. However, it can be used to improve the initial conditions on the lower bound; specifically, $P_L(8) = 26,496$ can be used instead of $P_L(4) = 24$.

An upper bound on the number of distinct overall permutations performable by the ADM is:

$$P_U(N) = P_U(N/2)^2 * P_0(N)$$

where $P_U(8) = P(8) = 26,496$ and $N \geq 16$. This case assumes that the composition of any input permutation with any stage 0 permutation (including all regular exchanges, all irregular exchanges, all $+2^0$, and all -2^0) yields a unique overall permutation.

For $N \geq 16$, $P(N)$ is strictly less than $P_U(N)$ because there are overall permutations for which multiple distinct input permutation and stage 0 permutation compositions result in the same overall permutation. For example, the overall permutation of input i to output $(i + 3)$ modulo N, $0 \leq i < N$, can be performed in three ways:

1. Stage 0 set to all $+2^0$, stage 1 set to all $+2^1$, and all other stages set to all straight (see figure 6-8).
2. Stage 0 set to all -2^0, stage 2 set to all $+2^2$, and all other stages set to all straight (see figure 6-10).

3. Stage 0 set to all regular exchanges, and all other stages set as if they were simulating the generalized-cube network doing this permutation based on the rules in an earlier section (see figure 6–18).

Therefore, the number of distinct permutations performable by a size N ADM network is bounded by:

$$P_L(N) \leq P(N) < P_U(N)$$

or

$$P_L(N/2)^2 * [P_0(N) - 3] \leq P(N) < P_U(N/2)^2 * P_0(N)$$

where $N \geq 16$ and $P_L(8) = P_U(8) = P(8) = 26,496$.

Tightness of Bounds and Comparison to Generalized-Cube Network

The suitability of these bounds as a measure of ADM network performance will depend on how tight the bounds are for various values of N. The smaller the difference between the upper and lower bounds the more useful they are as an indicator of ADM network performance. The tightness of the bound can be calculated as a function of the size of the network. Define the *spread* of the bounds, $S(N)$, to be

$$S(N) = \frac{P_U(N) - P_L(N)}{P_L(N)}$$

Using this formula and the bound results, table 6–2 is calculated. The number of permutations performable by the generalized-cube network is $2^{Nm/2}$, as shown in chapter 5. It is included in table 6–2 for comparison. As shown, the value of $S(N)$ is small for networks of considerable size. As a result, for practical values of N, the bounds given provide a useful approximation of the number of ADM-network-performable overall permutations.

Summary

This section has considered the number of permutations performable by the ADM/IADM network in a single pass. Counting the number of ADM-network-performable permutations is made difficult by the fact that the net-

Table 6–2
**Bounds on Number of Permutations Performable by a Size N
ADM Network**

N	$P_L(N)$	$P_U(N)$	$S(N)$	$Cube(N)$
4	24	24	0	16
8	26,496	26,496	0	4096
16	1.55×10^{12}	1.55×10^{12}	1.36×10^{-3}	4.29×10^{9}
32	1.17×10^{31}	1.17×10^{31}	2.74×10^{-3}	1.21×10^{24}
64	3.24×10^{75}	3.26×10^{75}	5.45×10^{-3}	6.28×10^{57}
128	5.90×10^{177}	5.97×10^{177}	1.09×10^{-2}	7.27×10^{134}
256	1.01×10^{409}	1.13×10^{409}	2.20×10^{-2}	1.80×10^{308}
512	1.22×10^{925}	1.28×10^{925}	4.44×10^{-2}	3.74×10^{693}
1024	1.50×10^{1957}	1.64×10^{1957}	9.09×10^{-2}	1.88×10^{1541}
2048	2.27×10^{4128}	2.70×10^{4128}	1.90×10^{-1}	6.34×10^{2585}

Note: $P_L(N)$ and $P_U(N)$ are the lower and upper bounds, respectively, on the number of permutations performable by a size-N ADM network. $S(N)$ is the spread of the bounds calculated as $[P_U(N) - P_L(N)]/P_L(N)$. Cube(N) is the number of permutations performable by a size-N generalized-cube network, given by $2^{Nm/2}$.

work has settings that do not yield a permutation and it has multiple settings for certain passable permutations. Using the partitioning theory (developed in the previous section) in a divide-and-conquer approach led to a lower and upper bound on the number of distinct overall permutations that an ADM network can perform.

Dynamic Rerouting

It was shown in an earlier section that both a positive dominant and a negative dominant route could be found between any pairs of processors (except where $S = D$, so $T = 0$). Other paths use both positive and negative links (as well as straight). For example, figure 6–34 shows all possible paths from source 10 to destination 23 in the ADM network for $N = 32$. The positive dominant and negative dominant paths are shown as solid and dashed lines, respectively. The dotted lines indicate other paths that can be used. The positive dominant route is straight, $+2^3$, $+2^2$, straight, $+2^0$. The negative dominant route is -2^4, straight, straight, -2^1, -2^0. A few of the mixed-sign routes are: (1) -2^4, -2^3, $+2^2$, $+2^1$, -2^0; (2) -2^4, straight, -2^2, straight, $+2^0$; and (3) straight, $+2^3$, $+2^2$, $+2^1$, -2^0. In all cases, when the values of the links in each path are added (straight contributes nothing), the result is either 13 or -19 (which is 13 modulo 32). All possible paths same source/destination pair in the IADM network for $N = 32$ are shown in figure 6-35.

To exploit the existence of multiple paths, several rerouting schemes that employ natural routing tags have been developed for each network; these schemes allow messages to change paths dynamically in an MIMD environment. As a result, messages can avoid busy or faulty switches and links whenever the required alternate path is available. It is assumed that there is a mechanism for detecting and indicating that a node is faulty. A node is considered busy if it is unable to receive a new message because it is processing another message. If both the original (natural) path and the alternate path is busy, the sending node can switch between the two choices until one is available. It is assumed that if two messages arrive at an available node simultaneously, one will be accepted and the other will find the node to be busy.

A variety of schemes are presented in this section to give the network implementer design flexibility and to give the reader insight into the logical structure of the ADM and IADM networks. This section is based on McMillen and Siegel (1982c), which was done as part of R.J. McMillen's Ph.D. dissertation research.

As a result of the reverse ordering of the stages, the rerouting methods for the ADM and IADM networks differ. First, methods for rerouting one-to-one communications in the ADM network are described, followed by methods for rerouting one-to-one communications in the IADM network. Then, rerouting broadcast communications is discussed. Finally, rerouting when the ADM or IADM network is partitioned is examined. The notation $w_{a/b}$ indicates bits $w_a w_{a-1} ... w_b$ of W, $a \geq b$.

Rerouting in the ADM Network

In this subsection, rerouting methods for the ADM network are presented. Following the description of each method are an example of its use and a proof that the method works correctly. The examples are based on source 10 sending a message to destination 23 in the ADM network for $N = 32$. The positive dominant tag for this is $D - S = 23 - 10 = +13 = 001101$, and the negative dominant tag is $(001101)' = 110011$, as shown in figure 6-34.

ADM REROUTE METHOD 1. In the ADM network, if a message becomes blocked by a straight link at stage i $(t_i = 0)$, $0 < i < m$, it can be sent on the nonstraight link whose sign is the same as that of the routing tag, if the low-order i bits of the tag are not all zero. The routing tag is then replaced by the equivalent tag of opposite dominance.

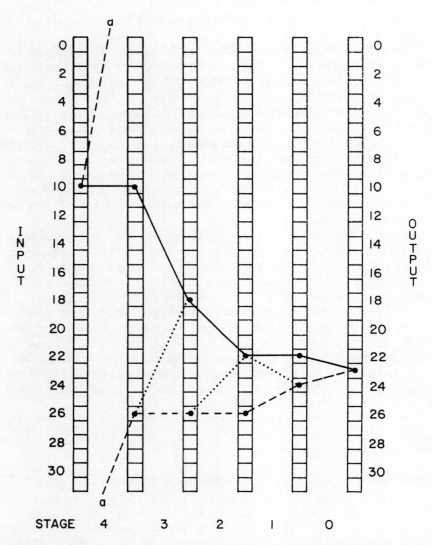

Note: The solid lines show the positive dominant path; the dashed lines show the negative dominant path.

Figure 6-34. All Possible Paths in the ADM Network for $N = 32$
Connecting Source 10 to Destination 23

Example. In figure 6–34, if a tag following the negative dominant path is unable to access the straight link in stage 3, it can take the dotted path shown (the -2^3 link) and then continue on the positive dominant path.

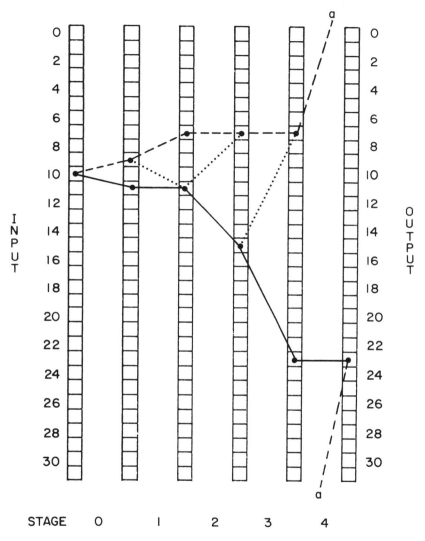

Note: The solid lines show the positive dominant path; the dashed lines show the negative dominant path.

Figure 6-35. All Possible Paths in the IADM Network for $N = 32$ Connecting Source 10 to Destination 23

Correctness proof. Intuitively, the message moves from one dominant path to the path of opposite dominance to avoid the blocked link. To understand mathematically why this method works, assuming routing tag $T = t_{m/0}, t_i = 0$, the straight link requested in stage i is unavailable, and so the message is sent on the $(-1)^{t_m}2^i$ link (that is, the link whose sign is the same as the tag). At stage i, the message is a distance of $\Sigma_{j=0}^{i}t_j2^j = \Sigma_{j=0}^{i-1}t_j2^j$ from its destination (the equality is due to the fact that $t_i = 0$). After the reroute at stage i, the distance between where the message was sent and the desired destination is $2^i - (\Sigma_{j=0}^{i-1}t_j2^j)$. The message needs to move this distance in the $-(-1)^{t_m} = (-1)^{\overline{t_m}}$ direction, because the 2^i reroute was in the $(-1)^{t_m}$ direction. By definition of two's complement, the distance is $(t_{i-1/0})'$. The two's complement of the whole routing tag can be taken because the sign bit needs to be complemented and the high-order $m - i$ bits have already been interpreted by the network (that is, the high-order $m - i$ bits are ignored by stages $i - 1$ to 0). The fact that the two's complement of T is the path of opposite dominance follows from the discussion in an earlier section of this chapter.

With this method, no routing information is lost because the new tag is equivalent to the original tag (as was shown earlier). A return tag can still be formed by complementing the sign bit. This method of taking the two's complement of the whole tag allows each node to perform the same operation when rerouting a message instead of two's complementing some subset of the bits based on the node's stage address. Because a new complete equivalent tag is formed, this rerouting method can be used by the same message as often as the stated conditions for rerouting are met. For example, consider figure 6–34. After the first reroute, the message is on the positive dominant path. If it is blocked by the straight link in stage 1, it can take the $+2^1$ link instead of the straight link and then use the negative path (in this case, the -2^0 link) to reach the destination.

The primary advantage to the method 1 scheme is that it is self-contained and consequently does not contribute to routing tag overhead. Specifically, the two's complement operation is performed by the node that reroutes the message and no other node is involved in the procedure. The drawback is that each node must contain enough extra hardware to perform the two's complement operation. In a VLSI implementation, where a high logic-to-pin ratio is desirable, this extra logic is easy to include and increases the ratio. In a discrete implementation, the extra hardware is more of a consideration. The next scheme requires less hardware but one extra bit in the tag.

ADM REROUTE METHOD 2. In the ADM network, if a message becomes blocked by a straight link at stage i ($t_i = 0$), $0 < i < m$, it can be sent on the nonstraight link whose sign is the same as that of the routing tag, if the low-order i bits of the tag are not all zero. To compensate for the reroute, an additional *reroute bit* t_{m+1} in the tag (initially 0), is set to 1 to indicate that a reroute occurred. Whenever $t_{m+1} = 1$, t_j, $0 \le j < i$, is given a new interpretation: if $t_j = 1$, route the message on the $-(-1)^{t_m}2^j$ link and reset the reroute bit to 0; if $t_j = 0$, route the message on the $-(-1)^{t_m}2^j$ link and leave the reroute bit set to 1.

Example. A message following this rerouting policy attempts to return to its original path (that of the same dominance) if rerouted. For example, in figure 6–34, the negative dominant tag is $(D - S)' = (001101)' = 110011$. Adding the reroute bit t_6, initialized to 0, makes the tag 0110011. If a message following the negative dominant path is unable to access the straight link in stage 3, it can be sent on the dotted path shown (the -2^3 link). The reroute bit of the tag will be set to 1, so the tag would now be 1110011. The stage 2 node in the path finds $t_{m+1} = t_6 = 1$, $t_m = t_5 = 1$, and $t_2 = 0$, so the message is sent on the $+2^2$ link and t_{m+1} is left unchanged. The stage 1 node in the path finds $t_{m+1} = t_6 = 1$, $t_m = t_5 = 1$, and $t_1 = 1$, so the message is sent on the $+2^1$ link and t_{m+1} is reset to 0, making the tag 0110011. At this point (stage 0) t_6 has its original value of 0 and the message is back on the negative dominant path.

Correctness proof. Intuitively, the following sequence is happening, assuming the message is originally on the negative dominant path. Because $t_i = 0$, -2^i would not be used to map the source address to the destination address (map in the sense discussed in chapters 2 and 3). Assume t_k is the next nonzero tag bit, $k < i$ (there is some -2^k, $k < i$, which is used in the mapping because the low-order i bits are not all zero). To avoid the blocked straight link in stage i, the -2^i and $+2^{i-1}$, $+2^{i-2}$, ..., $+2^k$ links are used, resulting in a -2^k contribution to the mapping (that is, $-2^i + (\sum_{q=k}^{i-1} 2^q) = -2^k$). The rerouting used by this method puts the message back on its original negative dominant path. To see this result mathematically, let $T = 0t_{m/0}$, and suppose $t_i = 0$ for a fixed value of i, $0 < i < m$. Assume the requested straight link in stage i is unavailable. According to method 2, t_{m+1} is set to 1 and the message is sent on the $(-1)^{t_m}2^i$ link. Consider the action taken in stage $i - 1$.

Case 1: $t_{i-1} = 1$.

The signed distance of the message from the source after being rerouted in stage i is $(-1)^{t_m}((\sum_{j=i+1}^{m-1} t_j 2^j) + 2^i)$. After the compensation is applied in stage $i - 1$, the distance from the source is:

$$\left[(-1)^{t_m}((\sum_{j=i+1}^{m-1} t_j 2^j) + 2^i)\right] - (-1)^{t_m}2^{i-1} =$$

$$(-1)^{t_m}((\sum_{j=i+1}^{m-1} t_j 2^j) + 2^{i-1})$$

Because $t_i t_{i-1} = 01$, the message is now where it would have been if the reroute had not occurred.

Case 2: $t_{i-1} = 0$ $(t_{i-2/0} \neq 0)$.

After the reroute in stage i, the signed distance of the message from the source is $(-1)^{tm}((\sum_{j=i+1}^{m-1} t_j 2^j) + 2^i)$. Assume t_k is the next nonzero tag bit, $k < i$. At each stage s, $k < s < i$, the $-(-1)^{tm} 2^s$ link is taken. Thus, when the message arrives at stage k, the signed distance of the message from the source is:

$$\left[(-1)^{tm}((\sum_{j=i+1}^{m-1} t_j 2^j) + 2^i)\right] - (-1)^{tm}(\sum_{s=k+1}^{i-1} 2^s) =$$

$$(-1)^{tm}((\sum_{j=i+1}^{m-1} t_j 2^j) + 2^{k+1})$$

Because $t_{i-1/k+1} = 0$ the net result is as though the message were first rerouted in stage $k + 1$. At this point case 1 applies because $t_{m+1} = 1$ and $t_k = 1$.

Rerouting method 2 can be repeated as often as the stated conditions for rerouting are met. This is because according to method 2, while rerouting is in progress, regardless of the value of the magnitude bits, nonstraight links are used. Because straight links must be requested for rerouting to occur, no further rerouting occurs while an earlier reroute is in progress. Rerouting terminates when the first 1 bit in the tag is encountered. When rerouting terminates, the message is back on the original path specified by the routing tag. Because there is no evidence of a previous reroute in the tag (the reroute bit t_{m-1} is reset to 0), rerouting can be repeated.

The following procedure is a variation on method 2. It allows a message in the process of a method 2 reroute to use a straight link instead of a $-(-1)^{tm} 2^k$ link if $t_k = 1$, thus avoiding the $-(-1)^{tm} 2^k$ link if desired. This process adds extra flexibility and power to method 2.

ADM REROUTE METHOD 2'. Assume a message was rerouted in stage i of the ADM network using method 2. If the reroute bit t_{m+1} is still set when this message arrives in stage k, $0 < k < i$, then if $t_k = 1$ (and the remaining low-order bits are not all 0), the message can be sent straight and the reroute bit left set to 1.

Example. Suppose the 0110011 tag following the negative dominant path in figure 6–34 is blocked by the straight link in stage 3. Using method 2, the -2^3 link is taken and the reroute bit $t_{m+1} = t_6$ is set to 1. At stage 2, the $+2^2$ link is taken, because $t_2 = 0$, $t_m = t_5 = 1$, $t_{m+1} = t_6 = 1$, and method 2 is being used (method 2' is not applicable because $t_2 = 0$). At stage 1, method 2' is applicable because $t_1 = 1$ and $t_{m+1} = t_6 = 1$. The straight link is taken, following the positive dominant path, because $t_1 = 1$ and $t_m = t_5 = 1$. At stage 0, method 2' is not applicable, so method 2 is used, sending the message on the $+2^0$ link because $t_0 = 1$, $t_m = t_5 = 1$, and $t_{m+1} = t_6 = 1$. The negative path is finally rejoined at the output node.

Correctness proof. For the intuition behind method 2 ′, consider a message following a negative dominant path that is rerouted onto the -2^i link at stage i using method 2. Assume the tag is such that $t_i = 0$, $t_k = 1$, and $t_j = 1$, $0 \le j < k < i$, and no other $t_r = 1$, $j < r < i$. Stages i through j should contribute $-2^k - 2^j$ to the mapping of the source address to the destination address. Assume the straight link is taken at stage k (method 2 ′), the $+2^j$ link is taken at stage j (method 2), and the $+2^r$ link is taken at stage r, $j < r < i$, $r \ne k$ (method 2). This process produces a contribution of:

$$-2^i + \left(\sum_{r=k+1}^{i-1} 2^r \right) + \left(\sum_{r=j}^{k-1} 2^r \right) = -2^i + 2^i - 2^{k+1} + 2^k - 2^j = -2^k - 2^j$$

Thus, the message is put back on its original path. To prove method 2 ′ works correctly, let the period between setting and resetting the reroute bit t_{m+1} be called a *reroute cycle*. The proof is by induction on the number of times the original rerouting is prolonged by method 2 ′ during the reroute cycle. The induction hypothesis is simply that method 2 ′ works correctly.

Basis: The action of method 2 ′ occurs once; thus, there are only two 1s, t_k and t_j, encountered in the magnitude of the routing tag during a reroute cycle, $0 \le j < k < i < m$. Recall $t_i = 0$ and the message was rerouted in stage i. At stage k, method 2 ′ can be applied, routing the message straight. Reroute bit t_{m+1} remains set to 1. The signed distance traveled from stage i to stage k is $d_{i,k} = (-1)^{tm} (2^i - \Sigma_{q=k+1}^{i-1} 2^q) = (-1)^{tm} 2^{k+1}$. Because the reroute bit is left set to 1 and $t_r = 0$, $k > r > j$, the message is routed on the $-(-1)^{tm} 2^r$ link in traveling to stage j (method 2). Thus the distance traveled to stage j is $d_{i,j} = (-1)^{tm}(2^{k+1} - \Sigma_{q=j+1}^{k-1} 2^q) = (-1)^{tm}(2^k + 2^{j+1})$. Method 2 contributes $-(-1)^{tm} 2^j$ and resets the reroute bit, terminating the cycle and making $d_{i,j-1} = (-1)^{tm}(2^k + 2^j)$. This is correct because $t_k = t_j = 1$ and $t_r = 0$, $j < r \le i$, $r \ne k$.

Induction step: Assume the induction hypothesis is correction when method 2 ′ is used $p - 1$ times; that is the action of method 2 ′ can be applied $p - 1$ times (p 1s are encountered in the magnitude of the tag during a reroute cycle). Suppose the action is applied p times ($p + 1$ 1s to be considered). Let t_k be the most significant 1 in the cycle and t_ℓ be the next most significant 1, $m > i > k > \ell > 0$. Calculate $d_{i,k} = (-1)^{tm}(2^i - \Sigma_{q=k+1}^{i-1} 2^q) = (-1)^{tm} 2^{k+1}$. Following the same procedure as in the basis, calculate $d_{i,\ell} = (-1)^{tm}(2^k + 2^{\ell+1})$. Now suppose that method 2 had been terminated in stage k when t_k was encountered. Compensation would have been complete, with a 2^k term generated in the distance $d_{i,k}$ calculated to that point; that is, $d_{i,k} = (-1)^{tm} 2^k$. If another reroute occurred in stage r (the reroute cycle began in stage r), $k > r > \ell$, the distance $d_{i,\ell}$ would be $(-1)^{tm}(2^k + 2^r -$

$\sum_{q=\ell+1}^{r-1} 2^q) = (-1)^{tm}(2^k + 2^{\ell+1})$. Thus from the viewpoint of a node in stage l, the reroute occurred at stage r and a tag with p 1s in the cycle is being processed. By the induction hypothesis, this case will be handled properly.

Method 2' can be applied whenever a method 2 reroute is in progress, $t_k = 1$, and the $(-1)^{tm}2^k$ link is blocked. At any time method 2' is being applied, if the straight link is busy, method 2 can be applied; the message can be sent on the $-(-1)^{tm}2^j$ $(0 \leq j \leq i)$ link, thus terminating the reroute. Thus, together, methods 2 and 2' provide many alternative routings. If method 2' is always used when possible, it simulates method 1, following the opposite dominant path.

In summary, the reroute methods in this section demonstrate the versatility of the ADM network. Furthermore, these reroute methods are based on the easily caculated natural routing tags. The overhead in terms of data paths is just one bit for methods 2 and 2'. The overhead in terms of switching-node complexity would make good use of a custom VLSI node implementation.

Rerouting in the IADM Network

In this subsection, rerouting methods for the IADM network are presented. As in the previous section, following the description of each method is an example of its use and a proof of its correctness. The first method to be described is analogous to ADM reroute method 1, in that it requires the same hardware in each node. The second method is a different procedure for rerouting, but it is still self-contained and does not require any extra bits. Finally, the third method is analogous to ADM reroute method 2 in that one extra bit is required, but hardware is saved.

IADM REROUTE METHOD 1. In the IADM network, if a message becomes blocked by a $\pm 2^i$ link, $0 \leq i \leq m - 2$, it can be sent on the oppositely signed link if the routing tag is replaced by the equivalent tag of opposite dominance.

Example. In figure 6–35, if a tag following the positive dominant path is blocked by the $+2^2$ link in stage 2, it can use method 1 and take the dotted path shown (the -2^2 link). It then follows the negative dominant path (shown in dashed lines).

Correctness proof. Intuitively, the message moves from one dominant path to the path of opposite dominance to avoid the blocked link. To prove the correctness of this method mathematically, assume routing tag $T = t_{m/0}$, $t_i = 1$, the $(-1)^{tm}2^i$ link is blocked, and the message is sent on the $-(-1)^{tm}2^i$ link (the link with opposite sign). The total distance the message has traveled after being rerouted (the distance of its node in stage $i + 1$ from the source address) is:

$$(-1)^{t_m}(\sum_{j=0}^{i-1} t_j 2^j) + (-1)^{\bar{t}_m} 2^i = (-1)^{\bar{t}_m}(2^i - \sum_{j=0}^{i-1} t_j 2^j) =$$

$$(-1)^{\bar{t}_m}(t_{i-1/0})'$$

The message, on being rerouted, arrives at the same node in the $(i + 1)$st stage it would have been sent to using the equivalent tag of opposite dominance. Having switched paths due to the reroute, the tag should be converted to its two's complement equivalent form to route the message correctly to the desired destination. As in ADM reroute method 1, no information is lost. (The $m - 2$ bound on i is based on the assumption that the $+2^{m-1}$ and -2^{m-1} links use the same physical connection.)

The advantages and disadvantages of this reroute method are the same as those discussed for the ADM reroute method 1, except that here there is no need to check for a lower-order 1 in the tag. The next IADM reroute method requires the switching nodes to be capable of performing integer addition modulo N.

IADM REROUTE METHOD 2. If at stage i in the IADM network a message is blocked by a $\pm 2^i$ link, $0 \le i < m - 2$, it can be sent on the oppositely signed link if 2^{i+1} is added to the magnitude portion of the routing tag (modulo N).

Example. In figure 6-35, for $N = 32$, the negative dominant tag to route from source 10 to destination 23 is $(23 - 10)' = (13)' = (001101)' = 110011$. If the -2^1 link in stage 1 is blocked, the message is rerouted on the $+2^1$ link and $2^{1+1} = 2^2$ is added to the magnitude portion of the tag. The new tag is 110111. Following the new tag, the message takes the -2^2 link in stage 2, rejoining the original negative dominant path. Because bits $t_{5/3}$ of the new tag equal bits $t_{5/3}$ of the original tag, the message properly completes its route on the negative dominant path.

Correctness proof. Intuitively, assuming the message is following a negative dominant path, the reroute contributes $+2^i$ to the mapping instead of -2^i, a difference of $+2^{i+1}$. By adding 2^{i+1} to the tag, the later stages of the network contribute an extra -2^{i+1}, compensating for the reroute. Once the compensation is complete, the message will rejoin its original negative dominant path. To prove the correctness mathematically, assume routing tag $T = t_{m/0}$, $t_i = 1$, the $(-1)^{t_m} 2^i$ link is unavailable, and so the message is sent on the $-(-1)^{t_m} 2^i$ link. The distance d between the node in stage $i + 1$ where the message is routed and the node where the message would have been sent is $d = (-1)^{t_m}2^i - [-(-1)^{t_m}2^i] = (-1)^{t_m}2^{i+1}$. The message is sent in a direction opposite that specified by the sign of the routing tag. To compensate for the effect of the reroute, it is only necessary to add 2^{i+1} (modulo N) to the magnitude of the routing tag. Because adding 2^{i+1} to the magnitude can potentially affect (as a result of carry propagation) only bits $i + 1$ through $m - 1$ of the tag, and the message resides in stage i at the time the compensation is added, it is possible for the network to send the message on the new route. (Again, the $m - 2$ bound on i is based on the assumption that the $+2^{m-1}$ and -2^{m-1} links use the same physical connection.)

A disadvantage of method 2 is that the modified tag cannot be used as a return tag from the destination back to the source. The next reroute method is a variation of IADM reroute method 2 that does not have this disadvantage. It implements the rerouting procedure without modifying the routing tag by adding an additional reroute bit t_{m+1}.

IADM REROUTE METHOD 3. Add a reroute bit t_{m+1} to the routing tag and initialize it to 0. If at stage i in the IADM network a message is blocked by a $\pm 2^i$ link, send the message on the oppositely signed link and set t_{m+1} to 1. Whenever $t_{m+1} = 1, t_j, i < j < m,$ is given a new interpretation: if $t_j = 1$ the message is routed straight and t_{m+1} remains set to 1; if $t_j = 0$ the message is routed on the $(-1)^{t_m}2^j$ link and t_{m+1} is reset to 0.

Example. Consider the example for IADM reroute method 2. The tag is initially 0110011. After the reroute at stage 1 the tag is 1110011. At stage 2, because $t_{m+1} = t_6 = 1, t_j = t_2 = 0,$ and $t_m = t_5 = 1$, the message is routed on the -2^2 link, and t_6 is reset to 0. The path followed by the message is the same as that for method 2.

Correctness proof. Method 3 works the same way as method 2. Rather than explicitly modifying the tag by adding 2^{i+1} to the magnitude of the tag, a carry bit (the reroute bit) is set. If $t_j = 1$, t_j plus the carry bit has a sum bit of 0 (so the message is routed straight) and has a carry-out of 1 (so the reroute bit is left set to 1). If $t_j = 0$, t_j plus the carry bit has a sum bit of 1 (so the message is routed $(-1)^{t_m}2^j$) and has a carry-out of 0 (so the reroute bit is reset to 0). Thus, the reroute bit is a carry flag that remains set to 1 until a 0 is encountered in the magnitude bits of the rerouting tag. Therefore, the bits of the routing tag are interpreted as though they had been modified as in method 2.

Using method 3, any rerouted tag will try to return to the original path (as with method 2) as opposed to remaining on the path of opposite dominance (as with method 1). The main difference between methods 2 and 3 is that method 2 requires a more complex switching node while method 3 requires an additional bit in the tag.

In summary, all three IADM reroute methods can be repeated as often as the stated conditions for rerouting are met. In methods 1 and 2, the compensation applied to the tag produces a new tag that is valid for its rerouted location. Thus, the rerouting procedure can be applied to the new tag. In method 3, if the reroute bit t_{m+1} is set to 1 and $t_j = 0$, $m > j > i$, rerouting can be repeated. Normally the tag would be routed on the $(-1)^{t_m} 2^j$ link and t_{m+1} set back to 0. Because carry propagation stops here, if the link is blocked, rerouting can be repeated (sending the message on the $-(-1)^{t_m} 2^j$ link) and t_{m+1} simply left set to 1.

As for the ADM network, the IADM reroute methods that have been described are based on the easily computed natural routing tags. IADM reroute methods 1 and 2 require two's complement or addition capability, respectively, at each node. Method 3 requires the reroute bit be added to the tag, but does not require tag modification. As with the ADM rerouting schemes, the increase in switching-node complexity needed to provide rerouting capabilities would make good use of custom-VLSI implementation.

Rerouting Broadcast Communications

In an earlier subsection of this chapter, 2^i-type broadcasting on the ADM and IADM networks was discussed. In this subsection the rerouting of this type of broadcast is considered. This rerouting method is an extension of the equivalent broadcast routing tag analysis described earlier. This rerouting method is applicable to both the scheme to broadcast to a power of two destinations and to the scheme to broadcast to an arbitrary number of destinations presented in that subsection.

The ADM and IADM networks can reroute a 2^i-type broadcast message when a node that performs a reroute is not also required to broadcast a message. If bit i of the broadcast mask is 0, the routing-control portion of the broadcast tag can be treated as in ADM reroute method 1 or IADM reroute method 1 of the previous subsections. This method converts the broadcast-routing tag to its equivalent form of opposite dominance. This process can be done in stage i even if it is after a stage where a broadcast has occurred as long as $b_i = 0$ (that is, in the remaining stages some copies of the message may be following the positive dominant broadcast path while others follow the negative dominant path). If the broadcast was to an arbitrary number of destinations, the reroute method must be modified so that the bits of the routing control that correspond to ones in the broadcast mask are left unchanged (to preserve the count field). After the message has been completely replicated any of the one-to-one reroute methods can be applied.

As an example, consider rerouting a positive dominant broadcast in an ADM network. The solid lines in figure 6–36 show the positive dominant

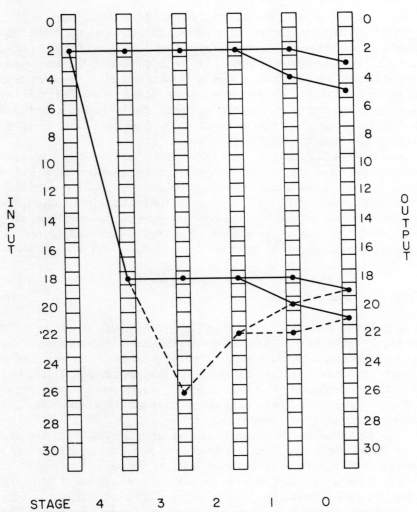

Note: The solid lines show the positive dominant broadcast path from input 2 to outputs 3, 5, 19, and 21, using the broadcast-routing tag $\{R = 00001, B = 010010\}$. The dashed lines show how the broadcast could be rerouted if the straight link at stage 3 from node 18 were faulty or busy.

Figure 6-36. Rerouting a Posititive Dominant Broadcast in an ADM Network with $N = 32$

broadcast path from input 2 to outputs 3, 5, 19, and 21 in an ADM network for $N = 32$ using the broadcast-routing tag $\{R = 000001, B = 010010\}$. The dashed lines show how the broadcast could be rerouted if the straight link at stage 3 from node 18 were faulty or busy. The new routing control is $R' = 111111$.

Rerouting in a Partitioned Network

The rules for partitioning the ADM and IADM networks into independent subnetworks were presented in an earlier section. As stated there, when partitioning a network of size $N = 2^m$ to form a subnetwork consisting of 2^q input/output ports, the addresses of all input/output ports in the partition must agree in the $m - q$ low-order bits. This rule implies that all routing tags used for communication among processors in the same partition will have 0s in their low-order $m - q$ bit positions. Under such an assignment, the partitioning is enforced by setting all switching nodes in the $m - q$ low-order stages of the network to straight. In all the rerouting schemes presented in this section, these stages remain set to straight. ADM reroute method 1 will not change the low-order 0 bits of a tag (a property of the two's complement operation); thus the corresponding stages will remain set to straight. ADM reroute methods 2 and 3, by definition, cannot change the route of a message in stages corresponding to low-order 0s in its routing tag. All the IADM reroute methods leave stages 0 to j completely unchanged if they are set to straight (that is, if $t_{j/0} = 0$). Thus, the rerouting rules are completely compatible with the partitioning rules. In other words, a message sent between an input port and an output port or ports in the same subnetwork can be rerouted using any of the preceding schemes and will still remain within its subnetwork.

Summary

Schemes for dynamically rerouting messages around known faulty or busy nodes in the ADM or IADM network were presented. Two methods for rerouting in the ADM network were described. ADM reroute method 1 required two's complement hardware at each node, whereas ADM reroute method 2 used less logic but needed an extra bit to be added to the tag. Three methods for rerouting in the IADM network were given. IADM reroute method 1 required two's complement hardware, method 2 needed the capability to perform modulo N addition, and method 3 used an extra tag bit and some simple logic. A method for rerouting 2^i-type broadcasts was presented. Finally, the ability to perform rerouting in a partitioned network was explained.

Conclusions

In this chapter various properties and capabilities of the augmented data manipulator (ADM) and inverse ADM (IADM) network were studied.

These networks are representative of a class of networks whose structure is that of a multistage series of PM2I interconnection functions.

First, the relationship of the topology of the ADM/IADM network to the PM2I interconnection functions was discussed. Then, the distributed control of the ADM/IADM network through the use of routing tags was examined. The fact that the ADM network's interconnecting capabilities are a superset of those of the generalized-cube network was proved. Ways in which the ADM/IADM networks could be partitioned into independent subnetworks were examined next, followed by an investigation of the number of distinct data permutations the ADM/IADM networks could perform and how they compared to the number performable by the generalized-cube network. Finally, dynamic rerouting schemes to take advantage of the multiple paths between most source/destination pairs were presented.

The ADM/IADM networks have all of the positive features of the generalized-cube network: simultaneous transfers by N devices are permitted; they can be controlled in a distributed fashion using routing tags; they can be partitioned into independent subnetworks of varying sizes under operating-system control or under user control (both through the use of routing tags); one device can broadcast to all or a subset of devices; a fault-tolerant variation (not discussed here) has been developed (McMillen and Siegel 1982a); and it can function in the SIMD, multiple-SIMD, MIMD, and partitionable-SIMD/MIMD modes of parallel processing. Thus, the ADM/IADM networks have all of the positive features of the generalized-cube network, plus the ADM network has all of the interconnecting capabilities of the generalized-cube network and much more data-permuting capability. (The IADM network can also perform all the connections that the generalized-cube network is capable of, by using a relabeling such as that in chapter 5 for relating the generalized-cube network to the STARAN flip and indirect binary n-cube networks.) In addition, the structure of the ADM/IADM networks allows dynamic rerouting around faulty or busy network switches. The tradeoff is that straightforward implementations of the ADM/IADM networks are more costly than those for the generalized-cube network (McMillen and Siegel 1982b).

In summary, the ADM/IADM networks could be used in any environment where the generalized-cube network could be used. The ADM/IADM networks would provide more capability, but at a possibly higher implementation cost. To decide between these two types of networks, a system designer would have to weigh any advantages of the ADM/IADM networks based on the system's intended operating environment against any difference in construction and maintenance costs. The information presented in this chapter, chapter 5, and the cited references will aid the designer in making this decision.

Summary and Further Reading

Alice asked:
"Would you tell me,
please, which way I ought
to go from here?"

The Cheshire Cat responded:
"That depends a good deal on
where you want to get to."

Lewis Carroll
Alice's Adventures in Wonderland

The goal of this book is to present tools and information that can be used in the analysis, comparison, evaluation, and design of interconnection networks for large-scale parallel processing systems. Chapter 2 defined the interconnection networks that were studied, and presented various organizations of parallel processing systems. The networks were compared in terms of their single-stage implementations in chapter 3. In particular, the ability of each network to perform the connections of the other networks was analyzed. Chapter 4 investigated the partitioning properties of the single-stage interconnection networks. The permutation cycle structures of the networks were used as a basis for this analysis. In chapter 5 a multistage implementation of cube/shuffle-exchange networks called the generalized-cube was presented. The multistage implementation of the PM2I network termed the data manipulator was explored in chapter 6. The features of these networks examined in chapters 5 and 6 included distributed routing control, relationships to other networks, partitionability, number of permutations performable by the network, and fault-tolerance. The knowledge gained from this study of an important class of interconnection networks can be used in the future design and analysis of large-scale parallel processing systems.

Where "to go from here . . . depends a good deal on where you want to get to." Using the background gained from this book as a basis, other books and articles related to one's particular interests in interconnection networks can be read. The references listed in this book are one source of information about such publications. Relevant technical journals include the *IEEE Transactions on Computers, Computer, Journal of the ACM,* and *Communications of the ACM.* The proceedings of the following conference series are also excellent sources: International Conference on Parallel Processing, International Conference on Distributed Computing Systems, and the International Symposium on Computer Architecture.

245

References

Abidi, M.A., and D.P. Agrawal, "On conflict-free permutations in multistage interconnection networks," *Journal of Digital Systems,* vol. 4, Summer 1980, pp. 115–134.

Adams, G.B., III, and H.J. Siegel, "On the number of permutations performable by the augmented data manipulator network," *IEEE Transactions on Computers,* vol. C-31, April 1982a, pp. 270–277.

————, "The extra stage cube: a fault tolerant interconnection network for supersystems," *IEEE Transactions on Computers,* vol. C-31, May 1982b, pp. 443–454.

Anderson, G.A., and E.D. Jensen, "Computer interconnection structures: taxonomy, characteristics and examples," *ACM Computing Surveys,* vol. 7, December 1975, pp. 197–213.

Baer, J.L., "Multiprocessing systems," *IEEE Transactions on Computers,* vol. C-25, December 1976, pp. 1271–1277.

————, *Computer Systems Architecture* (Potomac, Md.: Computer Science Press, 1980).

Barnes, G.H., R.M. Brown, M. Kato, D.J. Kuck, D.L. Slotnick, and R.A. Stokes, "The Illiac IV computer," *IEEE Transactions on Computers,* vol. C-17, August 1968, pp. 746–757.

Barnes, G.H., and S.F. Lundstrom, "Design and validation of a connection network for many-processor multiprocessor systems," *Computer,* vol. 14, December 1981, pp. 31–41.

Batcher, K.E., "Sorting networks and their applications," *AFIPS Conference Proceedings 1968 Spring Joint Computer Conference,* 1968, pp. 307–314.

————, "STARAN parallel processor system hardware," *AFIPS Conference Proceedings 1974 National Computer Conference,* May 1974, pp. 405–410.

————, "The flip network in STARAN," *1976 International Conference on Parallel Processing,* August 1976, pp. 65–71.

————, "The multidimensional access memory in STARAN," *IEEE Transactions on Computers,* vol. C-26, February 1977a, pp. 174–177.

————, "STARAN series E," *1977 International Conference on Parallel Processing,* August 1977b, pp. 140–143.

————, "Design of a massively parallel processor," *IEEE Transactions on Computers,* vol. C-29, September 1980, pp. 836–840.

————, "Bit serial parallel processing systems," *IEEE Transactions on Computers,* vol. C-31, May 1982, pp. 377–384.

Bauer, L.H., "Implementation of data manipulating functions on the STARAN associative processor," *1974 Sagamore Computer Conference on Parallel Processing,* August 1974, pp. 209–227.

Beneš, V.E., *Mathematical Theory of Connecting Networks and Telephone Traffic* (New York: Academic Press, 1965).

Bouknight, W.J., S.A. Denenberg, D.E. McIntyre, J.M. Randall, A.H. Sameh, and D.L. Slotnick, "The Illiac IV system," *Proceedings of the IEEE,* vol. 60, April 1972, pp. 369–388.

Briggs, F.A., K.-S. Fu, K. Hwang, and J. Patel, "PM4—a reconfigurable multimicroprocessor system for pattern recognition and image processing," *AFIPS Conference Proceedings 1979 National Computer Conference,* June 1979, pp. 255–265.

Briggs, F.A., K.-S. Fu, K. Hwang, and B.W. Wah, "PUMPS architecture for pattern analysis and image database management," *IEEE Transactions on Computers,* vol. C-31, October 1982, pp. 969–982.

Chen, P.-Y., D.H. Lawrie, P.-C. Yew, and D.A. Padua, "Interconnection networks using shuffles," *Computer,* vol. 14, December 1981, pp. 55–64.

Chen, P.-Y., P.-C. Yew, and D.H. Lawrie, "Performance of packet switching in buffered single-stage shuffle-exchange networks," *Third International Conference on Distributed Computing Systems,* October 1982, pp. 622–627.

Ciminiera, L., and A. Serra, "A fault-tolerant connecting network for multiprocessor systems," *1982 International Conference on Parallel Processing,* August 1982, pp. 113–122.

Couranz, G.R., M.S. Gerhardt, and C.J. Young, "Programmable RADAR signal processing using the RAP," *1974 Sagamore Computer Conference on Parallel Processing,* August 1974, pp. 37–52.

Crane, B.A., M.J. Gilmartin, J.H. Huttenhoff, P.T. Rux, and R.R. Shively, "PEPE computer architecture," *IEEE Computer Society Compcon 72,* September 1972, pp. 57–60.

Dennis, J.B., G.A. Boughton, and C.K.C. Leung, "Building blocks for data flow prototypes," *Seventh Annual Symposium on Computer Architecture,* May 1980, pp. 1–8.

Dias, D.M., and J.R. Jump, "Analysis and simulation of buffered delta networks," *IEEE Transactions on Computers,* vol. C-30, April 1981, pp. 273–282.

———, "Augmented and pruned N log N multistage networks: topology and performance," *1982 International Conference on Parallel Processing,* August 1982, pp. 10–11.

Enslow, P.H., Jr., "Multiprocessor organization—a survey," *ACM Computing Surveys,* vol. 9, March 1977, pp. 103–129.

Feng, T., "Data manipulating functions in parallel processors and their implementations," *IEEE Transactions on Computers,* vol. C-23, March 1974, pp. 309-318.

————, "A survey of interconnection networks," *Computer,* vol. 14, December 1981, pp. 12-27.

Feng, T., and C. Wu, "Fault-diagnosis for a class of multistage interconnection networks," *IEEE Transactions on Computers,* vol. C-30, October 1981, pp. 743-758.

Fishburn, J.P., and R.A. Finkel, "Quotient networks," *IEEE Transactions on Computers,* vol. C-31, April 1982, pp. 288-295.

Filip, A.E., "A distributed signal processing architecture," *Third International Conference on Distributed Computing Systems,* October 1982, pp. 49-55.

Flynn, M.J., "Very high-speed computing systems," *Proceedings of the IEEE,* vol. 54, December 1966, pp. 1901-1909.

Fountain, T.J., "CLIP4: progress report," in *Languages and Architectures for Image Processing,* ed. M.J.B. Duff and S. Levialdi (London: Academic Press, 1981), pp. 281-291.

Gentleman, W.M., "Some complexity results for matrix computations on parallel processors," *Journal of the ACM,* vol. 25, January 1978, pp. 112-115.

Gottlieb, A., R. Grishman, C.P. Kruskal, K.P. McAuliffe, L. Rudolph, and M. Snir, "The NYU Ultracomputer—designing an MIMD shared-memory parallel computer," *IEEE Transactions on Computers,* vol. C-32, February 1983, pp. 175-189.

Goke, L.R., and G.J. Lipovski, "Banyan networks for partitioning multiprocessor systems," *First Annual International Symposium on Computer Architecture,* December 1973, pp. 21-28.

Golomb, S.W., "Permutations by cutting and shuffling," *SIAM Review,* vol. 3, October 1961, pp. 293-297.

Gries, D., *Compiler Construction for Digital Computers* (New York: Wiley, 1971).

Herstein, I.N., *Topics in Algebra* (Lexington, Mass.: Xerox, 1964).

Higbie, L.C., "The Omen computer: associative array processor," *IEEE Computer Society Compcon 72,* September 1972, pp. 287-290.

Hoggatt, V.E., Jr., *Fibonacci and Lucas Numbers* (Boston: Houghton Mifflin, 1969).

Hockney, R.W., and C.R. Jeshope, *Parallel Computers* (Bristol, England: Adam Hilger, 1981).

Hunt, D.J., "The ICL DAP and its application to image processing," in *Languages and Architectures for Image Processing,* ed. M.J.B. Duff and S. Levialdi (London: Academic Press, 1981), pp. 275-282.

Hwang, K., and F. Briggs, *Computer Architecture and Parallel Processing* (New York: McGraw-Hill, 1984).

Jones, A.K., R.J. Chansler, Jr., I. Durham, P. Feiler, and K. Schwans, "Software management of Cm*—a distributed multiprocessor," *AFIPS Conference Proceedings 1977 National Computer Conference,* June 1977, pp. 657–663.

Johnson, P.B., "Congruences and card shuffling," *American Mathematical Monthly,* vol. 63, December 1956, pp. 718–719.

Kapur, R.N., U.V. Premkumar, and G.J. Lipovski, "Organization of the TRAC processor-memory subsystem," *AFIPS Conference Proceedings 1980 National Computer Conference,* June 1980, pp. 623–629.

Knuth, D.E., *The Art of Computer Programming: vol. 3. Sorting and Searching* (Reading, Mass.: Addison-Wesley, 1973).

Krygiel, A.J., "An implementation of the Hadamard transform on the STARAN associative array processor," *1976 International Conference on Parallel Processing,* August 1976, p. 34.

Kuck, D.J., "A survey of parallel machine organization and programming," *ACM Computing Surveys,* vol. 9, March 1977, pp. 29–59.

———, *The Structure of Computers and Computations, vol. 1* (New York: Wiley, 1978).

Kuck, D.J., and R.A. Stokes, "The Burroughs Scientific Processor (BSP)," *IEEE Transactions on Computers,* vol. C-31, May 1982, pp. 363–376.

Kuehn, J.T., H.J. Siegel, and P.D. Hallenbeck, "Design and simulation of an MC68000-based multimicroprocessor system," *1982 International Conference on Parallel Processing,* August 1982, pp. 353–362.

Lang, T., "Interconnections between processors and memory modules using the shuffle-exchange network," *IEEE Transactions on Computers,* vol. C-25, May 1976, pp. 496–503.

Lang, T., and H.S. Stone, "A shuffle-exchange network with simplified control," *IEEE Transactions on Computers,* vol. C-25, January 1976, pp. 55–66.

Lawrie, D.H., "Access and alignment of data in an array processor," *IEEE Transactions on Computers,* vol. C-24, December 1975, pp. 1145–1155.

Lawrie, D.H., and C. Vora, "The prime memory system for array access," *IEEE Transactions on Computers,* vol. C-31, May 1982, pp. 435–442.

Lawrie, D.H., T. Layman, D. Baer, and J.M. Randall, "Glypnir - a programming language for Illiac IV," *Communications of the ACM,* vol. 18, March 1975, pp. 157–164.

Lilienkamp, J.E., D.H. Lawrie, and P.-C. Yew, "A fault tolerant interconnection network using error correcting codes," *1982 International Conference on Parallel Processing,* August 1982, pp. 123–125.

Lin, S., *An Introduction to Error Correcting Codes* (Englewood Cliffs, N.J.: Prentice-Hall, 1970), p. 43.

Lipovski, G.J., and A. Tripathi, "A reconfigurable varistructure array processor," *1977 International Conference on Parallel Processing,* August 1977, pp. 165–174.

McCoy, N.H., *Introduction to Modern Algebra,* 3rd ed. (Boston: Allyn and Bacon, 1975).

McDonald, W.C., and J.M. Williams, "The advanced data processing test bed," *IEEE Computer Society Compsac,* March 1978, pp. 346–351.

McDonald, W.C., and T.G. Williams, "Evaluation of a multimicroprocessor interconnection network for a class of sensor data processing problems," *SPIE Real Time Signal Processing,* vol. 241, July 1980, pp. 238–248.

McMillen, R.J., G.B. Adams III, and H.J. Siegel, "Performance and implementation of 4×4 switching nodes in an interconnection network for PASM," *1981 International Conference on Parallel Processing,* August 1981, pp. 229–233.

McMillen, R.J., and H.J. Siegel, "The hybrid cube network," *Distributed Data Acquisition, Computing, and Control Symposium,* December 1980, pp. 11–22.

———, "Performance and fault tolerance improvements in the Inverse Augmented Data Manipulator network," *Ninth Annual Symposium on Computer Architecture,* April 1982a, pp. 63–72.

———, "A comparison of cube type and data manipulator type networks," *Third International Conference on Distributed Computing Systems,* Oct. 1982b, pp. 614–621.

———, "Routing schemes for the Augmented Data Manipulator network in an MIMD system," *IEEE Transactions on Computers,* vol. C-31, December 1982c, pp. 1202–1214.

———, *A Study of Multistage Interconnection Networks: Design, Distributed Control, Fault Tolerance, and Performance,* School of Electrical Engineering, Purdue University, Technical Report TR-EE 83-13, August 1983.

Masson, G.M., G.C. Gingher, and S. Nakamura, "A sampler of circuit switching networks," *Computer,* vol. 12, June 1979, pp. 32–48.

Mueller, P.T., Jr., L.J. Siegel, and H.J. Siegel, "A parallel language for image and speech processing," *IEEE Computer Society Compsac,* October 1980a, pp. 476–483.

———, "Parallel algorithms for the two-dimensional FFT," *Fifth International Conference on Pattern Recognition,* December 1980b, pp. 497–502.

Nassimi, D., and S. Sahni, "Bitonic sort on a mesh-connected parallel computer," *IEEE Transactions on Computers,* vol. C-28, January 1979, pp. 2–7.

———, "An optimal routing algorithm for mesh-connected parallel computers," *Journal of the ACM,* vol. 27, January 1980, pp. 6–29.

———, "Data broadcasting in SIMD computers," *IEEE Transactions on Computers,* vol. C-30, February 1981, pp. 101–107.

———, "Optimal BPC permutations on a cube-connected SIMD computer," *IEEE Transactions on Computers,* vol. C-31, April 1982a, pp. 338–341.

———, "Parallel permutation and sorting algorithms and a new generalized connection network," *Journal of the ACM,* vol. 29, July 1982b, pp. 642–667.

Nutt, G.J., "Microprocessor implementation of a parallel processor," *Fourth Annual Symposium on Computer Architecture,* March 1977a, 147–152.

———, "A parallel processor operating system comparison," *IEEE Transactions on Software Engineering,* vol. SE-3, November 1977b, pp. 467–475.

O'Donnell, and C.H. Smith, "A combinatorial problem concerning processor networks," *IEEE Transactions on Computers,* vol. C-31, February 1982, pp. 163–164.

Okada, Y., H. Tajima, and R. Mori, "A novel multiprocessor array," *Second Symposium on Micro Architecture,* 1976, pp. 83–90.

———, "A reconfigurable parallel processor with microprogram control," *IEEE Micro,* vol. 2, November 1982, pp. 48–60.

Opferman, D.C., and N.T. Tsao-Wu, "On a class of rearrangeable switching networks," *Bell System Technical Journal,* vol. 50, May-June 1971, pp. 1579–1600.

Orcutt, S.E., "Implementation of permutation functions in Illiac IV-type computers," *IEEE Transactions on Computers,* vol. C-25, September 1976, pp. 929–936.

Parker, D.S., and C.S. Raghavendra, "The gamma network: a multiprocessor interconnection network with redundant paths," *Ninth Annual Symposium on Computer Architecture,* April 1982, pp. 73–80.

Patel, J.H., "Performance of processor-memory interconnections for multiprocessors," *IEEE Transactions on Computers,* vol. C-30, October 1981, pp. 771–780.

Pease, M.C., III, "The indirect binary n-cube microprocessor array," *IEEE Transactions on Computers,* vol. C-26, May 1977, pp. 458–473.

Premkumar, U.V., R. Kapur, M. Malek, G.J. Lipovski, and P. Horne, "Design and implementation of the banyan interconnection network in TRAC," *AFIPS Conference Proceedings 1980 National Computer Conference,* June 1980, pp. 643–653.

Pradhan, D.K., and K.L. Kodandapani, "A uniform representation of single- and multistage interconnection networks used in SIMD Machines," *IEEE Transactions on Computers,* vol. C-29, September 1980, pp. 777–791.

Reeves, A.P., and R. Rindfuss, "The BASE 8 binary array processor," *1979 IEEE Computer Society Conference on Pattern Recognition and Image Processing,* August 1979, pp. 250–255.

Seban, R.R., and H.J. Siegel, "Performing the shuffle with the PM2I and Illiac SIMD interconnection networks," *1983 International Conference on Parallel Processing,* August 1983, pp. 117–125.

Sejnowski, M.C., E.T. Upchurch, R.N. Kapur, D.P.S. Charlu, and G.J. Lipovski, "An overview of the Texas reconfigurable array computer," *AFIPS Conference Proceedings 1980 National Computer Conference,* June 1980, pp. 631–641.

Shen, J.P., and S.P. Hayes, "Fault tolerance of a class of connecting networks," *Seventh Annual Symposium on Computer Architecture,* May 1980, pp. 61–71.

Siegel, H.J., "Analysis techniques for SIMD machine interconnection networks and the effects of processor address masks," *IEEE Transactions on Computers,* vol. C-26, February 1977, pp. 153–161.

———, "Partitionable SIMD computer system interconnection network universality," *Sixteenth Annual Allerton Conference on Communication, Control and Computing,* University of Illinois, October 1978, pp. 586–595.

———, "Interconnection networks for SIMD machines," *Computer,* vol. 12, June 1979a, pp. 57–65. Reprinted in *Tutorial: Distributed Processor Communication Architecture,* ed. K.J. Thurber (New York: IEEE, 1979), pp. 379–387, and *Tutorial on Parallel Processing,* ed. R. Kuhn and D.A. Padua (New York: IEEE Computer Society Press, 1981), pp. 110–119.

———, "A model of SIMD machines and a comparison of various interconnection networks," *IEEE Transactions on Computers,* vol. C-28, December 1979b, pp. 907–917.

———, "The theory underlying the partitioning of permutation networks," *IEEE Transactions on Computers,* vol. C-29, September 1980, pp. 791–801.

Siegel, H.J., and R.J. McMillen, "Using the Augmented Data Manipulator network in PASM," *Computer,* vol. 14, February 1981a, pp. 25–33.

———, "The cube network as a distributed processing test bed switch," *Second International Conference on Distributed Computing Systems,* April 1981b, pp. 337–387.

———, "The multistage cube: a versatile interconnection network," *Computer,* vol. 14, December 1981c, pp. 65–76.

Siegel, H.J., and P.T. Mueller, Jr., "A survey of interconnection methods for reconfigurable parallel processing systems," *AFIPS Conference Proceedings 1979 National Computer Conference,* June 1979, pp. 529–542. Translated into Japanese and reprinted in *Nikkei Electroncis,* no. 228, December 1979, pp. 49–82.

Siegel, H.J., and P.T. Mueller, Jr., "The organization and language design of microprocessors for an SIMD/MIMD system," *Second Rocky Mountain Symposium on Microcomputers,* August 1978, pp. 311–340.

Siegel, H.J., P.T. Mueller, Jr., and H.E. Smalley, Jr., "Control of a partitionable multimicroprocessor system," *1978 International Conference on Parallel Processing,* August 1978, pp. 9–17.

Siegel, H.J, L.J. Siegel, F.C. Kemmerer, P.T. Mueller, Jr., H.E. Smalley, Jr., and S.D. Smith, "PASM: a partitionable SIMD/MIMD system for image processing and pattern recognition," *IEEE Transactions on Computers,* vol. C-30, December 1981, pp. 934–947.

Siegel, H.J., and S.D. Smith, "Study of multistage SIMD interconnection networks," *Fifth Annual Symposium on Computer Architecture,* April 1978, pp. 223–229.

————,"An interconnection network for multimicroprocessor emulator systems," *First International Conference on Distributed Computing Systems,* October 1979, pp. 772–782.

Siegel, L.J., "Image processing on a partitionable SIMD machine," in *Languages and Architectures for Image Processing,* ed. M.J.B. Duff and S. Levialdi (London: Academic Press, 1981), pp. 293–300.

Siegel, L.J., H.J. Siegel, and A.E. Feather, "Parallel processing approaches to image correlation," *IEEE Transactions on Computers,* vol. C-31, March 1982, pp. 208–218.

Siegel, L.J., H.J. Siegel, R.J. Safranek, and M.A. Yoder, "SIMD algorithms to perform linear predicative coding for speech processing applications," *1980 International Conference on Parallel Processing,* August 1980, pp. 193–196.

Siegel, L.J., H.J. Siegel, and P.H. Swain, "Performance measures for evaluating algorithms for SIMD machines," *IEEE Transactions on Software Engineering,* vol. SE-8, July 1982, pp. 319–331.

Smith, S.D., and H.J. Siegel, "Recirculating, pipelined, and multistage SIMD interconnection networks," *1978 International Conference on Parallel Processing,* August 1978, pp. 206–214.

————, "An emulator network for SIMD machine interconnection networks," *Sixth International Symposium on Computer Architecture,* April 1979, pp. 232–241.

Smith, S.D., H.J. Siegel, R.J. McMillen, and G.B. Adams III, "Use of the Augmented Data Manipulator multistage network for SIMD machines," *1980 International Conference on Parallel Processing,* August 1980, pp. 75–78.

Stevens, K.G., Jr., "CFD—a Fortran-like language for the Illiac IV," *ACM Conference on Programming Languages and Compilers for Parallel and Vector Machines,* March 1975, pp. 72–76.

Stone, H.S., "Parallel processing with the perfect shuffle," *IEEE Transactions on Computers,* vol. C-20, February 1971, pp. 153–161.

———, *Discrete Mathematical Structures and Their Applications* (Chicago: Science Research Associates, 1973).

———, "Parallel computers," in *Introduction to Computer Architecture,* ed. H.S. Stone (Chicago: Science Research Associates, 1980, 2nd ed.), pp. 363–425.

Sullivan, H., T.R. Bashkow, and K. Klappholz, "A large-scale homogeneous, fully distributed parallel machine," *Fourth Symposium on Computer Architecture,* March 1977, pp. 105–124.

Swan, R.J., A Bechtolsheim, K. Lai, and J.K. Ousterholt, "The implementation of the Cm* multi-microprocessor," *AFIPS Conference Proceedings 1977 National Computer Conference,* June 1977, pp. 645–655.

Swan, R.J., S.H. Fuller, and D.P. Siewiorek, "Cm*: a modular, multi-microprocessor," *AFIPS Conference Proceedings National Computer Conference,* June 1977, pp. 637–644.

Thanawastien, S., "The shuffle/exchange-plus networks," *ACM Southeast Regional Conference,* April 1982.

Thompson, C.D., and H.T. Kung, "Sorting on a mesh-connected parallel computer," *Communications of the ACM,* vol. 20, April 1977, pp. 263–271.

Thurber, K.J., *Large Scale Computer Architecture: Parallel and Associative Pricessors* (Rochelle Park, N.J.: Hayden, 1976).

———, "Circuit switching technology: a state-of-the-art survey," *IEEE Computer Society Compcon,* September 1978, pp. 116–124.

———, "Parallel processor architectures—part 1: general purpose systems," *Computer Design,* vol. 18, January 1979, pp. 89–97.

Thurber, K.J., and G.M. Masson, *Distributed-Processor Communication Architecture* (Lexington, Mass.: Lexington Books, 1979).

Thurber, K.J., and L.D. Wald, "Associative and parallel processors," *ACM Computing Surveys,* vol. 7, December 1975, pp. 215–255.

Vick, C.R., and J.A. Cornell, "PEPE architecture—present and future," *AFIPS Conference Proceedings 1978 National Computer Conference,* June 1978, pp. 981–992.

Wah, B.W., and A. Hicks, "Distributed scheduling of resources on interconnection networks," *AFIPS Conference Proceedings 1982 National Computer Conference,* June 1982, pp. 697–709.

Warpenburg, M.R., and L.J. Siegel, "SIMD image resampling," *IEEE Transactions on Computers,* vol. C-31, October 1982, pp. 934–942.

Wen, K.Y., *Interprocessor Connections—Capabilities, Exploitation, and*

Effectiveness, Ph.D. thesis, report UIUCDCS-R-76-830, Computer Science Dept., University of Illinois, Urbana, October 1976.

Wester, A.H., "Special features in SIMDA," *1972 Sagamore Computer Conference,* August 1972, pp. 29–40.

Wilson, D.E., "The PEPE support software system," *IEEE Computer Society Compcon 72,* September 1972, pp. 61–64.

Wu, C., and T. Feng, "On a class of multistage interconnection networks," *IEEE Transactions on Computers,* vol. C-29, August 1980, pp. 694–702.

———, "The universality of the shuffle-exchange network," *IEEE Transactions on Computers,* vol. C-30, May 1981, pp. 324–332.

Wu, C., T. Feng, and M. Lin, "Star: a local network system for real-time management of imagery data," *IEEE Transactions on Computers,* vol. C-31, October 1982, pp. 923–933.

Wulf, W.A., and C.G. Bell, "C.mmp—a multi-miniprocessor," *AFIPS Conference Proceedings 1972 Fall Joint Computer Conference,* December 1972, pp. 765–777.

Yoder, M.A., and L.J. Siegel, "Dynamic time warping algorithms for SIMD machines and VLSI processor arrays," *1982 International Conference on Acoustics, Speech, and Signal Processing,* May 1982, pp. 1274–1277.

Index

About the Author

Howard Jay Siegel received the B.S. degree in electrical engineering and the B.S. degree in management in 1972 from the Massachusetts Institute of Technology. He received the M.A. and M.S.E. degrees in 1974 and the Ph.D. degree in 1977 from the Department of Electrical Engineering and Computer Science at Princeton University. In 1976, Dr. Siegel joined the School of Electrical Engineering at Purdue University where he is currently a professor specializing in parallel and distributed computing.

Dr. Siegel has published over 100 technical papers on parallel and distributed computer systems and has presented his work at conferences in the United States and Europe. He has received research grants or contracts from the Air Force Office of Scientific Research, the Army Research Office, the Ballistic Missile Defense Agency, the Defense Mapping Agency, IBM, NASA, and the National Science Foundation. Dr. Siegel is an associate editor of the new *Journal of Parallel and Distributed Computing,* has served as a guest editor of the *IEEE Transactions on Computers,* and was on the editorial board of the *Journal of Digital Systems.* He has consulted on parallel and distributed computing for a number of companies. From 1979 to 1982, Dr. Siegel was an IEEE Computer Society Distinguished Visitor, giving invited lectures across the country about his research.

Dr. Siegel is a senior member of the Institute of Electrical and Electronics Engineers (IEEE), and a member of the Association of Computing Machinery (ACM). He is chairman of the ACM Special Interest Group on Computer Architecture, has served as chairman of the IEEE Computer Society Technical Committee on Computer Architecture and as a vice-chairman of the IEEE Computer Society Technical Committee on Distributed Processing. Dr. Siegel was chairman of the Workshop on Interconnection Networks for Parallel and Distributed Processing in April 1980, general chairman of the Third International Conference on Distributed Computing Systems in October 1982, and program co-chairperson of the 1983 International Conference on Parallel Processing in August 1983. He is a member of the Eta Kappa Nu and the Sigma Xi honorary societies.